Intractable Dilemmas in the Energy-Rich Eastern Mediterranean

Intractable Dilemmas in the Energy-Rich Eastern Mediterranean

Edited by

Aris Petasis

Cambridge Scholars Publishing

Intractable Dilemmas in the Energy-Rich Eastern Mediterranean

Edited by Aris Petasis

This book first published 2016

Cambridge Scholars Publishing

Lady Stephenson Library, Newcastle upon Tyne, NE6 2PA, UK

British Library Cataloguing in Publication Data
A catalogue record for this book is available from the British Library

ISBN (10): 1-4438-8687-4
ISBN (13): 978-1-4438-8687-1

To democracy and the rule of international law

CONTENTS

LIST OF FIGURES

LIST OF TABLES

NOTES ON CONTRIBUTORS

Stephanos Constantinides has a BA in History and Literature from the University of Athens, an MA in the work of Demosthenes from the Sorbonne, Paris, a PhD in Political Sociology from the University of Paris I, and a PhD in Political Science from Sorbonne Panthéon-Assas University. At the Sorbonne he studied Thucydides under Jacqueline de Romilly. He has taught at Laval University, the University of Montreal, and the University of Quebec at Montreal, Canada, as well as being a collaborator with the University of Crete. He is Director of the Centre for Hellenic Studies and Research Canada (KEEK) and of the journal *Etudes helléniques/Hellenic Studies*. He has written and published extensively and his particular areas of interest include the European Union, Greece, Turkey, Cyprus, and the Greek diaspora.

George Georgiou studied Economics at Drew University, London School of Economics, University of Brussels, and George Washington University. He is Professor of International Economics at Towson University, University System of Maryland, US. He has had a long and distinguished career in teaching, research, and consulting, and has held faculty positions at National Defense University, George Washington University, University of Maryland University College, University of Baltimore, St. Mary's College of Maryland, and Marymount University. His expertise covers national economic policy in the context of a global economy and he has published extensively, presented papers, delivered lectures, and provided training on national and international economic policy issues to many diverse groups.

Solon Kassinis has a Diploma in Marketing from the Chartered Institute of Marketing in London, a BA in Business Studies from Philips College, Cyprus, and a BSc in Chemical Engineering from the University of Surrey. He is an Honorary Doctor of the National and Kapodistrian University of Athens, President of the Solon Kassinis Energy Training School and Research Centre at UCLan Cyprus, Member of the Cyprus Scientific and Technical Chamber, Chevalier of the Order of St. Stanislas of Warsaw, past adviser on energy matters to the ex-Prime Minister of Greece Antonis Samaras, past Executive Vice President of the Cyprus

National Hydrocarbons Company, past Director of the Energy Service (Government of Cyprus), and past President of the Cyprus Institute of Energy. He is Managing Director of Kassinis International Consulting.

Hilal Khashan has a BA from the University of Florida, and an MS and PhD from Florida State University, all in Political Science. He is a professor at the American University of Beirut and a visiting professor at a number of other universities. The holder of numerous awards, including visiting scholar at the Annenberg Research Institute in Philadelphia, he conducts editorial and referee work for several journals and is the author or co-author of numerous books, monographs, manuscripts, and articles. His work focuses on comparative politics (with an emphasis on Arab countries) and on minorities, democratization, civil society, Lebanese politics, the Arab–Israel peace process, and the performance of the public sector in the Middle East.

Theodoros Kyprianou has an MD from the University of Athens Medical School and a PhD from the University of Athens Department of Pulmonary and Intensive Care Medicine. He completed clinical fellowships in Pulmonary Medicine and Tuberculosis and Intensive Care Medicine in several University Hospitals in Athens. He is founding Head of the Department of Intensive Care at Nicosia General Hospital, Associate Professor at St Georges' University of London Medical Program delivered at the Medical School of the University of Nicosia, and is the current Chair of the Technology Assessment and Health Informatics trans-sectional Working Group at the European Society of Intensive Care Medicine. Along with a multidisciplinary research team and international collaborators, he has presented, published, and participated in over 100 scientific articles, posters, and presentations in congresses and peer-reviewed journals in the fields of ICU bio-signals and data management, intensive care education and training, critical illness pathophysiology, and other related areas.

William Mallinson has a PhD from the department of International History at the London School of Economics and Political Science. A former diplomat, he lectures on British history, literature, and culture at the Ionian University, Greece and is an occasional lecturer at the Greek National Defence School. He has also worked as European public affairs manager for multinational corporations. The author of numerous books and articles and a popular speaker, his research interests are Dutch foreign policy, Dutch–German relations, and German rearmament during the initial period of the building of European institutions and NATO, and the formative years of the Cold War.

Miguel Ángel Moratinos Cuyaubé has a degree in Law and Political Sciences from Complutense University of Madrid and also completed the programme in Diplomatic Studies at the Spanish Diplomatic School. He served in the Spanish Diplomatic Service and has held major positions including General Deputy Director for Northern Africa, Director of the Institute of Cooperation with the Arab World, General Director of Foreign Policy for Africa and the Middle East (he took part in the organization of the historic Middle East Peace Conference in Madrid in 1992), Spain's Ambassador in Israel, EU Special Representative for the Middle East Peace Process, Member of Parliament, Spanish Minister of Foreign Affairs and Cooperation, President of the United Nations Security Council, and chairmanships-in-office of the Organization for Security and Cooperation in Europe (OSCE), the Council of Europe, and the Council of the European Union.

Aris Petasis has a BBA (Bachelor in Business Administration) from the American University of Beirut, an MBA and an EdD from Drake University, Iowa, US, and was a postdoctoral Fellow at the University of Rhodesia. He completed all his tertiary-level education on merit-based scholarships/fellowships, and was Victor Ludorum at the American University of Beirut. He has lectured and/or provided consulting services at international level in more than 25 countries on four continents covering strategy, leadership, and organizational development. A founding member of the International Trustee Fund of the Tsyolkovsky Moscow State Aviation University, he is currently a Member of the fund's Presidential Council. He has written and published treatises on organizational development, strategy, politics, and leadership and is a popular public speaker and debater, as well as being the holder of numerous awards and recognitions.

ACKNOWLEDGMENTS

Over lunch in Nicosia with the late Tommaso Padoa-Schioppa, Italy's former minister of finance and to most people a founding father of the European single currency, our discussion turned to Altiero Spinelli, the Italian political theorist generally considered one of the fathers of the European Union. Tommaso had a comprehensive understanding of Spinelli's ideas and his burning desire to see the countries of Europe work together peacefully. He was a strong force in getting me to start thinking about the Eastern Mediterranean along the lines that Spinelli saw Europe (in his time) and, most importantly, to start questioning the status quo in the Eastern Mediterranean, which holds back all the countries in the region and does not allow them to achieve their potential. From this discussion it become clear to me that democracy and the rule of law would have to be the two pillars on which to build the new Eastern Mediterranean nations. Clearly, therefore, I owe a strong debt of gratitude to Tommaso for planting in my head the first ideas around the subject of this book. The same holds for Miguel Moratinos, former Spanish Minister of Foreign Affairs and one of the contributors here, who some time back proposed the idea of a High Energy Authority for the countries of the Eastern Mediterranean, which ultimately became a central theme of this book.

There is no need for me to search further than the chapters to follow to find seven thinkers to acknowledge for their contribution and to thank for all the great work they have done. A strong expression of gratitude therefore goes to my seven colleagues in this work, in chapter order: Stephanos Constantinides, William Mallinson, Solon Kassinis, George Georgeou, Hilal Khashan, Miguel Moratinos, and Theodoros Kyprianou. I find it difficult to use the right words of praise for these colleagues, whose seamless cooperation led to this work being completed on time and without a single hitch. I do not think that many editors can claim such good fortune.

Equally, I consider myself very lucky to have found Dr Sally Osborn to do the copyediting that improved the quality of the book immensely. Her contribution went beyond copyediting; she cared enough to make constructive comments on every matter that she thought deserved comment. I was indeed fortunate to work with a great professional. I was also lucky to have found Thomas Costi from Nicosia, Cyprus to help on page layout issues and to put the book together in the right format, ensuring that publisher requirements were met. I was always worried about this side of the project, but was fortunate enough to have heard that Thomas is in this business. Having spent a few months in the quiet and inspiring environment of the Stadtbibliothek Winterthur, Switzerland working on this book, I feel I also owe a word of thanks to this welcoming library for keeping its doors open not only to me, but to any scholar who wishes to use its facilities. My wife Sophie took the brunt of my ceaseless reference to what my colleagues and I were doing; she listened patiently and acted as a valuable sounding board. As a person greatly interested in spirituality and the after-life, I suspect that she must have found some parts of our discussion boring – certainly the discussion on the economics of the region!

With no hesitation I take full responsibility for any mistakes or omissions in the editorial work of this book.

PREFACE

The history of the Eastern Mediterranean in the last 100 or so years reminds one of British and French colonialism and the continued attempts by outside powers to exploit the resources of a region by exploiting its internal squabbles. The many conflicts in the Eastern Mediterranean have marked its history and continue to influence perceptions and attitudes to this day. In the last century the region has faced disturbing and unsettling events including conflict between Arabs and Israelis; continued Turkish occupation of 37 percent of Cyprus's territory; bullying of weak countries by their stronger neighbors; religious fundamentalism and violence; big-power games and proxy wars; brutality, coups, and counter-coups; and failed and ungovernable states. On the shinier side, and going a long way back in history, the Eastern Mediterranean reminds one that three of the world's major religions were founded in the Middle East; that the region has made immense contributions to civilization, the arts, the sciences, philosophy, and theology; that a hugely disproportionate percentage of the world's antiquities are to be found in this part of the world, led by Egypt and Greece; and that as well as its magnificent ancient history, the region is blessed with easy-going people, sandy beaches, warm weather, and a leisurely way of life. It is a region of contradictions.

The Eastern Mediterranean is gradually beginning to make a name for itself as a possibly significant oil and gas player. The potential energy finds in the region offer optimism, but that potential hangs to a large extent on the willingness of these countries to work together cooperatively. If all goes well, the region will at last free itself from big-power games and exploitation at economic, political, and military levels. Yet, its countries need first to assess the situation realistically and resolve to work together democratically to solve within the rule of law two burning issues: the Palestinian problem and the occupation of Cyprus.

Conflict and cooperation

The management of this new-found energy wealth is fraught with problems: inter-country rivalries, outsiders looking for opportunities to lay their hands on the region's wealth, and big-power rivalries being just a few. The bullying of the weak by the strong has already started, threatening the peaceful exploration and commercial utilization of the energy finds. Proxies are now being summoned to play their usual role of promoting the interests of outsiders. Predictably, the region is now seeing the presence of foreign warships – US, Russian, and British – there as a show of force but ready to arm twist as necessary. Time will tell where such developments will lead the region. Tensions are already manifesting themselves, with a powerful Turkey bullying a weak Cyprus in an attempt to muscle its way in to Cyprus's exclusive economic zone (EEZ) in violation of the Law of the Sea. The deafening silence of Cyprus's former colonial power, Britain, and its successor, the United States, lends encouragement to the aggressor and casts doubts over the prospects for true cooperation on a democratic platform.

Encouragingly, however, some of the countries in the region are beginning to work together for their common benefit. It is heartening to see Greece and Cyprus working amiably with Egypt and Israel on joint energy projects. Lebanon is expected soon to join the league of cooperating countries in the energy field, as might Jordan.

Cooperation and energy benefits

This book brings together the work of eight contributors who are deeply concerned about the future of the Eastern Mediterranean. They believe that the region finds itself at a fork in the road and needs to decide whether to cooperate in exploiting its energy resources for mutual benefit, or work alone or in small groups, raising the possibility of conflict and making the region dependent on bigger powers that will exploit that conflict for their own advantage. The difference in benefits between the two options could be massive.

Under the first option, the economics of the region stand to be catapulted to new heights, people's living standards immensely enhanced, and defense budgets slashed. Under the second option, most if not all countries in the region will end up in some form of disagreement with their neighbors, while their economies will suffer or continue to work greatly below potential, with defense budgets much above what is reasonable. The contributors to this book strongly recommend the adoption of the first option, while appreciating the great difficulties of getting all countries in the region to work together and to fully respect international law. Foremost is the creation of a High Energy Authority (HEA), just as Germany and France did in 1951, which in the end proved to be a great blessing for both (and others that joined the successor institution, the European Union).

The option of cooperation is a rational approach considering the many problems of the region, economic and otherwise, which hopefully can be remedied through collaboration. Some of these problems are as follows:

- All the countries are under varying threats of destabilization, particularly Egypt, Greece, Cyprus, Lebanon, and Jordan. Israel is continuously in an emergency situation and worried about its future and Turkey is threatened internally. Egypt is experiencing internal problems, particularly in the Sinai, many of which are instigated from abroad. Syria is an inferno and Lebanon has problems caused by its divisive and undemocratic constitution.
- Nearly all countries in the region have open conflicts of some sort and scale. Cyprus is in open conflict with Turkey, which is occupying 37 percent of its territory. Greece is in conflict with Turkey over Cyprus and the Aegean. Israel and the Arab countries are in a festering conflict over the Palestinian issue.
- Some of the countries are suffering economically and are in financial crisis: Cyprus is experiencing serious economic problems, as are Greece and Egypt. Turkey will probably follow the same route soon according to some predictions. Investor confidence is at an all-time low in some countries, business trust is generally low, and bad management is in evidence in many places. particularly in the public sector.
- Although all countries in the region view its energy reserves as crucial to their economic growth, they have failed to take the great leap toward cooperation. In fact, some are in open disputes with their neighbors over resources.
- Everyone in the region lives under conditions of uncertainty. Turkey does not know what will happen with the Kurds, who are now approaching 20 million by some estimates and will soon become the largest ethnic group given their high birth rate. Cypriots do not know what Turkey will do next to undermine the Republic of Cyprus and its government. In Lebanon no one is sure what the next day will bring, and Syria is a shambles. With continued uncertainty, people inevitably continue to pay a daily psychological tax.
- To varying extents, all the countries in the region are dictated to by the big powers, particularly the United States. The colonial demands of the past and those of today's colonial successor prevent them from formulating independent foreign policies.

- All countries in the region need security, which all depend on outsiders to provide. Turkey gets its security from the United States as a NATO member and America's policeman in the region. Israel also gets its security from America on account of the special relationship between the two countries. In exchange, both Turkey and Israel benefit hugely from economic and military assistance. The other countries in the region are continuously on the lookout for protection, but often with frustrating results.

All the countries in the Eastern Mediterranean feel insecure, which explains why they are so keen on alliances. Instead of looking to outsiders to protect them from their neighbors, they now have the option of closing ranks to free themselves from outside control. Improved security means reduced defense budgets, making money available for other, more beneficial causes. Strong economies are more likely than weak ones to bring about political stability. Thus all the countries in the region realize that energy monetization is critical to their economic future.

Inter-relatedness

This book is divided into nine chapters, each of which deals with one or more of the inter-related issues facing the Eastern Mediterranean:

- In Chapter 1, Stephanos Constantinides provides an in-depth analysis of the political dynamics of the Eastern Mediterranean and Middle East regions and examines the key political issues that affect each country. He also discusses the role in the region of the European Union, the United States, Russia, Iran, and China.
- In Chapter 2, William Mallinson examines the case of Greece and Cyprus and talks about their qualified independence, which does not allow them to chart their own sovereign foreign policy. Their situation forms a good paradigm for the region, given that hardly any country in the area is allowed a free hand in foreign policy. All are therefore keen to gain more independence via the region's potential energy wealth.
- In Chapter 3, Solon Kassinis covers energy and energy reserves in Cyprus and the region as a whole, and provides an in-depth but non-technical analysis of hydrocarbons and their exploration. This chapter shows vividly the immense benefits that the region could reap if its countries started working together within the rule of law.

- In Chapter 4, George Georgiou considers energy and the interdependence of countries using the paradigm of a partnership between Cyprus and Israel. He shows lucidly what happens when nations fail to cooperate and refuse to join forces. Failure to find peace in the region through cooperation unquestionably leads to countries trying to conclude mini-alliances to defend themselves against the dangers from neighboring countries.
- In Chapter 5, Aris Petasis traces the economic performance of each country as measured by various indices. He concludes that the countries in the region are not competitive (with the exception perhaps of Israel) and that much work needs to be done to bring their economies up to par. The best way forward would be to use income from energy to help in their reorganization and competitive improvement.
- In Chapter 6, Hilal Khashan puts energy into the historical context of the region and the enmities that past conflicts have created. He asks whether these countries are now ready to cooperate for the common good, and concludes that much work needs to be done to prepare them and put them on the path to cooperation. A period of lasting peace would have to start before the countries can begin to trust each other.
- In Chapter 7, Miguel Moratinos originates the idea of an HEA for the region that would get all countries working together for the common good. He introduces a note of optimism, in that he believes an HEA would liberate these nations from external dominance and avoid them squandering their wealth and impoverishing their citizens through conflict.
- In Chapter 8, Aris Petasis and Theodoros Kyprianou explain the concepts of holism and inter-relatedness and how they can be transferred from a theoretical level to a practical one to help the Eastern Mediterranean regain its luster. This chapter makes good use of one author's background in medicine and the other's in organizational development and strategy. The two put forward the position that a whole (the proposed HEA) made up of parts (countries in the region) can work efficiently if the same principles that govern the workings of the human body and/or manmade social systems (e.g., economies and business enterprises) are applied, maximizing efficiency through synergy and profiting from change by obeying the rule of dynamic homeostasis. The chapter offers an interesting and perhaps unique approach to cooperation between countries using holism and its underlying principles.

- In Chapter 9, Aris Petasis integrates the essence of all the chapters in the book and consolidates discussion of the issues that the countries in the region need to contend with in their attempt to work cooperatively through an HEA. He concludes that they stand to reap great benefits if they work together and in harmony, rather than operating alone in pursuit of their national interest. The chapter stresses that true cooperation rests on trust, which requires honesty and integrity at the highest level from cooperating countries.

The "if 'A' then 'B'" dictum that is inherent in holism explains why no action can be divorced from its consequences. Every single action (or decision) by one country will inevitably lead to consequences for its neighbors. It therefore behooves countries in the region to take decisions on energy jointly and in consultation, to avoid negative impacts as much as possible and to enhance positive outcomes for all. The HEA forms an ideal platform for joint decision making.

Challenges

This book brings to the fore the multiple challenges that the countries of the Eastern Mediterranean face and sheds light on the many problems that stand in the way of their full cooperation. Nevertheless, a serious attempt at inter-country cooperation needs to be made. The benefits to the region in terms of enhanced peace and the advancement of people's living standards should outweigh any concerns over national interests.

CHAPTER ONE

GEOPOLITICAL POKER IN THE EASTERN MEDITERRANEAN

STEPHANOS CONSTANTINIDES

The geopolitical balance in the Eastern Mediterranean (EM) is precarious, not least because of the new conflicts that the recent energy finds have brought to the region. Equally, the problems in Cyprus and Palestine continue to be major obstacles on the path to peace and cooperation between countries in the area. Not surprisingly, we now see Cyprus, Israel, Greece, Egypt, and Turkey engaging in uneasy diplomacy and posturing for position. In the meantime, the geopolitical developments in the Middle East and Eastern Europe, particularly the Ukrainian crisis, continue to affect the balance of power in the EM. Clearly, a new geopolitical and geoeconomic environment is beginning to form in the southeastern Mediterranean region.

The failure of the Arab Spring, the worsening situation in Palestine, instability in Iraq and Syria, and the appearance of the so-called ISIL, the jihadist group Islamic State of Iraq and the Levant, constitute the background to unfolding developments. In the meantime, Turkey, which has illegally occupied the northern part of Cyprus since 1974, now threatens the sovereignty of the Republic of Cyprus (RoC) and its hydrocarbon resources. In the complex EM strategic area, Turkey continues with new-found vigor its neo-Ottoman, aggressive, and expansionist foreign policy, adding to an already complex and combustive situation in the EM (Constantinides 1996, 2002). On the positive side, the area is now seeing a thaw in relations between the West and Iran.

A complex game of geopolitical poker is now in progress in the EM with the United States (US) and Russia as the main actors and Turkey as a menacing proxy player. While Ankara's foreign policy is putting Turkey on a path of diplomatic isolation, Turkish President Tayyip Erdoğan continues to look for reasons to assert Turkish power, with Cyprus falling as the country's first victim and Greece its second. Syria is no less a victim, as is Iraq though to a lesser degree maybe. Erdoğan is attempting to monetize Turkey's half-hearted (and often dubious) participation in the war against the jihadists by pressing for concessions on Cyprus in the belief that Washington will side with Turkey here, as it has done for the last 60 years. Luckily for Cyprus, several promising diplomatic possibilities at local and global levels are beginning to unfold, and these may prove fortuitous for the future of the island.

The regional geopolitical game

The year 2014 and the first half of 2015 have seen more than their fair share of extraordinary events. The often turbulent Middle East continues to receive increased attention, largely on account of the advent of ISIL, which replaced with astonishing speed the top jihadist organization al-Qaeda. Local tensions very quickly turned into international and in this way added to the already tense Syrian theater, which continues to attract much attention from foreign powers, most of which have failed to date to map out an effective strategy on the country.

Current conflicts are questioning the Sykes–Picot agreement of May 16, 1916, which in effect divided the Arab provinces (outside the Arabian Peninsula) that were under Ottoman Empire rule and put them under the effective control of the British and the French; in practice creating the borders we know today. Unfolding developments and conflicts make the breakdown of current boundaries in the region inevitable. Indeed, the Syrian conflict (and the displaced millions that it created), the Kurdish involvement in the war against ISIL, and the shifting alliances that are orchestrated largely by the powers of the Gulf, Iran, and Turkey make the fragmentation of current borders a strong probability. Iraq, Syria, and Libya could be the first to break up. The Kurds of Iraq, who have enjoyed a degree of autonomy for many years, ISIL and its supporters, as well as other factions that are close to Iran seem not to want a repeat of what was for some years an Iraqi secular autocracy under Saddam Hussein. The conflict that the Western powers with the help of local supporters started with the aim of countering and containing ISIL contrasts sharply with the inaction of the international community over the Syrian crisis, which has now morphed into a vicious civil war, proxies and all. Syria is fighting to keep its current borders intact, but it seems that the sectarian divide will ultimately determine the final outcome.

Turkey became embroiled in a complex game in Syria by first supporting ISIL, then later half-heartedly joining the coalition against it, while simultaneously fighting against the emergence of a Kurdish state on its doorstep. Although Turkey is preventing the flow of men and materiel into the Syrian Kurdish town of Kobani, it turns a blind eye to the transit of jihadists and oil to ISIL. Some accuse Turkey of outright support for the jihadists. Turkey is clearly playing a very dangerous game that has strong religious undertones and goes against Kemal Atatürk's secularism.

Cyprus risks becoming a sacrificial lamb on the altar of Western military and economic interests in the region, which Turkey supports. The US and Britain continue to favor a solution to the Cyprus problem that would be in the mold of the already rejected Annan Plan of 2004, which would have turned Cyprus into a Turkish protectorate. The Anglo-Americans and NATO (North Atlantic Treaty Organization) favor Cyprus becoming a Turkish dependency because, in their minds, that would safeguard Western interests in the region. This, of course, would in the end prove to be a calamitous miscalculation by the Anglo-Americans, adding one more bad decision to a long list of disastrous misjudgments.

A future Palestinian state might be created in the not too distant future, although this is by no means certain. Debates on the possibility of a two-state solution have been going on for many years, but no concrete steps have been taken to address the many unresolved issues, some of which date back to World War II. Some commentators argue that the creation of confessional states in the Middle East and beyond would facilitate the resolution of the many conflicts. Others argue that such a resolution could come about through more mundane change agents such as the energy resources that seem to abound in the region.

Populous Egypt is now governed by the military after a short experiment with free elections, for the first time in the country's modern history, which brought to power the Muslim Brotherhood. While Egypt and Tunisia took the same route to political change that put an end to the Ben Ali and Mubarak regimes, the two countries now follow different approaches to government, with both experiencing sporadic violence from the (politically) disaffected. Tunisia opted for a consensual constitution (which for now at least brought some semblance of peace despite the eruption of violence), while Egypt went for military government and firmness.

For fear of a dominant Iran, the Gulf monarchies opted for protection from the US and Western powers. The Gulf states chose to protect themselves against a very powerful and often meddling neighbor, but got stuck in a local cold war that one day might make them pay a heavy price considering the steady struggle between Sunni and Shiite powers in the EM and beyond. The regional power game in the Gulf is played with a prominent American presence, and with Russia making a gradual return to the area after an absence of a few years on account of the collapse of the Soviet Union. Russia is now actively fighting the extremists in Syria.

In this chapter an attempt is made to identify the major geopolitical issues in the region, assessing in parallel the economic impact that energy finds might have. Clearly, in the EM a new balance of power is emerging, in which two developments stand out: the European Union's (EU) policy of diversification of energy supplies to reduce reliance on Russian gas; and the threat posed by expanding Islamic extremism in the Mediterranean.

Turkey is at the center of matters because its geostrategic position is vital to the security of the EM and the Middle East. However, Turkey is at risk of isolation as the country is gradually seen as an unstable, cunning, and undependable Western ally. Inevitably other actors are also having a decisive influence on the evolution of a region in turmoil. The Middle East occupies a central position in the current international system because of its many conflicts, the global energy resource situation, and its unique geopolitical and geostrategic position, taking into account that the region straddles the continents of Europe, Asia, and Africa. Meanwhile, the Sunni–Shia clash is becoming an overarching narrative for the area. The current highly militarized rivalry between Iran and Saudi Arabia is likely to continue to escalate in the absence of any effort to reach a regional security arrangement. The US–Iran rapprochement that is now in progress is likely to create a new dynamic and will most likely add to the complexity of an already tense region.

Although the US remains the dominant external player in the region, it now finds itself caught between Iran (and Iran's possible new strategic ally, Iraq) and its traditional allies, particularly Saudi Arabia and Israel. However, the Sunni–Shia clash cannot explain all that is happening now. In Egypt, for example, the regime of the Sunni Muslim Brotherhood was toppled by other Sunni forces, the Egyptian military, with Saudi Arabian financial support. In Gaza, the Sunnis of Hamas clashed with the Sunnis of ISIL. Equally, al-Qaeda is at odds with ISIL.

It seems that the region is now facing a tripartite divide that will almost certainly emerge as Iranians, Turks, and Arabs all seek to revive their past (glorious) identities. Iranians will increasingly turn to Persianism, Turks to Ottomanism, and Arabs to intemperate Islamism. This divide will far surpass the existing Sunni–Shia split or the gap that currently divides extremist and moderate Muslims. A resolute Jewish state in the midst of these three forces and continued imperial rivalry among foreign powers will add to the unpredictability of what might finally happen in the region.

International players

Taking into account the importance of the region, the trained observer can now see a mix of players vying for position openly and/or surreptitiously. As might be expected, local players are trying to determine which way the tide might turn and are acting accordingly. Importantly (and ominously perhaps), the region is seeing major world powers making their presence felt with the intention of furthering their own interests and in the process adding to the risk of a fallout from big power antagonisms.

Turkey

From the day Islamists assumed power in Turkey in 2002 through the Justice and Development Party (AKP), Ankara started gradually to adopt a neo-Ottoman foreign policy. This moved Turkey steadily away from Kemalism and toward Islamism, while being reminiscent of the Ottoman Empire. Turkey's internal political landscape has also undergone radical change during this period. Islamists now hold all the levers of the state and are transforming the structures of society in the direction of Islamism. Even the army, which once controlled the political process, has been sidelined through a series of purges and trials of hundreds of military officers (retired and active), including dozens of generals. Thus, the world is now witnessing the end of an era that lasted for a nearly a century and the ushering in of a new Islamist–Ottoman age. Obviously, the revised political landscape is having a strong influence on Ankara's foreign policy.

Although there are elements of continuity in Turkish foreign policy, for the first time Turkey openly acclaims its Ottoman imperial past and aspires to become the world's Muslim leader. Not long ago, Turkish Prime Minister Ahmet Davutoğlu inaugurated Turkey's policy of "zero problems" with neighbors, but ended up having issues with practically everyone in the neighborhood. Davutoğlu also proposed the doctrine of "strategic depth" in an (imaginary) Ottoman space. As quoted by the Ministry of Foreign Affairs of Turkey on its website, the Davutoğlu doctrine ostensibly promotes peace with its neighbors:

> Aware that development and progress in real terms can only be achieved in a lasting peace and stable environment, Turkey places this objective at the very center of her foreign policy vision. This approach is a natural reflection of the "Peace at Home, Peace in the World" policy laid down by Great Leader Atatürk, founder of the Republic of Turkey. Besides, it is a natural consequence of a contemporary responsibility and a humanistic

foreign policy vision. (http://www.mfa.gov.tr/policy-of-zero-problems-with-our-neighbors.en.mfa)

The policy of "zero problems" is not novel; Mustafa Kemal had in the past adopted the motto "peace in the country, peace in the world." The difference between current and old versions of the same policy is that the newer version stresses neo-Ottomanism, which captures the Islamist vision of Turkey, whereas the old Kemal version deemphasized the influence of the Ottoman Empire. Kemal wanted to move Turkey toward Europe, while the Islamists want to bring back the boundaries of the Ottoman Empire of old.

As part of this neo-Ottoman policy, Ankara resumed ties with the Middle East, after half a century of isolation. Economic and trade exchanges with Arab states as well as with Iran increased, visa restrictions with its neighbors were lifted, and at one time Turkey even assumed the role of mediator in some of the most difficult conflicts in the region. Ankara negotiated the resumption of indirect talks between Syria and Israel, and between Pakistan and Afghanistan, and even encouraged dialogue between Palestinian political parties Fatah and Hamas. Moreover, Turkey offered its good offices to mediate between the West and Iran over the Iranian nuclear issue. This aimed at allowing Turkey to be at the heart of the negotiation process and to enable it to improve its position in the power equation with Tehran, considering that distrust between the two countries continues to create suspicion and enmity. Ankara is opposed to Iran's nuclear ambitions on the grounds that they would give Tehran military superiority in the region.

Turkey's neo-Ottoman policy failed miserably, partly because the status quo in the area was upset by the changes that the Arab Spring brought with it. Worse still, in his effort to approach the Arab Muslim world, Erdoğan broke Turkey's friendly relations with Israel. The deterioration in relations began in Davos in 2009. Here Erdoğan, Turkey's Prime Minister at the time, unleashed a vitriolic attack against Shimon Peres, then Israeli president, criticizing Israeli policies in the Gaza Strip. The bonds between the two countries came to breaking point on May 31, 2010 when Israel attacked MV *Mavi Marmara*, the ship that was trying to break the Gaza blockade, killing nine Turkish activists (Black, MacAskill, and Booth 2010).

The Arab Spring shook up Turkish foreign policy, forcing Ankara to interfere in the affairs of the Arab world, provoking reactions from Arab countries that had not yet forgotten the heavy Ottoman yoke of the past. Ankara struggled hard to adapt to the new reality and to accept that the region was not willing to tolerate the imposition of neo-Ottoman policy. In

Libya, before the fall of Gaddafi, Ankara had argued that it was not the West's responsibility to intervene in the country. In Syria, it broke its strategic alliance with Assad and pressed for his overthrow by supporting the most extremist of Islamic forces. Erdoğan also ignored friendly warnings about the alarming change that was taking shape in the Syrian opposition, which saw a moderate Muslim Brotherhood being replaced by al-Qaeda and in turn by ISIL.

As regards Egypt, Turkey tried in the beginning to develop a privileged alliance with Islamist president Mohamed Morsi by putting him under Turkish protection and in the process angering both Israel and Saudi Arabia. After the overthrow of Morsi, Ankara cut its ties with Egypt and engaged in a war of words against the Gulf monarchies for their refusal to support Morsi. Turkey even accused Israel of having collaborated in the coup that removed him (Cagaptay 2013). By then, neo-Ottoman diplomacy had reached its limits and as such began to have little influence.

Meanwhile, relations with the US also deteriorated on account of Ankara's reluctance to engage vigorously in the war against the jihadists of ISIL, who formed their own state in parts of Iraq and Syria. Turkey attempted to play the Islamic card by trying to win over Sunni Islamic forces, offering them the role of a protector. Erdoğan walked away from the West feeling that he had a sufficiently strong part to play and that it would have allowed him to impose his conditions on Western countries. After all, it was with the support of the EU that Erdoğan managed to win the contest against the Turkish Kemalist military establishment. Having pocketed the victory over the military and the Kemalist bureaucracy, he then tried to cash in on Turkey's geostrategic position by negotiating its participation in the alliance against the jihadists. He also tried to take advantage of US consent over Turkish actions concerning Cyprus by laying claim to Cyprus's energy resources. Erdoğan read well America's position that Turkey could be very useful in the US fight against ISIL in Syria and Iraq. At least, this is the analysis that is presented in Nicosia, concerning Cypriots' fears of being forced by the Americans into concessions to Ankara.

Recent remarks by US secretary of state John Kerry to the effect that America needed to talk to Syrian president Bashar al-Assad as expected prompted a strong reaction from Ankara. Speaking in an interview in March 2015, Kerry carefully avoided repeating the long-held US line that Assad had lost all legitimacy and must go (Hurriyet Daily News 2015c). Kerry also angered the Turkish when he praised the reforms of Egyptian president Abdel Fattah al-Sisi, who in 2013 overthrew the elected president Mohamed Morsi of the Muslim Brotherhood. Erdoğan and

Davutoğlu denounced Sisi on every possible occasion, regardless of the fact that they are alone in doing that. Kerry's remarks coincided with a number of US-origin editorials and reports accusing Turkey of drifting away from the Western NATO military alliance as regards the latter's position on fighting ISIL and other fanatics. Turkey is also accused for its middle-of-the-road stance on the conflict in Ukraine and the NATO–Russia standoff.

There is something wrong with Turkish policy in the Middle East and the EM, a Turkish commentator noted (Yetkin 2015). Up until five or six years ago, Turkey was mediating between Israel and Syria and entering a strategic partnership with Egypt. Today, it does not have an ambassador in any of these three countries. The failure, therefore, is strategic and not tactical in nature, because the ruling AKP's foreign policy for the region – as shaped by Erdoğan and Davutoğlu – supported the formation of a Sunni triangle that would rely on three power centers – Ankara, Damascus, and Cairo – and this has failed. At the time Cairo was not under democratic rule, considering that Hosni Mubarak was in power, and Damascus was not even under Sunni rule. Assad was the symbol of a Nusayri/Alevi autocracy over a Sunni majority, even when Erdoğan was calling him "my brother" while holding joint cabinet meetings and taking family holidays together (Yetkin 2015).

Responding to Kerry, Turkish Foreign Minister Mevlüt Çavuşoğlu warned the country's powerful ally the US about the rise of a Shiite wave in Iraq, which he said "contributed to the rise of ISIL because of the pressure on Sunnis." About this warning Yetkin (2015) noted, "There might be some truth in this warning, but it also signals that the AKP Party government has no intention of revising its foreign policy, which has been alienating Turkey in the area since the start of the Arab Spring."

At the same time, the sacred union between Erdoğan's party, the AKP, and the powerful religious movement of Fethullah Gülen was shattered. Since 2002 the AKP had enjoyed the strong support of the religious community of Fethullah Gülen, an influential religious leader who was exiled to the US and persecuted by Kemalists. Gülen shared the same goals as AKP, with both sides wanting an end to Kemalist rule and the establishment of an Islamic government. Once the army and the state bureaucracy, which were both loyal to Kemalist power, were subdued, the two partners found themselves face to face over control of the government machinery. Erdoğan suspected Gülen's supporters of infiltrating the police and the judiciary. Even as the establishment succeeded in convicting many generals in the Ergenekon trial of members of an alleged criminal network, in the process muzzling the army, Gülenists were weary of Erdoğan and the autocratic direction he was taking. They spoke out against the replacement of the old security–military complex with a new authoritarian system centered on Erdoğan. On December 17, 2013, prosecutors and police officers close to Gülen led a "coup" against Erdoğan's relatives, accusing them of corruption. This was apparently Gülen's response to Erdoğan's decision to close a vast network of educational centers that constituted the economic and social fiber of the Gülen movement. At any rate, since then both sides have been in an open war. For now Erdoğan is the winner of the first round, although coming out ethically weaker. However, he has lost the support of liberal intellectuals because of charges of corruption and authoritarianism. All of this has happened at a time when internationally Ankara feels isolated and faces a series of problems, even with Sunni regimes in the region.

Relations with the US also deteriorated due to Ankara's reluctance to engage actively in the war against the ISIL jihadists (Hurriyet Daily News 2015c). The Americans no longer put forward the "Turkish model" of democracy after Erdoğan's Islamic regime's repression of its opponents, particularly journalists and the Gezi Park protesters. Major US newspapers provided evidence of Turkish repression, causing consternation among Ankara's friends in Washington, who now struggle to defend the Turkish "point of view" (Taspinar 2014). Diplomatic cables released by WikiLeaks reveal that US diplomats were skeptical about the reliability of Turkey as a partner. Ankara's leaders are portrayed in these cables as divided and infiltrated by Islamists. Americans are also worried about the neo-Ottoman ambitions of Islamists. For some time now President Obama himself has avoided direct contact with Erdoğan; vice president Joe Biden was recently charged with the mission of maintaining contact with Turkey. One strong external sign of the deterioration of US–Turkish relations is the fact that the US sent only a low-level delegation to represent America at Erdoğan's inauguration ceremony as president. The fact that Turkey has now half-heartedly allowed the stationing in eastern Turkey of American military aircraft to attack and strafe fundamentalist positions in Syria and Iraq has not changed the overall picture.

Neither America nor Turkey wishes to push the relationship to breaking point. Washington needs Turkey to carry out the war against ISIL and more generally to support American efforts to achieve stability in the region. From its side Ankara knows that it cannot hope to achieve its ambitions of becoming a regional power without the direct or tacit support of the Americans. Turkish foreign policy always oscillates between partnership with the West, which needs Turkey as a NATO member, founding member of the Council of Europe, candidate for the EU, and

major business partner of many EU member states; and with the Middle
East, in which Turkey features first and foremost as Muslim and also as
bearer of the Ottoman heritage.

A leading American analyst and president of the Council on Foreign
Relations (CFR), Richard Haas, set the record straight when he declared:

> We are still allies [with Turkey] technically and legally, but strategically
> we are not on the same page. We've got real differences in how we assess
> the situation and what should be done.

Going further, he added, "Kurds today are the primary US partner in Iraq
and Syria" (Özer 2014). Little did Haas suspect at the time that the US
would stay on the sidelines as Turkey initiated its violent suppression of
the Kurdish people in Turkey, Syria, and Iraq.

The latest developments in the Arab world are also disturbing for
Turkey. A Turkish journalist noted:

> The perception of Turkey among Arab nations has taken a dramatic turn
> for the worse because of the harsh diatribes and meddlesome shortsighted
> policies adopted by Turkish leaders. This in turn has started to take a toll
> on political relations, with adverse impact on the Turkish economy and a
> decision by the 22-member Arab League to revisit its ties with Turkey ...
> to the detriment of Turkey's national interests, Erdoğan and his allies in the
> government, including Prime Minister Ahmet Davutoğlu, succeeded in
> turning both Saudi Arabia and Egypt, two powerhouses in the Arab
> League, into a united enemy that is determined to thwart Turkish overtures
> not only in the Arab and Muslim world but also in global politics. The last
> casualty of this sad picture is the decisive defeat Turkey experienced in the
> race to secure a seat on the United Nations Security Council as a non-
> permanent member, in which it managed to secure only 60 votes, as
> opposed to 150 five years ago. (Bozkurt 2014)

Obviously, Erdoğan's arrogance cannot hide Turkey's weaknesses in the
current geopolitical context of the Middle East. The three biggest issues
facing Turkey today are the Kurds, Syria, and the economy. The Kurdish
problem is now more complicated than before because of the strategic
importance that Westerners ascribe to the Kurdish factor in the stability of
the region. In fact, Kurds in Iraq and Syria have become the centerpiece in
the fight against Islamist extremism. Turkey does not take kindly to this
development, fearing that the creation of a more autonomous Kurdish
region in Syria and Iraq would awaken separatist or autonomist tendencies
in Turkish Kurds. Turkey is worried that the issue of Kurdish
independence may find its way into the peace process that began two years

ago between the Turkish government and the Kurdish leader Abdullah Öcalan to resolve the issue of Kurdish rights in Turkey. This process ultimately collapsed and went nowhere (Akgönül 2014). Turkey has been negotiating with the Kurds for over five years with little progress. For the first time since the beginning of the "Eastern Question," the Kurds in the region and more so those of Iraq and Syria can now hope for an independent Kurdish state, even if their hopes were dashed recently. Understandably, Turkey hates to see the strengthening of Kurdish armed elements on its borders.

As regards Syria, Ankara's major objective of overthrowing Assad has not been achieved on account of the strong support that Syria receives from Russia and Iran, but also because neither the Americans nor the Israelis wish to see Assad leave because of the Islamist threat to the region.

Erdoğan paid a visit to Tehran soon after Iran and the West reached agreement, on April 2, 2015, over Iran's nuclear program. Not long ago, and in a bizarre twist, Erdoğan blamed Iran for the destabilization of the Middle East and sided fully with the Sunni anti-Iran coalition in Yemen. He even declared that Turkey stood ready to provide logistical military support to the coalition.

In a sense, Erdoğan's visit to Tehran was a desperate effort to lead his country out of isolation. However, it was also a question of economic interests, considering the importance of trade between the two countries. As Turkey was in fact excluded from the coalition of war against Yemen's Houthi rebels, Erdogan turned to Tehran (İdiz 2015). Turkey was not invited to contribute soldiers to the Saudi operation, as this was considered an inter-Arab issue that needed to stay within the "family." However, this does not explain why Pakistan was invited to take part in the coalition but not Turkey. The reason was that (even if the Turks are reluctant to admit it) the Ottoman legacy and its negatives are still fresh in the memory of the Arab people (İdiz 2015).

In the emerging regional order, Erdoğan and Davutoğlu are clearly trying to carve out a new niche for Turkey in the Middle East to enable it to regain some of its lost influence in the region. Yet, as positions keep changing, Erdoğan's grand vision of Turkey leading the Middle East is becoming a pipedream. This frustrating truth is causing Turkey to become more aggressive over weak and defenseless Cyprus.

Although it has been glorified for some time, Turkey's emerging economy (as defined by the International Monetary Fund) is not going as well as first thought and is now more vulnerable than ever, leading some analysts to believe that its decline is only a matter of time. A leading US think tank warns that authoritarianism threatens the growth of the Turkish economy; a statement by the Bipartisan Policy Center warns of Turkey's "shaky economy" and that "rising authoritarianism, restrictions on journalists and the media, and rising claims of institutional corruption all threaten the economic balance" (BGN News 2015; Deliveli 2015).

Professor Kemal Kirişci, who now works at Brookings Institution as a TUSIAD senior fellow, introduced the concept of a "trading state" to explain one of the factors that transformed Turkey's foreign policy in the 2000s from one that depended on "regional coercive power" to one relying on "benign" if not "soft power." Kirişci substantiated his thesis by providing key statistics about Turkey's foreign trade. In 1975 overall trade accounted for 9 percent of GDP. In 1995 it reached 23 percent. By 2005, trade made up 39 percent of GDP, and by 2007 42 percent of GDP. This, according to Kirişci, explains the degree to which Turkey was integrating into the world economy.

The AKP came to power a few months after the term BRICS (Brazil, Russia, India, China, and South Africa) was coined and became the symbol of the apparent shift in global economic power away from the developed G7 economies and toward the developing economies. As the Western world started suffering the effects of the financial crisis, the "West and the Rest" equation began to tilt, making the latter a more attractive proposition for investors and business (Yinanç 2015).

The AKP government's declared policy of zero problems with neighbors and the lifting of visa requirements as per its plan contributed to another transformation of Turkey's trading practices. Turkey diversified its trading partner list, with Europe's share falling and that of the Middle East and other regions steadily rising. However, in 2010 the tide began to turn against trade with the Middle East. Kirişci summarized the external dimension of the change as "the gradual return of the West and the decline of the Rest." He also talked about the rise of chaos in Turkey's neighborhood and the consequential loss of markets. Looking at the statistics, one can see clearly the drop in Turkey's trade with the Middle East (Yinanç 2015).

The deterioration of relations with its neighbors turned out to be very costly for Turkey, because it negatively affected its trade relations with Israel, Syria, Egypt, and beyond. The government is still in a mood of denial over its own mistakes on these issues and prefers to blame "the interest rate lobby" or the "Gülen movement." However, instead of chasing ghosts, Turkey would do better to start thinking hard of ways to emerge from its costly loneliness. As one way out, Kirişci suggests that Turkey ought to reemphasize its ties with its traditional Transatlantic

Community partners. He makes this simple point: as instability in Turkey's neighborhood continues to erode its export markets and capital inflow position, it needs to turn its focus to Transatlantic Community business. In this respect, and despite the standstill in its drive for accession to the EU, Turkey ought to keep the EU as an anchor for its business. In Kirişci's view, Turkey should therefore revive its reform agenda to enable continuation of the accession process, while not neglecting to upgrade its customs union ties with the EU (Yinanç 2015).

Another area that needs Turkey's urgent attention is the Transatlantic Trade and Investment Partnership (TTIP) that is now being negotiated between the EU and the US. While Turkey's exclusion from the TTIP is likely to be extremely costly, its inclusion would prove highly difficult. Turkey, the US, and the EU need to find a win–win solution on this important issue. Turkey therefore needs to stop criticizing the West at every turn and start behaving as an ally rather than a foe (Yinanç 2015). The Turkish lira hit historic lows against the dollar in 2015, leading Erdoğan to issue diatribes, for instance saying in February that the Central Bank's monetary policy was "unsuited to the realities of the Turkish economy" after it failed to meet his demand for interest rate cuts. He queried whether the bank was under external influence (Hurriyet Daily News 2015a, b; Today's Zaman 2015c).

Turkey's unemployment rate as at December 2014 stood at 10.9 percent, a four-year high, and above November's rate of 10.7 percent, according to figures released by the Turkish Statistics Institute (TurkStat). Opposition Republican People's Party deputy Hurşit Güneş said in a written statement that Turkey's economy was the most troubled among developing countries (Today's Zaman 2015d).

The current growth rate of the Turkish economy is around 3 percent, with an inflation rate above 5 percent (7.62 percent in February 2015; Hurriyet Daily News 2015d; Today's Zaman 2015a; Inflation.eu n.d.). Turkey's economy is also facing the dangers of an escalating dollarization that will see movement away from the lira in favor of the dollar, with a general weakening of the industrial sector, negatively affecting the country's growth rate and helping escalate unemployment. Turkey makes the list of countries whose currencies are frail and vulnerable against the US dollar. Indicatively, in the period between the start of the year and March 6, 2015, the Indian rupee gained 1.5 percent in value against the dollar. The South African rand lost 4.1 percent and the Indonesian rupee lost 4.5 percent in value. In the same period, the Turkish lira lost a staggering 11.4 percent against the dollar. Several domestic and international commentators attribute the problems of the Turkish lira to

Erdoğan's pressure on the Central Bank to lower interest rates and the loss in confidence that this has triggered. Turkey now faces increased risk premia that in turn will also weaken the Turkish lira in relation to the dollar (Sönmez 2015).

The recognition of the Armenian genocide by a host of countries on its 100th anniversary further isolated Turkey. The years-long vigorous and aggressive campaign by the Armenian diaspora to get the genocide recognized by more and more countries yielded results in 2015. Pope Francis lit the fuse when he described the 1915 massacres of Armenians by the Ottoman army as genocide and in this way made the entire Catholic world aware of this carnage. The European Parliament, the Austrian Parliament, the German Bundestag, German President Joachim Gauck, and Russian President Vladimir Putin, among others, lined up to use the "G-word," at the risk of drawing Turkey's wrath.

When the AKP assumed power the Islamist Erdoğan turned to Europe in the hope that Turkey would be anchored to the EU, thus giving the country in turn the ability to claim the role of spokesperson of the Muslim world. At this early stage Islamists also needed the EU's firm support to help avoid any slippage in their struggle with the Turkish military. With European and American support, the Islamists came to dominate Turkish politics. Turkey's objective of EU membership came to nothing, however. The Europeans, and especially the Germans, are very reluctant to accept Turkey in the Union, fearing an upset in the fragile balance in Europe. The Cyprus issue has obviously been another major obstacle for Turkey in its march toward Europe. Ankara wants strategic control of the island and as such was only willing to make some frivolous and meaningless concessions, aimed to fool the EU rather than solve the problem of Cyprus. Turkey tried, but failed, to remove from the EU agenda the intractable obstacle of Cyprus. The country's neo-Ottoman policy toward Cyprus is summarized as follows by Islamist Turkish Davutoğlu:

> Cyprus cannot be ignored by any regional or world power that makes strategic calculations for the Middle East, the Eastern Mediterranean, the Aegean Sea, the Suez Canal, the Red Sea and the Persian Gulf. Cyprus is in ideal distance of all these regions and taking into account this parameter it affects them all directly. Turkey must not use the advantage gained in Cyprus in the 70s, as part of a Cypriot defensive policy aimed at preserving the status quo, but as a fundamental support for an aggressive maritime strategy, of a diplomatic character. (Davutoğlu 2001)[1]

Turkish academic Taşpinar wrote about the three main grand strategic visions in Turkey's foreign policy, namely Kemalism, neo-Ottomanism and Turkish Gaullism. Neo-Ottomanism is closely associated with the strategic vision of the late Turkish President Turgut Özal and the AKP. It seeks to restore Turkey's imperial "strategic depth" in the territories formerly occupied by the Ottoman Empire using "soft power." The main objective of neo-Ottomanism is to improve economic, cultural, political, diplomatic, and military relations with Turkey's Muslim neighbors and the Balkan countries. Neo-Ottomanism differs from Kemalism in the sense that it puts a premium on rebalancing toward the Islamic world. Since the inception of the modern Turkish Republic, Kemalist foreign policy has been obsessed with Turkey's Western identity and has neglected the Middle East and North Africa (Taşpinar 2015).

While Kemalism and neo-Ottomanism are fairly well-known policies, Turkish Gaullism is still a mystery for most analysts trying to make sense of Turkish foreign policy. The simplest way to describe it would be to point out areas of convergence between neo-Ottomanism and Kemalism. Despite the important differences between Kemalists and neo-Ottomans, both share a strong sense of attachment to Turkish nationalism. Neo-Ottomans are religious nationalists who are inspired by the Turkish–Islamic synthesis rather than by Islamism alone and are determined to reconstruct an imagined *umma* (community of Muslim believers). In that sense, one can argue that neo-Ottomanism has successfully internalized the Kemalist paradigm of Turkish nationalism (Taşpinar 2015).

Seen from the prism of rising Turkish self-confidence, thanks largely to considerable economic growth under AKP governments in the past 12 years, Turkish Gaullism represents a synthesis of Kemalism and neo-Ottomanism. A sense of Turkish nationalism, grandeur, glory, independence, national prestige, sovereignty, and self-confidence are all at its heart. Above all, Turkish Gaullism seeks respect from the West and refuses to be taken for granted as a loyal NATO ally. Another advantage of Gaullism is that it transcends the over-emphasized "secular versus Islamic" or "East or West" divide in the foreign policy analysis of Turkey in Western circles. Turkish Gaullists unite behind the pursuit of Turkish national and strategic interests in a pragmatic and realistic way without giving much premium to ideology (Taşpinar 2011, 2015). Ömer Taşpinar, director of the Turkey program at the Brookings Institution in Washington, DC, says that Turkey's role reflects not so much the country's desire to improve relations with its Muslim neighbors, but rather its wish to achieve "Turkish national pride and a sense of grandeur," and he continues, "there is a new self-confidence bordering on hubris" (Slavin 2011).

There is no doubt that the AKP's neo-Ottoman vision of leadership in the Middle East and the EM has failed. The situation in Egypt and Syria clearly showed that democratic change will not come easily to entrenched autocracies. Turkey itself is moving toward an Islamic authoritarianism that has nothing to do with Gaullism.

Indeed, the elections of June 7, 2015 reduced somewhat the power of the AKP and all but put paid to Erdoğan's dream of a strong presidential system in Turkey.

Iran

Iran is expected to play a key role in the future balance of power in the region if its rapprochement with the West finally succeeds. The comprehensive nuclear agreement with Iran of April 2, 2015 is an important step in this direction. The P5+1 Nuclear Agreement with Iran included the US, United Kingdom (UK), France, Germany, Russia, China, and the EU. A successful conclusion of negotiations would confirm Iran's new important strategic role in the region.

Shiite Iran could be a privileged ally of the West against Sunni Islamism and against ISIL, which threatens the West as well as Iraq and Syria, both privileged allies of Tehran (Ciboulet 2015). A West–Iran axis could in part downgrade the strategic importance of Turkey, as Ankara would be wedged between Shiite Iran and Sunni Egypt. Is the world, therefore, about to see a new strategic rivalry in the Middle East between Iran and Turkey? The ingredients are there and the outcome remains to be seen. What is certain is that the Americans will exploit any rivalry between Iran and Turkey, particularly if Turkey and its Islamists refuse to commit solidly to the American fold.

Iran's potential is enormous and its oil reserves rank fourth largest in the world (Photius.com n.d.). Iran boasts a relatively young and comparatively well-educated population, with a median age of 29.8 years. It also appears that despite Shiite Islamic power, Iranians are open to the world and are much more focused on some secular aspects of life than are the Sunni Islamist clerical elites in other countries of the region. It also seems that the Iranian Shiite religious interpretation is more inclusive than the alternative Sunni interpretation. It is a fact, for example, that in Sunni sharia law a Shia must die as an apostate, while in Shia Sunnis are just another form of Muslims who are wrong on a few issues. The other strategic asset in Iran's arsenal is its undisputable leadership of Shiites in the region, if not of Shiites worldwide. The Shiite axis holds considerable strategic importance and could have a decisive influence on the evolution and redrawing of the Middle Eastern map. Iran is now present in Iraq, Syria, and Lebanon and has most recently made advances into Yemen.

Significantly, Iran has considerable influence on Shiite minorities in different Gulf monarchies that recognize it as a protector and natural leader. Iran influences events even within Sunni Islam, with the Palestinians (Hamas) being a case in point. Moreover, many of those who are uncomfortable with the social conservatism of some Sunni regimes, especially that of Saudi Arabia, do not mind allying with Iran.

To overcome the foreign embargo that was imposed after the revolution, Iran developed its own military industry, producing its own tanks, armored personnel carriers, guided missiles, submarines, military vessels, guided missile destroyers, radar systems, helicopters, and fighter planes. In recent years, official announcements have highlighted the development of weapons such as the Hoot, Kowsar, Zelzal Fateh-110, Shahab-3, and Sejjil missiles, and a variety of unmanned aerial vehicles (UAVs). The Fajr-3 (MIRV) is currently Iran's most advanced ballistic missile; it is a liquid fuel missile with an undisclosed range that was developed and produced domestically (Fox News 2005; Payvand Iran News 2006; Press TV 2009; IRNA n.d.).

In the current context of the fight against the jihadists of ISIL, Iran could be a close ally of the West. The Americans are not wrong when they try to make peace with this country. It remains for the two to settle the nuclear issue and for Iran to tone down its anti-Israeli rhetoric. Many observers are convinced that sooner or later Iran will become a nuclear power. Therefore, some commentators reason, it might be better to do this under Western monitoring rather than unmonitored. Iran hopes to establish its regional hegemony as a country with a nuclear capability; just as France and India have done in the past.

Iran's anti-Israeli discourse falls more into the rhetorical realm because Iran has no real desire to destroy Israel. One has to recall that this kind of language did not prevent cooperation between Tehran and Tel Aviv in the past, although that remained secret for a long time. It is a well-known fact that during the Iran–Iraq war Israel supplied arms to Iran, especially spare parts for American equipment that was bought by the previous Iranian regime. The Americans, Iraq's allies at the time, had placed an embargo on these types of spare parts.

According to Ronen Bergman (2008, 40–48), Israel sold Iran $75 million worth of arms from stocks of Israel Military Industries, Israel Aircraft Industries, and Israel Defence Force stockpiles in Operation Seashell in 1981. The material included 150 M-40 antitank guns with 24,000 shells for each gun, spare parts for tank and aircraft engines, 106 mm, 130 mm, 203 mm, and 175 mm shells, and TOW missiles. This material was transported first by air by Argentine airline Transporte Aéreo

Rioplatense and then by ship (after the 1981 Armenia mid-air collision). Arms sales to Iran totalled an estimated $500 million from 1981 to 1983, according to the Jafe Institute for Strategic Studies at Tel Aviv University (see also Parsi 2007; Crooke 2009).

So it was Israel, the cherished US ally in the region, that came to the rescue of Iran in its hour of need. There is enough evidence to prove that Iran does not intend to hurt its former benefactor. Once Iran's relations are normalized with the West, the common interest will prevail and Iran will start respecting international rules. Interestingly, Republican senators wrote to the Iranian leaders warning them that any agreement between the two sides will not make it through the US Congress. That the letter was signed by 47 US Senators, all from the Republican Party, is further evidence of what we already knew: namely, that there is no unified US domestic policy on Iran and that America has become increasingly polarized and dysfunctional over foreign policy.

The letter makes it clear to Iranian leaders that the deal being negotiated is only a mere "executive agreement" and that "the next president could revoke such an executive agreement at the stroke of a pen, and future congresses could modify the terms of the agreement at any time." Predictably, the White House reacted strongly, with Obama saying, "It's somewhat ironic to see some members of Congress wanting to make common cause with the hard-liners in Iran" (Jaffe and Sullivan 2015).

Even if Israeli–American relations are at their lowest point in recent history, the fact remains that American support for Israel appears to be unwavering. This provides conspiracy theorists with the opportunity to argue, perhaps absurdly, that a Jewish cabal runs American foreign policy as it has always done. The reality is that there are insurmountable differences between the US administration under Obama and the right wing of Israeli politics. At the heart of the divergence is Obama's determination to deal with Iran's nuclear ambitions in terms of American national security interests rather than those of Israel.

Although details of the emerging deal with Iran are still not clear, the deal is driving the Israeli leadership crazy because they feel that it will limit Iranian uranium enrichment, but will not totally stop or eradicate its nuclear program. In that sense, the deal does not meet Israel's maximalist position. It will bring strict limits to Iran's nuclear program for the next 10 years and establish a strict inspection regime to monitor centrifuge activities. The length of the breakout capacity period in the event of Iran deciding to achieve threshold status is less clear. The Israeli side contends that this deal only postpones the development of an Iranian bomb.

Israel

Barring minor exceptions, Israel has ranked as America's most important strategic ally in the Middle East since the state's creation. In line with this alliance, the US has been giving Israel a protective umbrella through huge financial and military aid programs. Undoubtedly, the US would come to the aid of Israel if it were in danger. Mutatis mutandis and taking account of population size, no other country ever received so much American help. Recently, however, the US elite is beginning to feel that this strategic relationship is one-sided and needs to be rebalanced to better serve the broader US interests in the region. This explains Obama's revisionist stance in recent years, which attempts to redefine American policy in the Middle East. The predominance of the right wing in the political affairs of Israel and the perceived intransigent attitudes that some hold regarding the Palestinian question encouraged Obama to revisit American policy vis-à-vis Israel.

The fact that it took two and a half days for Obama to pick up the phone and congratulate Benjamin Netanyahu on his last electoral victory is indicative of the soured relationship. This fact speaks for itself and shows that in the relationship between Israel and its financial supporter and protector, not all is well, to say the least. Some observers suspect that a further deterioration in relations between the two countries could still follow.

We "will need to reevaluate our policies after the new positions of Prime Minister [Netanyahu] and his comments regarding the two-state solution," said a White House official, speaking to Reuters on condition of anonymity. The words "new positions" refer to the pledge by Netanyahu, one day before the polls opened, that as Prime Minister he is never going to accept the creation of a Palestinian state. Quoting unnamed Israeli sources, Israeli TV stations said that the US president made it clear that he did not believe Netanyahu was genuinely supportive of a two-state solution to the Palestinian conflict, and he indicated that the US would no longer automatically support Israel at the United Nations (Times of Israel 2015).

In a fresh rebuke of Netanyahu, Obama said that the Israeli leader's pre-election disavowal of a two-state solution to the Israeli–Palestinian conflict makes it "hard to find a path" toward serious negotiations to resolve the issue (Dunham 2015). In an interview with the *Huffington Post*, Obama scolded Netanyahu over his remarks on the Israeli Arab vote, making it clear that the deep rift in relations between Israel and the United States will not be ending any time soon. He also expressed dismay over

Netanyahu's election-day warning to his supporters about Arab Israeli voters going to the polls "in droves," saying:

> We indicated that that kind of rhetoric was contrary to what is the best of Israel's traditions, that although Israel was founded based on the historic Jewish homeland and the need to have a Jewish homeland, Israeli democracy has been premised on everybody in the country being treated equally and fairly. (Stein 2015)

The most recent episode in US–Israeli relations came with the disclosure of spying by Israel on talks on Iran. As the *Wall Street Journal* revealed

> soon after the U.S. and other major powers entered negotiations last year to curtail Iran's nuclear program, senior White House officials learned Israel was spying on the closed-door talks. The spying operation was part of a broader campaign by Israeli Prime Minister Benjamin Netanyahu's government to penetrate the negotiations and then help build a case against the emerging terms of the deal, current and former U.S. officials said. In addition to eavesdropping, Israel acquired information from confidential U.S. briefings, informants and diplomatic contacts in Europe, the officials said. (Entous 2015)

This act of espionage did not upset the White House as much as Israel's sharing of inside information with US lawmakers and others to drain support from a high-stakes deal intended to limit Iran's nuclear program. A senior US official briefed on the matter said:

> It is one thing for the U.S. and Israel to spy on each other. It is another thing for Israel to steal U.S. secrets and play them back to U.S. legislators to undermine U.S. diplomacy. (Borger, Zonszein, and Siddiqui 2015)

In Israel, former officials of the army and security services fear that this quarrel may undermine the country's central strategic role in US policy in the region. It is clear that the failure to resolve the Israeli–Palestinian conflict, particularly after Israel's capture of Jerusalem in June 1967, helped the expansion of Sunni and Shiite Islamist extremism. The situation was exacerbated after the failure of Arab nationalism and the emergence of authoritarian Arab regimes in the region. These developments weakened the secular leadership of the Palestinians in favour of the Islamists of Hamas.

The current strategy of the US administration is to fight (as a matter of priority) ISIL in Iraq and Syria. In this regard, the Americans acknowledge that Iran makes a significant military contribution to the Iraqi army, which seeks to reclaim the Sunni population areas north of Baghdad with the support of additional US military instructors. Since the end of the Cold War, America has relied on four major countries to stabilize the Middle East: Turkey, Israel, Saudi Arabia, and Iran. America is well aware that Iran's influence runs through an axis from Iraq and Syria to Lebanon and also northern Yemen and Bahrain. Hence the American desire to see a deal signed that would ensure that Iran conforms to the Non-Proliferation Agreements signed in Tehran. Clearly, America wishes to have Iran on its side. Israel is concerned about the rise of Iran in its immediate vicinity and sees this as a priority danger. Netanyahu had opposed the US government during the tenure of Bill Clinton at the time of the Israeli–Palestinian negotiations in the 1990s. Now he opposes the Obama administration even more stridently.

On the other side of the debate, the opposition, led by the Zionist Union, which includes the Labour Party led by Yitzhak Herzog and the Hatnua party led by former Prime Minister Tzipi Livni, considers it a priority to maintain relations with the US, Israel's strategic ally. In fact, Israel is divided in two on this issue. The old guard of immigrants who came from Europe and built an Israel driven by socialist ideals is now weak. The right wing prevails in alliance with religious parties. The former gives priority to the alliance with the US, the latter opposes the American policy that seeks a solution to the Palestinian problem on the basis of two states. With the rise of Iran and the Sunni fundamentalist ISIL, Israel now fears becoming strategically irrelevant as regards US policy in the Middle East. Israeli politicians and many in the military and security services are trying hard to put Israel at the center of US interests in the region and in this way ensure its viability. For the moment, Israel does not seem to have a personality with sufficient stature and authority to bring the country out this dangerous impasse (Aggiouri 2015).

Egypt

Egypt is at the center of political developments in the EM and the Greater Middle East. As the largest Arab country, Egypt has always played a leading role in the Arab world. It is also an indisputable leader of the Sunni world and has served as an antipode to Turkey. Unlike the Turkish Sunnis, the Egyptian Sunnis are Arabs and form part of the larger Arab world. Egypt is of great geostrategic importance in the region and the Suez Canal (now expanded) lends it much importance. Egypt remembers well the colonial struggles over the control of this most significant waterway and as such is ready to defend Suez with all its might (Friedman 2012).

Today, nevertheless, the canal does not have the same importance as it did
in 1956 when the British and French waged a humiliating war against
Egypt after Nasser nationalized the canal. Britain's disgrace at Suez
marked the end of the country's presence as a major power in the area and
the emergence of the US as its successor. The Suez Canal continues to play
a large role in navigation and provides Egypt with much-needed revenues.

Egypt has been through turmoil in the last ten years or so and
continues to experience serious economic and social problems. The
overthrow of the Muslim Brotherhood, the first democratically elected
party in power, has not improved the country's international image. The
new Egyptian leader, Abdel Fattah al-Sisi, was able in a short time after
the overthrow of the Muslim Brotherhood to build alliances and get his
country out of isolation. The Americans' haste to form an alliance with the
Muslim Brotherhood once it came to power makes them suspect in the
eyes of the Egyptian military that overthrew Morsi, even as relations
between the two countries are beginning to improve. Egypt is too
important for the US, irrespective of who runs the country. America needs
Egypt as an ally in its current struggle against Islamic extremism, but
Egypt is fittingly weary of America. Saudi Arabia did not see eye to eye
with the Muslim Brotherhood and viewed it as a powerful social
movement that could become contagious and threaten its doctrinaire
kingdom. In response to the American stance, Egypt turned to Saudi
Arabia for financing and to Russia and France for military hardware.
Russian president Vladimir Putin went to Cairo and was received with
enthusiasm. French president François Hollande was also well received in
Cairo. Paris and Moscow are keen to sell weapons to Egypt, with the
finance coming from Saudi Arabia.

Egypt, Greece, and Cyprus have had close relations for a long time.
Not surprisingly, the former Greek Prime Minister Antonis Samaras and
Nicos Anastasiades, president of Cyprus, were both warmly welcomed in
Cairo. The three countries are now ready to form a political alliance
against neo-Ottoman expansionist Turkey. The potential alliance of
Cyprus and Greece with Egypt is seen as a red flag by Ankara, whose neo-
Ottoman drive was stopped at the gates of Cairo. The Egyptian president
also improved relations with Israel, which had suffered a setback after the
rise in power of the Muslim Brotherhood. By contrast, Egypt's relations
with the Palestinians, and particularly with Hamas, deteriorated sharply
due to Hamas's rapprochement with Turkey and the suspicion that Hamas
is supporting Islamist extremists fighting against the Egyptian government
in Sinai. The close relationship between Israel and Nicosia also causes
frustration and anger in Ankara. That said, Ankara still has the military

means to continue to violate the sovereignty of Cyprus in its exclusive economic zone (EEZ). Clearly, Cyprus cannot counter Turkish aggression by diplomatic means only and is militarily weak.

Sisi convened a major economic conference, the Egypt Economic Development Conference, in Sharm El-Sheikh in March 2015, which brought billions of dollars to Egypt in aid and investment. On the final day of the conference, he commented, "Some people thought my country had died, but Egypt is a country that God created so it can forever live" (Today's Zaman 2015b). Investors committed $10.7 billion to the Egyptian project, which came a day after Gulf Arab nations had announced a $12.5 billion aid package for the country. The three-day gathering in the Sinai resort showed to the outside world that Egypt is again open for business and is ready to welcome investors after four years of instability and turmoil following the 2011 Arab Spring uprising that ousted long-time autocrat Hosni Mubarak (Shenker 2015).

Cyprus

Sitting behind the Arabian Gulf and the Suez Canal, Cyprus unsurprisingly holds a privileged position in the EM.[2] Despite its strategic importance in a region in turmoil, the country is in a weak position because of Turkey's occupation of its northern part, but also because of the collapse of its economy and its banking system that is now in tatters. Nevertheless, its rapprochement with Israel could hopefully act as a buffer to regular threats from Ankara. Cyprus's rapprochement with Israel is diplomatically complemented by traditionally friendly relations with Egypt, although the latter came under threat after the coming to power of the Muslim Brotherhood. Under pressure from Turkey, then Egyptian president Morsi initiated a process that would have repudiated the agreement that delineated the EEZ between Cyprus and Turkey. The tripartite meeting in Cairo of November 8, 2014 between Egypt, Cyprus, and Greece is considered a major diplomatic success for Cyprus. Cyprus views it as a blessing to have a large and highly influential Arab Muslim country standing by its side against Turkish expansionism.

Cyprus also cooperates with Egypt on a project that aims to transport Cypriot gas to Egyptian terminals. The Cypriot minister responsible for natural resources made an official visit to Cairo and held talks with his Egyptian counterpart, aiming to establish the modalities of this cooperation. In Cairo on February 16, 2015 they signed a protocol that opens the way for an international agreement to be concluded soon. This assumes that a pipeline will be built to transport Cypriot gas to Egypt, an alternative that flies in the face of US and Western pressure to transport Cypriot gas via Turkey. The government-owned Egyptian Natural Gas Holding Company and the National Oil Company of Cyprus signed a memorandum of cooperation on March 13, 2015. The situation might change fast, however, if the existence of massive offshore gas finds in Egypt's EEZ is confirmed.

Cyprus ought to build alliances if it is to counter the perpetual threat of Turkey. Nicosia has learned from its terrible past experiences that flimsy and unreliable alliances with the US and Britain do not protect it against Turkish aggression. Indicatively, the Americans and the British did not lift a finger to protect Cyprus against the latest aggression from Turkey when it invaded Cyprus's EEZ. In fact, both countries washed their hands of the problem and asked victim and aggressor "to refrain from acts that can worsen the situation." Even the pro-American current president of Cyprus, Anastasiades, suggested that Washington's promises regarding the security of Cypriot energy resources were hollow. In this context, he paid an official visit to Moscow in February 2015, rekindling relations with Russia (Cyprus's traditional friend) that had cooled because of his pro-American policies.

Cyprus is renewing relations with Moscow because Russia supports Cyprus consistently in the United Nations (UN) Security Council and maintains good relations with the island. During the official visit to Moscow, talks also centered on Cyprus's economy, considering Russia's investments that at one time stood at $33 billion and made up a large portion of the total investments from outside the country. Clearly, Russia is Cyprus's privileged economic partner. Russian tourism to the country keeps increasing steadily: in 2014 there were visits from more than 600,000 Russians (nearly the population of Cyprus). Russians and Cypriots agreed to examine the possibility of Russian companies participating in the exploration and exploitation of Cypriot gas resources. This constitutes a major positive development for Cyprus, considering the lukewarm position of Europe and America whenever its EEZ is threatened by Turkey.

What really caught the attention of British and American planners is the agreement between the two countries that gives Moscow the right to use a number of civilian and military facilities in Cyprus, such as ports for the resupply of Russian warships. The agreement is ostensibly designed to help the Russian fleet "participate in international efforts" to fight terrorism, the trafficking of weapons of mass destruction, and piracy. What is more, the agreement allows Russian warships to dock at the Cypriot ports of Limassol and Larnaca and in this way formalizes an understanding between the two countries that dates back many years. Russia has maintained a naval base in Tartus, Syria since 1971 and now hopes to strengthen its position in the EM through these port facilities in Cyprus.

The Cypriot government spokesman said that one of the outcomes of Anastasiades' visit to Russia was the signing of agreements that defined "the context for economic and commercial cooperation between the two countries together with the energy sector." Russia, he added, demonstrated a willingness to enhance economic and commercial cooperation through (yet unspecified) proposals. Cyprus's energy minister, who was also interviewed on Cypriot CyBC Radio, said that the two countries had held "exploratory" talks on possible cooperation in developing the energy finds in Cyprus's EEZ. He continued that they will engage in dialogue to "see where we are with our planning … because we showed that Cyprus is in a position to host the interests of Russian companies that would like to start operations in the wider Eastern Mediterranean." On the same issue, Putin said that "energy is an important part of our cooperation," adding that "prospects exist."

Anastasiades' visit to Moscow is a spanner in the works of Western countries that are currently at loggerheads with Moscow over the Ukrainian issue. Westerners were disturbed when the Cypriot government spokesman said in February 2015 that Cyprus could consider granting Russia the right to use the Andreas Papandreou military airbase in Paphos for humanitarian purposes as and when required. The spokesman went on, "If [the use of the air base] is requested for humanitarian situations, Nicosia's approach will be positive." The rumor surrounding the opening of military bases to the Russian military spread on the island the week before Anastasiades' trip to Russia and gave hope to many in Cyprus. Nicosia was sending the message in all directions that rapprochement with Moscow had started in earnest. Asked if other countries had reacted to these agreements, the Cypriot government spokesman replied dryly: "The Republic of Cyprus … decides its own business, like any other country" (Cyprus Business Mail 2015). To give comfort to America and Britain, the government reiterated that Cyprus remains well entrenched in the West.

It is common knowledge that Cyprus has failed to exploit its membership of the EU. In particular, it has not brought to bear its institutional powers inside the EU to get its partners to lean on Turkey to recognize the Republic of Cyprus and to cease threatening the island; or, most importantly, to end its occupation of the northern part. Cyprus has been under pressure from the West to be conciliatory toward Turkey and not to block its negotiations with the EU, even if Turkey continues to occupy Cypriot territory. Nicosia's European card was practically neutralized when Turkey started pretending to support the inter-community dialogue in Cyprus and making pronouncements that included vague but hypocritical promises of cooperation. It behooved those EU countries that have strong economic interests in Turkey to pretend to believe it and to hide behind Turkish pronouncements. It must be said that it is not merely the pressure from its supposed Western allies that prevented Nicosia from using the European card to its advantage. Some of the most serious setbacks for Cyprus came from successive RoC governments that failed to press Cyprus' case because they were cowed and browbeaten. Even now, Nicosia makes believe that the two sides in Cyprus are freely negotiating, while fully understanding the realities of the situation. Turkey, with American assistance, is controlling the negotiations behind the scenes with the interlocutors from the occupied area simply acting as its surrogates.

Some respected analysts believe that only Israel can give realistic security assurances to Cyprus considering the deterioration of relations between Turkey and Israel. For the first time an Israeli Prime Minister, Netanyahu, visited Cyprus in February 2012. This visit was preceded by that of Israeli president Shimon Peres. The relationship between the two countries was also boosted by numerous visits at ministerial level. Under pressure from the US, cooperation on energy between the two countries stalled and the building of the planned liquefied natural gas (LNG) terminal at Vasilikos in Cyprus never took off, even when gas prices were riding high (Evripidou 2013). The subsequent fall in energy prices did the rest. It was the best option for Cyprus, according to a preliminary report by the Massachusetts Institute of Technology and the Cyprus Institute (Paltsev et al. 2013). Worryingly, George Georgiou notes in Chapter 4 of this volume that the relationship between Cyprus and Israel will remain problematic because partnerships include disparate factors that are never easy to manage; the mutually beneficial energy relationship between the two countries is a case in point. Nevertheless, he correctly notes that, "it might no longer be a matter of choice for Cyprus but a national and economic necessity" (this volume, p. 97), given its weak political position and considering that all hope for reviving its economy now appears to lie with the future development of its potential oil and natural gas resources. Greece has always had a privileged position in the EM region (Lesser 2011). In recent times, former Prime Minister Costas Simitis, a technocrat and in the view of many the possessor of a limited political horizon, tried to give the country a totally European bent and moved it away from the EM region and the Middle East. As a result, its traditionally good relations with the Arab world deteriorated. The only positive of this era was the marginal upgrading of relations with Israel. The two countries now have common cause, considering the deterioration of Israeli relations with Turkey and the new developments in the region. Europe is happy to see Greece and Israel work together, but is also protective of Turkey considering Europe's economic interests.

Greece's shift away from the EM was a calculated action by the Simitis government because he wished to disengage from Cyprus and wash his hands of the problem. After the accession of Cyprus to the EU in 2004, the Simitis government considered that any debt, moral or otherwise, that Greece owed to Cyprus was repaid in full through this accession. Cypriots' massive rejection in 2004 of the Annan Plan (which ostensibly was to "solve" the Cyprus problem), despite pressure to accept it first by the Simitis government and later by the government of the Panhellenic Socialist Movement (PASOK), aggravated the situation. Cyprus's decision was a powerful slap in the face of those politicians (in Greece, Cyprus, and the West) who did not mind having an undemocratic constitution forced on the hapless people of Cyprus merely to end the problem (see Constantinides 2010).

The economic crisis that started in 2009, which has since devastated Greece's economy, gave the final blow to the Greek presence in the important strategic area of the EM. Nevertheless, one has to recognize former Prime Minister Antonis Samaras and his government's feeble attempts to revive Greek influence in the EM and the wider Middle East, directed primarily at Egypt and Israel. Taking advantage of the crisis that Turkey created in Cyprus's EEZ, Samaras took part in the Tripartite Conference in Cairo on November 8, 2014 with the Cypriot and Egyptian Presidents (Daily News Egypt 2014; see also Damiras 2014). The new Greek government that won the January 2015 elections appears to be continuing this policy, but it is still early days for a conclusive assessment. Although Athens is engrossed in the country's economic problems and its crippling debt, Foreign Minister Nikos Kotzias is working hard to forge a multidimensional foreign policy that will also encompass the EM and the Middle East.

One ought to recognize the efforts of the pre–economic crisis government of Kostas Karamanlis to develop relations between Greece and Russia. These efforts were sabotaged inside the country by government elements, most strikingly by the then Greek Foreign Minister and more generally by the pro-American political elite in Greece. The Americans, as would be expected, did everything in their power to scuttle the growing relationship between Athens and Moscow. They also opposed the building of the Burgas–Alexandroupolis pipeline planned to channel Russian energy to the Greek market and from there to Europe. America even insisted on limiting Russian gas supplies to Greece (Moscow Top News n.d.; Hope 2006).

Despite Greece's dependence on the financial support of Berlin and Brussels, the Greek government of Alexis Tsipras continues the drive toward improved relations with Moscow. Kotzias chose Moscow for one of his first international visits, where he met Russian counterpart Sergei Lavrov. Tsipras's trip to Moscow followed soon after, in April 2015. The climate that was created by Greece's economic crisis does not help the country's drive to make friends outside the West. For now, it is roped firmly to the EU chariot, and particularly to Berlin.

Natural gas helped unite Israel and Cyprus (and by extension Greece) into a potentially lucrative economic and political alliance. Energy, in combination with the recent animosity and breakdown in relations between Turkey and Israel, appears to have facilitated the relationship between these two countries; at least for now. The formation of a geostrategic triangle between Greece, Israel, and Cyprus, one would hope with the blessing of the US, may have been accelerated by the Arab Spring, but is also based on geopolitical expediency. Given Turkey's neo-Ottoman ambitions to become the Muslim world's leading power and the ongoing instability in the Arab world, Israel's only politically safe and culturally friendly passage to the West is through Greece. Moreover, the relationship could see natural gas transported to Europe via Greece rather than via a wily Turkey.

Turning a blind eye to the fact that Greece's security problems originate in Turkey, Greek governments of all persuasions supported Turkish ambitions for EU membership. This goodwill has come to naught, considering that both Greece and Cyprus continue to experience Turkey's menacing behavior on an almost daily basis.

United States

After the end of World War II the US replaced Britain as the hegemonic power of the West in the Middle East. The transition saw its fair share of friction and antagonism, as the former colonial powers in the region, Britain and France, found it hard to relinquish control and come to terms with the fact that they were in decline and that their colonial adventures were coming to an end. America opposed the Anglo-French intervention in Suez in 1956, in which Britain and France suffered national humiliation. Soon after this the UK tried eagerly to develop a privileged strategic relationship with the US. In fact, it offered the US its role and influence in the region on a plate. France under General de Gaulle continued to challenge American hegemony in the area, but with little success. De Gaulle's successors gradually put their country back into the Western fold under American tutelage.

American policy in the EM and more particularly in the Middle Eastern region passed through various stages and adjustments. Throughout the period from the end of World War II to the present, America has considered Israel and Saudi Arabia its two pillars for control of the region. The privileged relationship with Israel proved to be the most stable option for American foreign policy. The relationship with Saudi Arabia was built largely on that country's enormous energy resources; America's need for energy and Saudi Arabia's need for security were the driving forces behind this alliance. The US appreciates that Saudi Arabia is also one of the gateways to the rest of the Arab world (Amir-Aslani 2013).

On February 14, 1945, just at the end of World War II, a historic meeting took place aboard USS *Quincy* in the Suez Canal, at which president Franklin D. Roosevelt signed an agreement with the king of Saudi Arabia, Abdul Aziz Ibn Saud. This agreement provided for unwavering US support to the Saudi royal family and Aramco (Saudi Oil Company), thus securing the uninterrupted flow to the West of Saudi "black gold." The relationship lasts to this day, despite its ups and downs. The Israeli–Palestinian conflict and more recently Islamic extremism guarantee its continuity (Lippman 2005).

The loss of Iran after the Islamic revolution in 1979 was a great blow to the US, because up to that time Iran had been a priceless strategic partner. Due to Iran's importance to American interests, the US continuous to this day to plug Iran into its foreign policy equation. Turkey has been its other major strategic partner in the Middle Eastern region, particularly in the EM. Throughout the Cold War Turkey held invaluable geopolitical and geostrategic importance. However, this relationship was complicated by the shaky relations between Turkey and Greece, which features as another important (but weaker) strategic partner of the West in the area. Starting in the 1950s, the Cyprus issue began to stand between Greece and Turkey, forcing the US to manage the rivalry mostly one-sidedly. Later more problems were added to this tottering relationship, particularly the new disputes over the Aegean.

US relations with the Arab world are turbulent because of America's privileged relationship with Israel and because of Arab nationalism, which wishes to see an end to Arab dependence on the West. Serious problems arose with Egypt in the era of Gamal Abdel Nasser because Egypt at the time supported pan-Arabism, which led to major crises in the region that drew in Jordan and Lebanon. The Palestinian problem has always been a major problem between the Arab countries and the US because of the latter's unwavering support for Israel.

Unsurprisingly, America was annoyed by the developing relationships between some Arab countries and Russia, considering that 40 percent of global energy resources, which America wishes to control, are in the Middle East. The present renewed relationship between Russia and Egypt is particularly irksome to the Americans because of Egypt's pivotal position in the region. America still remembers that Egypt created problems for the US in the past through its leadership position in the Non-Aligned Movement during the Cold War.

The Cyprus problem and disputes in the Aegean created problems on NATO's southeastern flank. In an effort to secure order and most importantly to serve its own strategic interests in the region, America tried unsuccessfully to put an end to these disputes by siding, often unabashedly, with Turkey. It came out in favor of the 2004 Annan Plan for the "solution" of the Cyprus problem, which would have led to the dissolution of the internationally recognized RoC and rendered Greek Cypriots defenseless fodder for Turkey.

With the end of the Cold War, America reordered its foreign policy priorities and turned its attention to isolating Iran. As the big thorn in the side of American policy, Egypt was placated by some gains it made through the agreements it signed with Israel at Camp David under US sponsorship. To punish and hurt Iran, America supported Iraq in its war against Iran. US defense secretary Donald Rumsfeld visited Baghdad in December 1983 as a representative of Ronald Reagan and in more than one way voiced America's support for Saddam Hussein and his war. When Saddam used chemical weapons against the Kurds and the Iranian army, Washington covered him by talking vaguely and with a forked tongue (Battle 2003). Later, America changed its position and attacked its former ally Iraq, twice devastating the country and in the process turning it into a powder keg for further violence and fundamentalism. Unwittingly this meant that America helped Iran, considering that the Shiites are probably the biggest beneficiaries of Iraqi rivalries. Iraq is now divided into three sectors, with the Kurdish sector turning out to be America's most important strategic ally in the region. Nevertheless, as politics is a nasty and hypocritical business, America has as yet stayed silent about Turkey's attacks on Iraqi Kurds.

Gaddafi's overthrow in Libya added to the unruliness and that country remains essentially ungovernable, under the control of various factions and Islamists. It has descended into chaos and ominously that instability is spilling across the region. It should not be forgotten that the US helped sow the seeds of anarchy in Libya in several ways, including direct military intervention against Gaddafi (practically all the bombing of Libya from the sea came from American navy ships). Most intriguingly, and as confirmed by a group of CIA officers, America armed al-Qaeda to help topple Gaddafi (Washington's Blog 2014).

The Arab Spring also contributed to the redistribution of the deck of cards. The failure to overthrow Assad in Syria led to a civil war that continues and has seen thousands dead and more than four million refugees. The dynamics of the region were changed by two unexpected twists. The first was the emergence of ISIL, which essentially replaced al-Qaeda, created state structures, and controls large swaths of Iraqi and Syrian territory. The jihadists of ISIL are to a large extent the outcome of Sunnis losing power in Baghdad. Equipped and supported by America and the West to fight Assad in Syria, they later turned against their Western supporters. Failing to overthrow the Syrian president, who is supported by Iran and Moscow, the Islamists resolved to set up their own state and to fight the West, which was a barrier to their aims. Just like al-Qaeda before it, ISIL is now the main threat to Western interests in the Middle East, the broader Arab region, and Africa. In retaliation, the US and the West have mounted air strikes against the fundamentalists, hoping to halt their march toward Baghdad and to improve the position of the Kurds of Syria and Iraq, who are also threatened by the advance of the Islamists. Obama sought approval from Congress to send limited land forces (an action that in the past had proved ineffective). A few Western forces are now operating in Iraq as military trainers of the Iraqi army and the Kurdish fighters with an extra ten thousand American troops arriving shortly.

The second major twist in the region was the recent rapprochement between the US and Iran. The Americans seem determined to reach an agreement with Tehran that will allow Iran to return to the region as a major player and influencer. Although officially negotiations are being conducted with a view to limiting Iran's nuclear capability, in reality the objective is the restoration of the West's relations with Iran in the interests of the former. So, we now see the Shiites as Western allies against Sunni Islam, especially ISIL, which is viewed as the greatest danger to American interests in the area. The US–Iran rapprochement is likely to redefine the energy map when sanctions against the latter are lifted, allowing the flow of Iranian oil to the West (Le Monde 2014).

America's newest policy toward Iran created problems between the US and its traditional allies, Israel and Saudi Arabia, which have been pillars of US foreign policy in the Middle East since World War II (Energy Information Association n.d.). Both these countries vehemently oppose America's rapprochement with Iran. Netanyahu tried to convey his country's opposition through a speech to the US Congress in March 2015, in which he controversially compared Iran to ISIL, although at the moment the Iranians are fighting against ISIL (National Post 2015; see also Rogin 2015).

Washington's new approach is creating problems with Turkey, which fears Iranian competition for its hegemonic ambitions in the region. Ankara provided steady support to the underground ISIL and opposed American aid to the Kurds in the region. The Americans' intention to negotiate with Assad also creates additional headaches for Ankara, which is now in some form of isolation. The attempt to revive its relations with Saudi Arabia has not borne fruit, as the Saudis asked Ankara to mend its relations with Cairo first. Ankara refused to approach Egypt because of Turkey's close relationship with former Muslim Brotherhood leader Morsi.

US foreign policy in the Middle East aims to restore Iran as an active player in the politics of the region without spoiling traditional alliances. Although the management of this policy is difficult, it remains within the realms of possibility. Israel and Saudi Arabia know that they cannot give to the US what Iran can and both realize that they need US protection. If successful, the new US policy will redefine the entire map of the Middle East. Questions remain as to the future of both Syria and Iraq and the potential for the creation of a Kurdish state. This policy is likely to bring to the forefront the interests of the Shiites and the Kurds, while simultaneously downgrading Sunni influence.

Russia

The Soviet Union's collapse stalled its substantial role in the troubled Middle East and gave America a free hand. However, very quickly after Putin came to power, Russia assumed an ever-increasing role in the region (Stergiou 2012; Office of the Historian n.d.). Westerners did everything they could, including veiled intimidation, to limit Russia's role. European and American interests in the southeastern Mediterranean, but also in the Greater Middle East, more often than not conflict with those of Russia. Iranian and Syrian support for Russia was critical to the latter's revived role in this geographic area. Russia's friendly relations with the Greeks are likely to add to its resurgence in the region.

Iran needed Russian support to repel constant attempts by the US to isolate it by imposing punishing sanctions. The relationship between Russia and Iran proved to be of great importance to the mutual interests of both. The Russian umbrella was critical to Iran's survival and Iranian support helped consolidate Russian influence. Moreover, the economic relations between the two countries also benefited both. For Iran, Russia provided an exit from isolation; and for Russia, Iran was a good market. In the end, Westerners realized that without Russian cooperation it would be impossible to achieve anything in the direction of stopping Iran from building nuclear weapons.

The second country to facilitate Russia's return to the Middle East was Syria. Faced with Western sanctions and political isolation, Syria turned decisively toward Moscow just as it did during the Soviet era. The Russian umbrella was vital for the regime's survival, considering that Russia remained Syria's main weapons supplier. Moscow benefited from the use of a naval base in Tartus that allowed the Russian fleet in the Mediterranean region to resupply. Later, when the civil war broke out in Syria, Assad's regime survived mainly because it had Russian support including air and naval backing. The fall of Gaddafi, which Moscow appears not to have opposed, resulted in Russia losing its influence in that country. The Libyan lesson taught Russia to stand firm on the side of Assad. It is common knowledge that Moscow prevented the bombing of Syria by America using skillful diplomacy that enabled Damascus to give up its chemical weapons. With the passage of time and the emergence of ISIL, Russia's position in favor of Assad seems to have been vindicated.

Syrian oil minister Suleiman Abbas signed on behalf of his government a 25-year deal with Russian SoyuzNefteGaz to explore for oil in the country's territorial waters off the Mediterranean coast. SoyuzNefteGaz is headed by Russia's former energy minister, Yuri Shafranik, and its main shareholder is the Central Bank of Russia. This agreement covers an area spanning 845 square miles (2,188 square kilometers) stretching southward from the government-controlled city of Tartus, where Russia has its only naval base in the Mediterranean. The rights extend to Banias, and about 45 miles into the sea in the Syrian EEZ. SoyuzNefteGaz has been involved for a number of years in onshore oil projects in Syria (Engdahl 2014).

Russia's return to the EM and especially to the Middle Eastern region is reflected through developments in two other countries as well: Turkey and Cyprus. Russia's relationship with Turkey strengthened after the collapse of the Soviet Union and once the so-called communist threat had disappeared. Nevertheless, relations between the two countries are fundamentally economic in character. Turkey imports more than 60 percent of its gas from Russia, while its export trade in the other direction has grown considerably in recent years. Moreover, there are further plans for the building of a pipeline through Turkey's EEZ that will transport Russian gas, thus lessening Europe's dependence on Ukrainian transport routes. But, the downing of a Russian jet by Turkey changed everything.

Moscow has for decades been using its natural gas exports as the principal means of projecting economic and political influence in Europe. Selectively allowing or denying access has given Moscow considerable leverage over the political and security stance of countries that are dependent on its energy supplies. With this in mind, the reader can see clearly the importance for Turkey and Russia of signing an agreement in December 2011 for the development of the South Stream natural gas pipeline through Turkey's EEZ. This agreement is now in doubt.

At a purely political level, these two countries have many differences that separate them, and their relationships are competitive both in the Turkic countries of the former Soviet Union, and in Georgia and the Ukraine. Even the support that Moscow provides to the RoC annoys Ankara. Differences between the two countries, however, take a back seat when it comes to the many mutual economic benefits from trading with each other. Recently, however, the relationship took a turn for the worse.

Moscow's relations with Cyprus have always been unique. In the Soviet era the support that Russia gave to the Republic of Cyprus was meant to create problems in the southeastern wing of NATO, whose faultlines were tested by the rivalry between Turkey and Greece. Yet even after the fall of the Soviet Union, Russia's support for Cyprus continues to create problems. In the post-Soviet period, Cyprus has managed to become an important magnet of economic activity for Russia in the EM region and the broader Middle East. Hundreds of Russian companies settled in Cyprus and enormous sums of Russian capital were invested in various sectors of the economy, more particularly in Cyprus's banking system and property market. Cyprus now boasts a sizable Russian community that maintains excellent relationships with the Cypriots. Even after the collapse of Cyprus's banking system and the haircut given to Russian deposits, Russian presence in the Cypriot economy remains vital. Cyprus's membership of the EU has been very positive for Russia. Cyprus and Greece have proven sound allies of Russia in the EU, often countering Eastern European countries' hostile attitudes toward Russia. The concessions to Moscow of Cypriot military facilities have bolstered an already strong relationship, much to the annoyance of Washington and other Western capitals.

Moscow strengthened its diplomatic and economic relationships with other countries in the region, taking advantage of the discontent of many with American policies. Even Israel upgraded its relationship with Moscow. Indicatively, Israel abstained from voting against Russia over Ukraine in the UN General Assembly, in the process annoying and irritating America (Forward 2014). Official visits were exchanged at a high level, with Netanyahu visiting Moscow and Putin Tel Aviv (Jaulmes 2012).

As regards Egypt, Russia managed to take advantage of Cairo's distrust of the Americans after Washington held back the military portion of a $1.5 billion planned US assistance package to Egypt in an attempt to demonstrate American disapproval of Sisi's overthrow of Morsi. Putin paid an official visit to Cairo, the first Russian leader to do so since the fall of the Soviet Union (Kingsley 2015). Moscow also revitalized its relationship with Saudi Arabia, which was dissatisfied with Washington's policy in the Arab world and is even contemplating buying Russian arms.

Countries renewing and strengthening their relationships with Russia fundamentally wish to send a signal that they should not be taken for granted and that they no longer wish to have their foreign policies dictated by others – meaning the US. Putin wishes to display Russia's network of alliances now that the country has been vilified by the West over Ukraine. In conclusion, Russia returned successfully to the EM and the Greater Middle East, and in the process sent a powerful signal to the West that Russia's cooperation in the solution of regional problems (i.e., Syria and Iran) is absolutely necessary.

China, Britain, France, and the European Union

China, Britain, France, and the EU have a presence and special interests in the region. China is speedily building bridges to serve its economic interests; for its relationship with Greece see China.org.cn (2015), and on its strategy more generally, CSIS (n.d.) and Lin (2011, 2013).

Britain maintains a foothold in the region from the past (Lewis 1995), but is integrating its regional policies with America's transatlantic position, as are France and the EU (Thomas 2009).

Conclusion

In summarizing the situation in the EM and the broader Middle East, one could support the idea that the time has come for countries in the region to redefine alliances and the balance of power. Cosmogonic developments are now taking place. The borders that were drawn in 1918 by Britain and France on the ruins of the Ottoman Empire are about to collapse. The legacy of states that were artificially carved up by colonizers is being strongly challenged. Political order is collapsing in Iraq, Libya, Syria, and Yemen. The very essence of Syrian and Iraqi nationhood has been corrupted by the dominance of sectarian and ethnic identities. The establishment of an independent Kurdistan no longer threatens regional stability as more and more sects and groups try to carve up territories for themselves. A new order is taking shape by force in the Middle East. This new geopolitics started with the end of the Cold War. The first wave began with the collapse of the Ottoman Empire following World War I. The second trailed World War II when the European colonial order collapsed. According to some analysts, "the contemporary Middle East is the product of these three geopolitical waves. Among the humiliating consequences of these waves is the rise of the extremist group calling itself the Islamic State" (Amirahmadi 2015).

The key features of the emergent third wave of Middle Eastern geopolitics are failed states, humiliated peoples, crippled economies, extreme inequality and poverty, devastated environments, plundered resources, conflicted geographies, inter-state conflicts, foreign intrusions and killings, political chaos, revolt, and violent radicalism. The struggles are more social and political than religious. The declared jihadists are certainly using religion to justify their political cause rather than the other way around. Islam is what gives the jihadists their identity as a distinct imagined community with a seemingly glorious past. This identity should not make one view the struggle by ISIL as Islamic, but rather as political, aimed at reversing demonization and humiliation and regaining the dream of the past (Amirahmadi 2015).

In 2006, the US *Armed Forces Journal* published a map with the new borders of the Middle East, in the center of which there was a new country named Free Kurdistan, consisting of territories of Syria, Iraq, Iran, and especially Turkey. This article provoked angry reactions and denials, and was officially marked as the personal opinion of Colonel Ralph Peters (Nazemroaya 2006; see also Judis 2014). When on April 13, 2015, a two-page spread in the *Wall Street Journal* was accompanied by a similar map, no one reacted angrily, because developments in Iraq, Syria, and Yemen had in the meantime changed the dynamics of the area as well as people's perceptions.

Ankara's offer of assistance to the Kurds is too little, too late. The limited autonomy that Erdoğan and Davutoğlu allegedly proposed to the PKK cannot in any case satisfy Turkey's Kurds. Since 1991 there has been a de facto independent Kurdish state in northern Iraq, on Turkey's southern border, and a new de facto independent Kurdish state in northeastern Syria emerged in late 2011. The violent Kurd versus jihadist conflict in Syria and Iraq cancels out Erdoğan's attempts to present his ruling AKP as the common denominator of political Islam and Sunni Muslims regardless of national identity. By investing in the risky caliphate of ISIL, Ankara is unwittingly encouraging full emancipation of the Kurds in Iraq and Syria.

The Kurds' desire to win an independent state in what is now eastern Turkey and northern Iraq was endorsed by the short-lived Treaty of Sevres, in the 1920 pact between the Western Allies and the Ottomans. That treaty was promptly repudiated by Turkish nationalists led by Mustafa Kemal Atatürk, the founder of the modern Turkish state. Until recently, in fact, Turkey denied the very existence of a separate Kurdish ethnicity.

The Kurds, who live scattered across Iraq, Turkey, Syria, and Iran, have already enjoyed decades of virtual independence. Under an autonomous government in northern Iraq – the mountainous part of what was once the Ottoman province of Mosul – Iraqi Kurds enjoy de facto autonomy. Kurds have also established three autonomous "cantons" in northern Syria.

Washington is trying to reorient its policy in the region via rapprochement with Tehran; if successful, this could rearrange alliances, but it has been begun against the wishes of both its traditional allies in the region, Saudi Arabia and Israel. The US also had to contend with Turkish irritation, although Ankara was much more discreet in its opposition because of its close trade relations with Tehran. The resurgence of Iran on the world stage in the form of an explicit or tacit alliance with the West will almost certainly limit Turkish influence. Iran will probably become the most important regional power and as such will cut many of Ankara's ambitions down to size. That being said, Turkey will continue to play an important role in the region. Kurdish independence is likely to feature high on the list of issues to be resolved. The signs on the horizon give hope to the Kurds despite the expected opposition from nearly all countries in the area, but particularly from Iran and Turkey.

An open Palestinian problem surely raises concerns about stability. The reelection of Netanyahu and the power of the right worry the Palestinians. Will Palestinian recognition by 100 countries force Israel to negotiate in the direction of a two-state solution? Most commentators believe that the answer lies with Washington, which up to now has provided unconditional support for Israel. The Arab world is suspicious of the Americans and their intentions considering their past behavior and the mess they brought to the region. US policy in Iraq has been a total failure, while the conflict in Syria drags on. The Libyan state virtually ceased to exist after the Western intervention and the overthrow of Gaddafi. Only Tunisia is still on its feet despite the many economic, political, and social challenges it now faces. Nevertheless, it is too early to draw any definite conclusions. As for Cyprus, the election in the Occupied Area of a seemingly moderate leftist leader, as the representative of the Turkish Cypriots, could prove a blessing for Turkey, considering the non-existent, confused, and shambolic strategy of Nicosia and Athens. Cyprus is likely to go through the same experiences as it did when another seemingly moderate leader was elected in the Occupied Area in 2004 and raised false hopes. The most likely outcome of the current negotiations is a new deadlock that will a priori be blamed on the Greeks, courtesy of their naive approach to the problem.

In conclusion, the deck of cards in the EM and the Middle East is being reshuffled, with energy resources playing a decisive role. Forecasting how the new map of the region will look is both risky and tricky. The military and diplomatic turmoil and the shifting alliances in the area make accurate prediction impossible.

Notes

1. In *The Strategic Depth* Davutoğlu also expresses the Turkish neo-Ottoman imperial policy. He believes that in the post-Ottoman region, from the Balkans to the Middle East, Turkey not only has a duty to act as a leader, but has a "natural right" to do so as a former imperial power. See also the later edition (Davutoğlu 2009: 275), where he says that "even if there were no Turks on the island, Turkey should have an interest in Cyprus," precisely because of its strategic importance. This admission debunks the argument that Turkey is in Cyprus to protect the Turkish Cypriot community.
2. One of the major challenges of the Mediterranean basin lies in its "belt North," and more precisely its eastern lock. This is protected by the geostrategic complementarity of Greece, Turkey, and Cyprus, as well as by the pivotal position of Iran, which extends the Turkish territory. With specific regard to Cyprus, the island holds a privileged position in the EM, at the rear of the Persian Gulf and the Suez Canal. Cyprus is located near areas of Near Eastern tensions and therefore welcomes defense and surveillance covering the Levantine façade. This geographically eccentric island continues since the Cold War to provide strategic coverage for Israel, to the extent that it opens up a potential maritime relay for that country. In addition, non-antagonistic Nicosia shares Western values with Tel Aviv. The Cypriot area is therefore likely to be an access to the sea for Israeli forces, whose territory does not have sufficient strategic depth. Cyprus is also positioned on the main axis of the

southern Turkish defense, which could pose a possible and immediate danger for Turkey in the case of conflict with Israel. At the same time, the Cypriot territory holds timely geostrategic advantages for Russia, which is trying to get closer to the Mediterranean states to counterbalance the influence of the US in the region. Cyprus lies 75 km from the Turkish coast, is bordered by the Levantine front to the east and south, is located near the Suez Canal and close to the Russian military base in Tartous on the Syrian coast, and, moreover, occupies a very strategic geographic position at the hinge end of the eastern basin of the Mediterranean. In this, it remains an important issue for American and Russian strategy in the region (Mirante-Psaltakis et al. 2011).

References

Aggiouri, Nicolas. 2015. "Benyamin Nétanyahou et la crainte de 'l'inutilité stratégique.'" Boulevard Extérieur, March 6.
http://www.boulevard-exterieur.com/Benyamin-Netanyahou-et-la-crainte-de-l-inutilite-strategique.html. Accessed November 2015.
Akgönül, Samim. 2014. "La Turquie désorientée." Orient XXI, October 9.
http://orientxxi.info/magazine/la-turquie-desorientee,0716.
Accessed November 2015.
Amirahmadi, Hooshang. 2015. "Dark New Geopolitics of the Middle East." Cairo Review of GlobalAffairs, March 30.
http://www.thecairoreview.com/tahrir-forum/dark-new-geopolitics-of-the-middle-east/. Accessed November 2015.
Amir-Aslani, Ardavan. 2013. "Les Chinois à Ryad et les Américains à Téhéran, nouvelle donne des relations entre Arabie Saoudite et États-Unis?" Atlantico, October 27.
http://www.atlantico.fr/decryptage/chinois-ryad-et-americains-teheran-nouvelle-donne-relations-entre-arabie-saoudite-et-etats-unis-ardavan-amir-aslani-881921.html#0iklsd2HEirjbhMp.99. Accessed November 2015.
Battle, Joyce (Ed.). 2003. Shaking Hands with Saddam Hussein: The U.S. Tilts toward Iraq, 1980–1984. National Security Archive Electronic Briefing Book No. 82. February 25. Washington, DC: National Security Archive.
Bergman, Ronen. 2008. The Secret War with Iran. New York: Free Press.
BGN News. 2015. "US Think Tank Warns That Rising Authoritarianism Threatens Turkish Economy." BGN News, March 15.
http://politics.bgnnews.com/us-think-tank-rising-authoritarianism-threatens-turkish-economy-haberi/4314. Accessed November 2015.

Black, Ian, Ewen MacAskill, and Robert Booth. 2010. "Gaza Flotilla Attack: Turks Killed by Israeli Soldiers Given Heroes' Funeral." The Guardian, June 4. http://www.theguardian.com/world/2010/jun/03/gaza-flotilla-attack-turkey-funeral. Accessed November 2015.

Borger, Julian, Mairav Zonszein, and Sabrina Siddiqui. 2015. "US Accuses Israel of Spying on Nuclear Talks with Iran." The Guardian, March 24. http://www.theguardian.com/world/2015/mar/24/israel-spied-on-us-over-iran-nuclear-talks. Accessed November 2015.

Bozkurt, Abdullah. 2014. "Turkey Loses Arab World." Today's Zaman, November 14. http://www.todayszaman.com/columnist/abdullah-bozkurt/turkey-loses-arab-world_364401.html. Accessed November 2015.

Cagaptay, Soner. 2013. "Erdogan's Empathy for Morsi." Washington Institute, September 14. http://www.washingtoninstitute.org/policy-analysis/view/erdogans-empathy-for-morsi. Accessed November 2015.

Center for Strategic and International Studies (CSIS). n.d. "China and the Middle East." http://csis.org/program/china-middle-east. Accessed November 2015.

China.org.cn. 2015. "China, Greece Agree to Promote Ties, Deepen Cooperation." China.org.cn, March 27. http://www.china.org.cn/china/Off_the_Wire/2015-03/27/content_35176691.htm. Accessed November 2015.

Ciboulet, Thomas. 2015. "L'Iran: Menace internationale ou partenaire stratégique." Sowt al Arab, February. http://sowtalarab.com/liran-menace-internationale-ou-partenaire-strategique. Accessed November 2015.

Constantinides, Stephanos. 1996. "Turkey: The Emergence of a New Foreign Policy; The Neo-Ottoman Model." Journal of Political and Military Sociology, Winter: 323–334

—. 2002. "The Emergence of a New Ottoman Model: A New Foreign Policy in Turkey." in The New Balkans: Disintegration and Reconstruction, edited by George A. Kourvetaris Victor Roudometof, Kleomenis Koutsoukis, and Andrew Kourvetaris, 379–400. Boulder, CO: East European Monographs.

—. 2010. Cyprus: Fragments of an Era. Nicosia: Agaion (in Greek).

Crooke, Alastair. 2009. "Quand Israël et l'Iran s'alliaient." Le Monde diplomatique, February.

Cyprus Business Mail. 2015. "Cyprus Says No Airbase Deal with Russia, Humanitarian Use Possible." Cyprus Business Mail, February 26.

Daily News Egypt. 2014. "Greece, Cyprus to Represent Egypt's Interests in EU." Daily News Egypt, November 8.

http://www.dailynewsegypt.com/2014/11/08/greece-cyprus-represent-egypts-interests-eu/. Accessed November 2015.

Damiras, Vassilios. 2014. "Greece, Cyprus and Israel in an Era of Geostrategic Friendship and Geoeconomic Cooperation." Bridging Europe, December 5.
http://www.mediterraneanaffairs.com/en/events/greece-cyprus-and-israel-in-an-era-of-geostrategic-friendship-and-geoeconomic-cooperation.html. Accessed November 2015.

Davutoğlu, Ahmet. 2001. Stratejik Derinlik (The Strategic Depth): Türkiye'nin Uluslararası Konumu, Istanbul: Küre Yayınları.

Davutoğlu, Ahmet. 2009. The Strategic Depth. Athens: Poiotita Publishing. (Greek ed.)

Deliveli, Emre. 2015. "Economic Data Signal SOS." Hurriyet Daily News, April 3. http://www.hurriyetdailynews.com/economic-data-signal-sos.aspx?pageID=449&nID=80515. Accessed November 2015.

Dunham, Will. 2015. "Obama Says It Is Now 'Hard to Find a Path' on Israeli-Palestinian Peace." Thomson Reuters, March 21.
http://www.reuters.com/article/2015/03/22/us-usa-israel-obama-idUSKBN0MH0RP20150322. Accessed November 2015.

Energy Information Association. n.d. Saudi Arabia. EIA.
http://www.eia.gov/countries/cab.cfm?fips=sa. Accessed November 2015.

Entous, Adam. 2015. "Israel Spied on Iran Nuclear Talks with U.S." Wall Street Journal, March 23. http://www.wsj.com/articles/israel-spied-on-iran-talks-1427164201. Accessed November 2015.

Evripidou, Stefanos. 2013. "Experts Agree That an LNG Plant Is Best Option for Cyprus." Cyprus Mail, November 23. http://cyprus-mail.com/2013/11/23/experts-agree-that-an-lng-plant-is-best-option-for-cyprus/. Accessed November 2015.

Forward. 2014. "Israel Abstains from U.N. Resolution Slamming Russia Takeover of Crimea. Jewish State Fails to Back U.S. Effort to Isolate Russia. Forward, March 28. http://forward.com/articles/195444/israel-abstains-from-un-resolution-slamming-russia/#ixzz3VpqoY5iJ. Accessed November 2015.

Fox News. 2008. "Iran Launches Production of Stealth Sub." Fox News, May 10. Accessed February 2008.

Friedman, George. 2012. "Egypt and the Strategic Balance." Stratfor, December 4. https://www.stratfor.com/weekly/egypt-and-strategic-balance. Accessed November 2015.

Hope, Kerin. 2006. "Russia Seeks Pipeline Deals with Greece." Financial Times, September 4. www.ft.com/cms/s/0/d5576350-3bb1-11db-96c9-0000779e2340.html. Accessed November 2015.

Hurriyet Daily News. 2015a. "Turkish Lira Hits Record Low on Central
Bank Worries." Hurriyet Daily News, February 27.
http://www.hurriyetdailynews.com/turkish-lira-hits-record-low-on-
central-bank-worries.aspx?pageID=238&NID=78952.
Accessed November 2015.
—. 2015b. "Turkish Central Bank Governor Dismisses Resignation
Rumors." Hurriyet Daily News, February 27.
http://www.hurriyetdailynews.com/turkish-central-bank-governor-
dismisses-resignation-rumors.aspx?pageID=238&nID=78970.
Accessed November 2015.
—. 2015c. "Kerry Says US Will Have to Negotiate with Syria's Assad."
Hurriyet Daily News, March 15.
http://www.hurriyetdailynews.com/kerry-says-us-will-have-to-
negotiate-with-syrias-assad.aspx?pageID=238&nID=79711.
Accessed November 2015.
Hurriyet Daily News. 2015d. "Turkey Needs Higher Growth, Reforms to
Avoid Middle Income Trap, Says Minister." Hurriyet Daily News,
March 15. http://www.hurriyetdailynews.com/turkey-needs-higher-
growth-reforms-to-avoid-middle-income-trap-says-minister-
.aspx?pageID=238&nID=79694. Accessed November 2015.
İdiz, Semih. 2015. "What Does Erdoğan's Iran Visit Tell us?" Hurriyet
Daily News, April 9. http://www.hurriyetdailynews.com/what-does-
erdogans-iran-visit-tell-us.aspx?pageID=449&nID=80773.
Accessed November 2015.
Inflation.eu. n.d. "Inflation Turkey – Current Turkish Inflation." Inflation.eu.
http://www.inflation.eu/inflation-rates/turkey/inflation-turkey.aspx.
Accessed November 2015.
IRNA. 2011. "Iran's Doctrine Based on Deterrence." IRNA.
http://www2.irna.com/en/news/view/line-24/0804185731142306.htm.
Accessed June 2011.
Jaffe, Greg, and Sean Sullivan. 2015. "47 GOP Senators Write to Iran."
Washington Post, March 10. http://www.pressreader.com/usa/the-
washington-post1047/20150310/281500749722033/TextView.
Accessed November 2015.
Jaulmes, Adrien. 2012. "L'Imposante visite de Vladimir Poutine en Israël."
Le Figaro, June 25.
http://www.lefigaro.fr/international/2012/06/25/01003-
20120625ARTFIG00750-l-imposante-visite-de-vladimir-poutine-en-
israel.php. Accessed November 2015.
Judis, John B. (2014). "The Middle East That France and Britain Drew Is
Finally Unravelling." New Republic, June 26.

http://www.newrepublic.com/article/118409/mideast-unravelling-and-
theres-not-much-us-can-do. Accessed November 2015.
Kingsley, Patrick. 2015. "Vladimir Putin's Egypt Visit Sends Message to
US. Russian President's Arrival in Egypt Allows Both Countries to
Signal That Their Foreign Policies Are Not to Be Dictated by Others."
The Guardian, February 9.
http://www.theguardian.com/world/2015/feb/09/vladimir-putin-egypt-
visit-message-us-russia. Accessed November 2015.
Le Monde. 2014. "L'Iran possible allié des Etats-Unis contre l'EIIL en
Irak." Le Monde, June 13. http://www.lemonde.fr/proche-orient/
article/2014/06/13/l-iran-possible-allie-des-etats-unis-contre-l-eiil-en-
irak_4437744_3218.html. Accessed November 2015.
Lesser, Ian I. 2011. "Greece's New Geopolitical Environment." Washington,
DC: Wilson Center, July 7.
https://www.wilsoncenter.org/publication/greeces-new-geopolitical-
environment-0. Accessed November 2015.
Lewis, Bernard. 1995. The Middle East: A Brief History of the Last 2,000
Years. New York: Scribner.
Lin, Christina. 2011. "The New Silk Road: China's Energy Strategy in the
Greater Middle East." Policy Focus #109. Washington, DC:
Washington Institute for Near East Policy, April.
—. 2013. "China's Strategic Shift toward the Region of the Four Seas:
The Middle Kingdom Arrives in the Middle East." Middle East
Review of International Affairs, 17: 32–55.
http://www.rubincenter.org/2013/03/chinas-strategic-shift-toward-the-
region-of-the-four-seas-the-middle-kingdom-arrives-in-the-middle-
east/. Accessed November 2015.
Lippman, Thomas W. 2005. "The Day FDR Met Saudi Arabia's Ibn
Saud." The Link, April–May: 1–14.
Mirante-Psaltakis, Fotini Katy, Stephanos Constantinides, Thalia Tassou,
and Christos Iacovou. 2011. "The Republic of Cyprus: 50 Years
After." Études helléniques/Hellenic Studies, 19: 23–62.
Moscow Top News. n.d. "Karamanlis and Putin Discuss Greek-Russian
Plans." Moscow Top News.
www.moscowtopnews.com/?area=postView&id=1010.
Accessed November 2015.
National Post. 2015. "Transcript of Benjamin Netanyahu's speech to U.S.
Congress." National Post, March 3.
http://news.nationalpost.com/2015/03/03/benjamin-netanyahu-iran-
and-isis-are-competing-for-the-crown-of-militant-islam/.
Accessed November 2015.

Nazemroaya, Mahdi Darius. 2006. "Plans for Redrawing the Middle East:
    The Project for a 'New Middle East.'" Global Research, November 19.
    http://www.globalresearch.ca/plans-for-redrawing-the-middle-east-the-
    project-for-a-new-middle-east/3882. Accessed November 2015.
Office of the Historian. n.d. "A Guide to the United States' History of
    Recognition, Diplomatic, and Consular Relations, by Country, since
    1776: Saudi Arabia." Office of the Historian.
    http://history.state.gov/countries/saudi-arabia. Accessed November 2015.
Özer, Verda. 2014. "Kurds Are the Primary US Partner in Iraq and Syria."
    Hurriyet Daily News, November 15.
    http://www.hurriyetdailynews.com/kurds-are-the-primary-us-partner-
    in-iraq-and-syria.aspx?PageID=238&NID=74344.
    Accessed November 2015.
Paltsev, Sergey, Francis O'Sullivan, Nathan Lee, Anna Agarwal, Mingda
    Li, Xuejing "Michelle" Li, and Nestor Fylaktos. 2013. Interim Report
    for the Study Natural Gas Monetization Pathways for Cyprus:
    Economics of Project Development Options. Boston, MA: MIT Energy
    Initiative/Cyprus Institute.
    https://mitei.mit.edu/system/files/Cyprus_NG_Report.pdf.
    Accessed November 2015.
Parsi, Trita. 2007. Treacherous Alliance: The Secret Dealings of Israel,
    Iran and the United States. New Haven, CT: Yale University Press.
Payvand Iran News. 2006. "Iran's Defense Spending 'a Fraction of
    Persian Gulf Neighbors'." Payvand Iran News, November 22.
    http://www.payvand.com/news/06/jun/1011.html. Accessed June 2011.
Photius.com. n.d. "Iran Oil and Gas Industry." Photius.com.
    http://www.photius.com/countries/iran/economy/iran_economy_oil_an
    d_gas_industry.html. Accessed November 2015.
Press TV. 2009. "Advanced Attack Chopper Joins Iran Fleet." Press TV,
    May 24. http://edition.presstv.ir/mobile/detail.aspx?id=95824.
    Accessed June 2013.
Rogin, Jose. 2015. "Republicans Warn Iran – and Obama – That Deal
    Won't Last. Bloomberg View, 9 March.
    http://www.bloombergview.com/articles/2015-03-09/republicans-
    warn-iran-and-obama-that-deal-won-t-last. Accessed November 2015.
Shenker, Jack. 2015. "Sharm el-Sheikh Rumbles with Grand Promises of
    the International Elite." The Guardian, March 15.
    http://www.theguardian.com/world/2015/mar/15/egyot-sharma-el-
    sheikh-rumbles-grand-promises. Accessed November 2015.

Geopolitical Poker in the Eastern Mediterranean 45

Geopolitical Poker in the Eastern Mediterranean   45

Slavin, Barbara. 2011. "Turkey Relishes Role as Mr. Fixit." ipsnews.net, April 6. http://www.ipsnews.net/2011/04/mideast-turkey-relishes-role-as-mr-fixit/. Accessed November 2015.
Sönmez, Mustafa. 2015. "Will a 3-Lira Dollar Lead to an Economic Crisis in Turkey?" Hurriyet Daily News, March 16. http://www.hurriyetdailynews.com/will-a-3-lira-dollar-lead-to-an-economic-crisis-in-turkey.aspx?PageID=238&NID=87395&News. Accessed September 2015.
Stein, Sam. 2015. "Obama Details His Disappointment with Netanyahu in First Post-Election Comments." Huffington Post, March 21. http://www.huffingtonpost.com/2015/03/21/obama-iran-deal_n_6905634.html. Accessed November 2015.
Stergiou, Andreas. 2012. "Russian Policy in the Eastern Mediterranean and the Implications for EU External Action." Paris: Institute for Security Studies. http://www.iss.europa.eu/publications/detail/article/russian-policy-in-the-eastern-mediterranean-and-the-implications-for-eu-external-action/. Accessed November 2015.
Taşpinar, Ömer. 2011. "The Rise of Turkish Gaullism: Getting Turkish-American Relations Right." Washington, DC: Brookings Institution. http://www.brookings.edu/research/papers/2011/01/turkey-taspinar. Accessed November 2015.
Taşpinar, Ömer. 2014. "New Turkey Unveiled by the Washington Post and New York Times." Today's Zaman, November 2. http://www.todayszaman.com/columnist/omer-taspinar/new-turkey-unveiled-by-the-washington-post-and-new-york-times_363321.html. Accessed November 2015.
—. 2015. "From Neo-Ottomanism to Turkish Gaullism." Today's Zaman, March 15. http://www.todayszaman.com/columnist/omer-taspinar/from-neo-ottomanism-to-turkish-gaullism_375325.html. Accessed November 2015.
Thomas, Daniel C. (Ed.). 2009. Making EU Foreign Policy: National Preferences, European Norms and Common Policies. London: Palgrave Macmillan.
Times of Israel. 2015. "Obama Left PM 'with Impression US Will Abandon Israel at UN.'" Times of Israel, March 20. http://www.timesofisrael.com/us-mulling-reassessment-of-un-support-for-israel-for-4-months/#ixzz3VAmP4hnv. Accessed November 2015.
Today's Zaman. 2015a. "Finance Minister: Turkey Needs Higher Growth and Reforms to Avoid 'Middle Income Trap.'" Today's Zaman, March 14. http://www.todayszaman.com/business_finance-minister-turkey-

needs-higher-growth-and-reforms-to-avoid-middle-income-trap_375248.html. Accessed November 2015.

—. 2015b. "Egypt's President Boisterous after Major Economic Conference." Today's Zaman, March 15. http://www.todayszaman.com/anasayfa_egypts-president-boisterous-after-major-economic-conference_375287.html. Accessed November 2015.

Washington's Blog. 2014. "Confirmed: U.S. Armed Al Qaeda to Topple Libya's Gaddaffi." Washington's Blog, April 24. http://www.washingtonsblog.com/2014/04/confirmed-u-s-armed-al-qaeda-topple-gaddaffi.html. Accessed November 2015.

Yetkin, Murat. 2015. "Understanding the Failure of Erdoğan's Syria and Egypt Policies." Hurriyet Daily News, March 17. http://www.hurriyetdailynews.com/understanding-the-failure-of-erdogans-syria-and-egypt-policies.aspx?pageID=449&nID=79755. Accessed November 2015.

Yinanç, Barcin. 2015. "The Rise and Demise of the Turkish Trading State." Hurriyet Daily News, March 17. http://www.hurriyetdailynews.com/the-rise-and-demise-of-the-turkish-trading-state.aspx?pageID=449&nID=79756. Accessed November 2015.

Chapter Two

Greece and Cyprus
as Geopolitical Fodder

William Mallinson

A truly independent Greece is an absurdity. Greece can either be English
or Russian, and since it cannot be Russian, it is necessary that she be
English. (Sir Edmond Lyons, British minister to Greece, 1841)

This quote, well known and well worn though it may be, is still valid
today, whatever lip service is paid to the concept of the free West and the
importance of national sovereignty. While no right-minded politician
would speak in such honest terms today, the fact remains, as we shall see,
that Greece and Cyprus are on the periphery of world affairs when it
comes to independence of action. Greece can even be described as a client
state in some respects, particularly when one takes into account the Troika
straitjacket into which it has been forced, admittedly through the folly of
its own alleged leaders as much as through the greed of financial interest
groups. Dramatic it may sound, but financial terrorism is a new and
unwelcome factor in the geopolitical cesspit of the Eastern Mediterranean
(EM), as Cyprus well knows. The whole farrago of the current instability
in the Middle East – Syria, Lebanon, Turkey, and the Palestine–Israel
open wound – has recently been enhanced by events in Ukraine, while the
involvement of Greece and Cyprus with Israel on the gas front has
bedeviled and possibly put at risk their relations with an increasingly
powerful Russia.

Before looking at modern Greece and Cyprus from a historical angle,
within the context of their political geography and the obsession with
Russia, I shall bully off by setting out my approach with a brief critique of
geopolitics and the dangers of the misuse of international relations theory,
introducing my geohistory as a more viable and mature method of analysis
and evaluation. As such, I shall offer a simple cerebral underpinning, but
certainly not a conceptual framework, the latter being the preserve of
international relations theorists seeking their pot of gold at the end of a

rainbow. Then I shall consider Greece and Cyprus as geopolitical fodder, bearing in mind the British and US obsession with Russia within the context of the EM geopolitical laboratory, before concluding.

Geocrudity

As Lin Yutang wrote, putting human affairs into exact formulae shows a lack of a sense of humor and therefore a lack of wisdom, while humankind's love for definitions is a step toward ignorance. The more he defined, aiming at an impossible logical perfection, the more ignorant he became (Yutang 1976, 9 and 404). So it is with much post-1960s international relations (IR) theory,[1] but especially with geopolitics, a "primitive form of IR theory," as Christopher Hill (2003, 168) calls it. Geopolitics as a modern label is closely associated with the obsession of big powers to gain yet more power, through the control of resources. Despite its close association with the imperialist-minded Halford Mackinder and Nazi adviser Karl Haushofer, it was Henry Kissinger, of all people, who helped to slide the term back into current international relations terminology, by using it as a synonym for balance-of-power politics (O'Tuthail, Dalby, and Routledge 1998, 1). The term is often used by politicians, who sometimes ignorantly interchange it with "geostrategy." With the increasingly desperate struggle for the world's resources, oil and gas pipelines almost become geographic maps. Old-style borders, encompassing culturally and homogenous groups of people, become less relevant in the eyes of the geopolitician. As Hill writes (2003, 169) the random way in which frontiers are superimposed on the world means that states vary enormously in size, mineral wealth, access to the sea, vulnerability, and cohesiveness. A look at a map of the Middle East is enough to show how cynically Britain and France carved up much of the area following the Sykes–Picot deal, to suit their geopolitical lusts. The medium- and long-term results have been tension in the area ever since. The very foundation of the modern state of Greece, let alone that of Cyprus, was based on a compromise between the big powers as much as on love of Greek freedom, as we shall see later.

The maelstrom of theories

There is nothing wrong with theorizing per se. Indeed, it can often aid analysis and even evaluation. The problem comes with the fact that many theories clash with each other, frequently the result of a thinker setting out to explain, and even to try to solve, an international relations problem by making a model. The problem there is that he then imprisons himself mentally in his model, and ceases actually to think freely. On top of that, he often selects – usually subliminally rather than dishonestly – only those pieces of information that suit his model and "prove" his theory. In this sense, most models tend to be Procrustean, since they must be made to fit. All this is bedeviled by the clash between realists and behavioralists, further enriched by structuralism, modernization theory, dependency theory, world-systems analysis, positivism, constructivism, critical theory, postmodernism, normative theory, pluralism, and functionalism. Most of these also have their sub-divisions, and are even connected to each other, to a greater or lesser extent. The problem is that there is no single nirvana theory that explains and solves everything.

Matters can sometimes reach a farcical level: for example, Francis Fukuyama dramatically wrote about the end of history, and on being proven mistaken he then turned to "masculine values" being rooted in biology as playing a central role, writing that female chimps have relationships, while male chimps practice Realpolitik (Bell 2006). Much the same can be said of Samuel P. Huntington's "Clash of Civilizations," with its simplistic and sometimes inaccurate and mistaken pigeonholing of history. Add to this IR theoreticians' obsession with categorizing the categories, and then sub-categorizing, serious reflection disappears, and thought processes become enslaved in nice-sounding labels, to the detriment of real substance and free thought.

Geohistory

My notion of geohistory, in contrast, means that far from packaging thoughts, ideologies, concepts, and events into personal interpretations of history to suit one's own wishes, or those of others, history becomes a neutral continuum that remains perforce entirely unaffected by any interpretation. Historicism, and even historiography, is discarded. The past is simply the past, which blends into the future as we write. Events alone can of course be interpreted (indeed, we all have our mental filters), although the very act of interpreting does tend to create dispute in the form of what we can term "different colors." We can nevertheless say that the same things have been happening, and will continue to happen, whichever way we choose to package and interpret them, simply because they are predicated on immutable human characteristics. History does not however repeat itself precisely; rather, the behavior of the human species manifests itself ad infinitum with different colors to suit our own selfish desires, new technology, and allegedly new ideas. Therefore, it can be argued that

G.W.F. Hegel and Karl Marx, for example, were banging their heads against the wall in using (their view of) history to argue in favor of, for example, German superiority, or materialism.

When one has looked behind the stage of relations between states – in other words, when one has scrutinized government documents over a number of years, as they are released – one finds that fundamental policy alters surprisingly little, whatever the public messages that governments put out. Indeed, one finds remarkable consistency. Thus, despite the Russian Revolution of 1917 and the dismantling of the Soviet Union in the early 1990s, a fundamental ingredient of Russian policy today is still to have some influence over events in its own back garden, and to have access to the EM. In the case of Greece, but particularly Cyprus, it is clear that it has for hundreds of years never been complete master of its own destiny. This is where Britain and the United States (US) come in. We shall now begin to home in on our theme, through geohistory.

Greece's qualified independence

A myth abounds that in 1832, a new and sovereign monarchical Greece was created. Sovereign it was up to a point, but as a protectorate of the major powers, the very powers involved in agreeing to its existence. Let us look briefly at how this came about.

By the time of the struggle for Greek independence, Greece had become a mere geohistorical tool of the British Empire, the latter even owning some Greek lands, the Ionian Islands. It is to Russia, not Britain, that Greece owes its qualified freedom (although revolutionary and Napoleonic France also has an intellectual claim), and it was despite, not because of, Britain that the 1821 revolution ended in independence. It was the Anglo-Russian Protocol of April 4, 1826 that did the trick: it stated that Britain would mediate to make Greece an autonomous vassal of the Ottoman Empire, but that if this proved impossible, Britain or Russia could intervene jointly or *separately*. Russia intervened, and by 1829, Greece, or at least some of it, was free. When the philhellenic Admiral Codrington and his French and Russian homologues sank the Egypto-Ottoman fleet at Navarino, the foreign secretary, the Duke of Wellington, is well known for having described the battle, in typical English understatement, as an "untoward event," while his ally Clemens von Metternich described it as a "dreadful catastrophe." Somewhat arrogantly and cynically, the latter had also, when speaking of the Greeks, said: "Over there, beyond our frontiers, three or four hundred thousand individuals hanged, impaled, or with their throats cut, hardly count" (Sked 1979, 7, quoting de Bertier de Sauvigny 1962, 251).

Whatever the simpering protestations of well-paid designer academics in both Britain and Greece, British policy has been essentially antithetical to Greek interests since the very inception of the modern Greek state. Apart from a few flashes in the pan, and a few individuals like George Canning, the only help that Greece has received has been from private individuals such as Lord Byron, or public individuals who were brave enough to go against official British policy, such as Codrington. Britain was forced into helping Greece to keep a finger in the Mediterranean pie, for fear of Russia ending up as Greece's main sponsor and weakening Britain's Ottoman friends. The Don Pacifico Affair is an example of Britain's attitude, when Britain actually threatened Greece with gunboats; while during the Crimean War, Britain, with its then French poodles, blockaded Piraeus. In 1916, Britain and France even interfered militarily in Greece, being beaten back by the king's forces, and then getting their revenge by backing the controversial and Britain-friendly Eleftherios Venizelos, who favored war; he blindly led Greece into a war that was to lead to the famous catastrophe.

The next war is another example of Britain's disdain. Despite the fact that Greece stood alone with Britain against all the odds, for several months the help that Britain sent was minimal, and the British did not engage in too much hard combat with the Germans, confusing many of the tough Greek fighters who had already earned their spurs against the Italian invaders. The Greek civil war is an even worse story: having supported the strongest anti-German resistance, ELAS, Britain then turned against it, ending up supporting those Greek forces that had been closest to the German occupiers and fueling a destructive civil war. As Francis Noel-Baker (1946, 43) wrote: "Instead of making Greek resistance more moderate, more democratic, more truly representative of the mass of Greek opinion, we drove it to extremes."

Extracts from a Foreign Office paper prepared for the Foreign Minister Anthony Eden in June 1944 show how Britain betrayed its main anti-German Greek resistance allies, essentially because of its obsession with, and distrust of, the Soviet Union:

> Nor can any accusation be levelled against the Russians of organising the spread of communism in the Balkans. ... The Soviet Government's support of the Communist-led elements in these countries is not so much based on ideological grounds as on the fact that such elements are most responsive to and are the most vigorous in resisting the axis. ... Furthermore, if anyone is to blame for the present situation in which the Communist-led

movements are the most powerful elements in Yugoslavia and Greece, it is
we ourselves. Russia's historical interest in the Balkans has always
manifested itself in a determination that no other Great Power shall
dominate them, as this would constitute a strategical threat to Russia. ...
whereas in the nineteenth century we had Austro-Hungary as an ally to
counter these Russian measures there is no one on whom we can count to
support us this time. ... As a result of our approach to the Soviet
Government, however, the latter have now agreed to let us take the lead in
Greece.[2]

Apart from the clear evidence that the British obsession with Russia (and
Britain's schizophrenic support for the communists in Yugoslavia and the
anti-communists in Greece) and the EM had not changed, we see here that
Winston Churchill's and Joseph Stalin's infamous "percentages agreement"
at Yalta a few months later, whereby Greece would be 10 percent Russian
and 90 percent English, already existed in essence. Greece was merely a
tool for Britain, which was soon to replace Austro-Hungary with the US to
counter Russia. Some of the main ingredients of the Greek civil war were
Churchill's obsession with the return of an unpopular Greek king,
Britain's obsession with Russia, and thus the way in which Britain helped,
whether by default or design, to polarize the forces in Greece. In this
sense, the Cold War began in the Balkans, since as we can see the Foreign
Office was already doing its utmost to keep the Soviet Union well away
from Greece long before the struggle for Germany had begun. Indeed, the
Allies had only just landed in Normandy. The Joint Planning Staff wrote
in December 1945:

> Our strategic interest is to ensure that no unfriendly power, by the acqui-
> sition of Greek bases, can threaten our Mediterranean communications. On
> the other hand, we wish to liquidate our present military commitment as
> soon as possible.[3]

In 1947, Britain handed Greece to America, thus introducing US and
future NATO (North Atlantic Treaty Organization) power into the
Balkans. The Truman Doctrine and massive deliveries of military
hardware – as well as the Tito–Stalin disagreement – put an end to the
civil war by 1949, and a bitter and exhausted Greece was now free to join
NATO, as it did in 1952. Yet the divisions caused by the civil war lived on
in the party political system. Shades of it still exist today.

The civil war heritage apart, Greece can today be described as an
economic – and by extension political – hub. The shenanigans surrounding
the so far failed attempts to privatize the Greek natural gas company
DEPA are but one of many examples of competing foreign interests,

underpinned by US/European Union (EU) attempts to ward off Russian economic influence in Greece (Michaletos 2011). And now China has entered the fray: one incisive analyst has written about reported interest from 10,000 Chinese citizens in acquiring real estate in Greece, at an average of $350,000 per unit (Michaletos 2014), which would apparently allow them a five-year residence permit. He adds that along with business networking, this could be a coup for Chinese intelligence services in Europe.

Cyprus's qualified independence

The year 1947 was certainly a defining one for Cyprus, and indeed for the EM. The Truman Doctrine was all the rage in Greece and Turkey, while the first Macarthyist tendencies were being exported from America. The Foreign Office, as well as the Colonial Office, which was responsible for Cyprus, considered whether to cede Cyprus to Greece. The factors favoring the latter were the Atlantic Charter and the Universal Declaration of Human Rights; impending decolonization, for example in India, Transjordan, Burma, and Ceylon; the handing of the Dodecanese by Italy to Greece (via the British Military Administration); and the natural feeling of the Greek Cypriots that they were in fact Greek, just as Greek Cretans had felt Greek. A senior under secretary in the Foreign Office argued strongly that giving up Cyprus would contribute to Greek morale and British influence (the civil war was in full swing) and prevent future strife in Cyprus.[4] However, other forces, including the War Office, argued that with a communist Greece, to give up Cyprus would be a serious mistake (Mallinson 1999, 31). There was a whiff of hypocrisy in this argument, since the massive arms deliveries by America were on the agenda, and the US had entered the picture courtesy of Britain. What can be said is that, whether by design or default, the Greek civil war was used as an excuse to hang on to Cyprus.

The story of the bitter fighting that led to Cyprus's qualified independence is too well known to repeat here. Suffice to say that the British colluded with Turkey, brought it into the equation illegally (in contravention of Article 16 of the Treaty of Lausanne), and were finally pressurized by the US to do a deal whereby Britain would keep some of Cyprus, allied to various other rights; rights that made a mockery of true sovereignty. Thus, Cyprus's alleged independence in 1960 was predicated on the British retaining both Cypriot territory and various other rights, mainly in the military field. Disraeli's words in 1878 are still valid today:

> If Cyprus can be conceded to your majesty by the Porte, and England at the same time enters into defensive alliance with Turkey, guaranteeing Asiatic Turkey from Russian invasion, the power of England in the Mediterranean will be absolutely increased in that region and your Majesty's Indian Empire immensely strengthened. Cyprus is the key of Western Asia. (Buckle 1920, 291)

Perhaps one difference today is that US power has increased in Cyprus, as the British bases are in all but name NATO ones, and since the US shares British electronic intelligence gathering. Even when Britain tried to give up its bases in the wake of the Turkish invasion, Kissinger simply said no. However, as late as 1977 a secret Ministry of Defence paper was stating that the government's preferred policy was to withdraw completely from the bases.[5] By 1980 the idea was dead, and a Thatcherite administration put paid to any idea of upsetting Britain's American sisters. Since then, we have seen Cyprus used by Greece (the Sampson coup), Turkey (the occupation), and even Russia, when it sold S-300 defense systems to Cyprus, in the possible knowledge that this would cause problems for NATO. In the end, Cyprus succumbed to Turkish bombing threats and the system ended up on Crete. Before now turning to the obsession with Russia, let us remember that in 1957, Henry Kissinger (1957, 165) wrote of Cyprus as a "staging area for the Middle East." And so it is today.

The Russian obsession

That both Greece and Cyprus have been, and are, political footballs in a frenetic match between outside players is a fact of life of the EM geopolitical laboratory. Fear of Russia still abounds, just as it always did:

> The most serious consequence of all would be that our withdrawal would lead to the ultimate establishment of Soviet influence on the island. Though this is perhaps not very likely, it is not impossible that an independent Cyprus Government, deprived of the economic benefits of our bases, might bring it upon themselves by seeking Soviet aid.[6]

That was in 1964. By 1975, the Cold War was at the base of British and American thinking on Greece and Cyprus:

> We must also recognise that in the final analysis Turkey must be regarded as more important to Western strategic interests than Greece and that, if risks must be run, they should be risks of further straining Greek rather than Turkish relations with the West.[7]

The already mentioned sale of S-300s is but one example of Russian involvement. Another example, perhaps more serious, was Russia's rejection at the UN Security Council of last-minute Western attempts to make the infamous Annan Plan look acceptable. Today, nothing has changed. Russia simply wants a demilitarized Cyprus to be the price of reunification.

Now

Greece and Cyprus will continue to be geopolitical fodder for the foreseeable future. The Ukraine debacle has enhanced this likelihood. Despite a cheap Russian loan to Cyprus, recently Greece, Cyprus, and Israel have irritated Russia by presenting their cooperation on gas exploration and potential production as a way of reducing EU dependence on Russian gas. On April 9, 2014, Cypriot president Nicos Anastasiades told Reuters that the discovery of gas within Cyprus's economic zone would facilitate international efforts to solve the Cyprus problem and provide an alternative energy supply source to Europe, thus decreasing its dependence on Russian gas imports (Cyprus Newsletter 2014).

Israel's finger in the geo-laboratorial pie of Greece and Cyprus, enhanced by its US-sponsored strategic cooperation with Turkey, is also a complicating factor, and a potentially destabilizing one at that. Apart from irritating Russia, various military exercises between Greek, Cypriot, and Israeli forces are hardly likely to please Moscow, in that they give Israel a connection with NATO. American vice president Joe Biden's visit to Cyprus in May 2014 demonstrated increasing US involvement in Cyprus, essentially to "show the Russians." As expected, he emphasized Cyprus's potential help to the EU on the gas front, and even linked gas to a solution to the Cyprus problem. The timing of his visit, just before the controversial presidential elections in the Ukraine, spoke volumes.[8] Cyprus can expect to be pressurized into another Annan Plan. Yet whatever happens, it will be a "solution" predicated on the British bases, meaning that Cyprus will not have its own foreign and military policy, whatever the semantics. In this regard, readers may well remember how, in the frenetic negotiations on the Annan Plan, the US and Britain, in their desperation to secure the future of the bases, tried to get Greece, Turkey, and Cyprus to sign a so-called Foundation Agreement, which would have reaffirmed the validity of the 1960 treaties – treaties that had been shown to have failed, and were in many respects disregarded. On top of that, the plan would have obliged Greece and Cyprus to support Turkey's accession to the European Union. Thus, the bases were seen as the main objective of the US and Britain, along with getting Turkey into the EU, just as a quarter of a century before. At the end of 1980, having completely succumbed to the master–butler relationship, a senior Foreign Office official wrote:

> The benefits which we derive from the SBAs [Sovereign Base Areas] are of major significance and virtually irreplaceable. They are an essential contribution to the Anglo-American relationship. The Department have regularly considered with those concerned which circumstances in Cyprus are most conducive to our retaining unfettered use of our SBA facilities. On balance, the conclusion is that an early "solution" might not help (since pressures against the SBAs might then build up), just as breakdown and return to strife would not, and that our interests are best served by continuing movement towards a solution – without the early prospect of arrival.[9]

The only difference today is that the US is pushing hard for a "solution," worried at the prospect that as long as unoccupied Cyprus has its own foreign policy, there will always be a danger that it will move closer to Moscow. At the same time, it is important to bear in mind that Turkish–Israeli strategic cooperation in the Middle East, particularly on Syria, is an even greater priority to the US than a reunified Cyprus. Although Turkish–Israeli relations have been adversely affected by Erdoğan's anti-Israel rhetoric on the Palestinian question, the US-sponsored effort to use Turkey and Israel (as well as Greece and Cyprus) to exclude the Russians is still very much there.

Another annoyance for Russia was the Burgas–Alexandroupolis oil pipeline farrago, when Russia realized that Greece was simply becoming a US and German client state par excellence. In 2008, according to the Greek Intelligence Service (EYP), then Greek Prime Minister Kostas Karamanlis's life was threatened. Nineteen Russian Federal Security Bureau (FSB) operatives were reported to have followed Karamanlis. According to the FSB, the reason for their presence was the attempted tapping of the telephones of Russian president Vladimir Putin, Bulgarian Prime Minister Sergei Stanishev, and Karamanlis (GR Reporter 2012). What makes the story credible is the fact that the Greek public prosecutor opened an investigation. The longer he fails to come up with an answer, the more credible the story becomes. At any rate, Karamanlis went on to lose the elections the following year, and the pipeline was put on hold or killed off, depending on one's perspective.

However, Cyprus, perhaps because of its geographic and geohistorical position, may be less of a client state than Greece. Should Russia consider guaranteeing its security, then it would be tempting for some sections of the Cypriot political spectrum to offer Russia a long-term naval and airforce base. That would certainly put the cat among the pigeons. It would also mark a step away from the official Russian position on Cyprus; namely, that it will never accept a united Cyprus, unless it is non-aligned, forbidden to join NATO, and the Americans allow Britain to give up its bases. Current shifts in Russian policy caused by NATO's obsession with the Ukraine's resources and its proximity to Russia could well see Russia adopting a firmer line on Cyprus, and even on Greece and Turkey. Its Mediterranean navy is increasing in size.

Conclusion

Can one ever really conclude anything connected to relations between states? In 1969, the US State department wrote:

> No solution is permanent. A glance at the last 3,500 years of Cypriot history demonstrates that the Phoenician, Greek, Assyrian, Macedonian, Egyptian, Persian, Roman, Byzantine, Saracen, Frankish, Venetian, Genoese, Turkish and British solutions were not permanent, regardless of how permanent they may have been at one time.[10]

Despite the simplicity and superficiality of the categorizations (for example, the separation of the Greeks from the Macedonians), the contention that no solution is permanent holds a fair amount of water if one looks at history. The real factors that determine the state of our world are human behavior and characteristics, both individual and collective. Thus, the title of this chapter, cruel though it may be and even it if may upset the more nationalistic Greeks and Cypriots, is valid. Worse, it may even be taken to imply that Greeks and Cypriots are themselves geopolitical fodder. This is of course hardly something that is restricted to Greeks and Cypriots. After all, Britain and Saudi Arabia are client states par excellence, and Ukraine is now being fought over by all manner of external forces.

The recent and curiously sudden appearance of ISIL (Islamic State of Iraq and the Levant) in Iraq and Syria is fortuitous for American and Israeli policy to control the Middle East, since ISIL can be used to topple Syrian president Bashar al-Assad's government, which would give the US a freer hand in Iran. Of course, plenty of bombs and missiles have been dropped and launched against ISIL, but to some observers it looks suspiciously like window dressing. Russia is undoubtedly aware of the US's Janus-like strategy, and continues to arm Syria.

The whole Middle East quagmire is now rebounding on Europe, with Muslims attacking bastions of European freedom of expression, such as French magazine *Charlie Hebdo*. This is leading to incipient US-style clampdowns on freedom of expression, and of course to increased sales pressure by American–Israeli security companies, which already have a large chunk of the European market.

Thus Greece and Cyprus need to be somewhat careful in their enthusiasm for military, and even oil energy, cooperation with Israel, particularly since they are crossroads of illegal immigration, with a large number of Jihadist-minded Muslims, some of whom may be exploitable fanatics. To keep out of the unpleasantness currently affecting France, Belgium, and Britain, Greece and Cyprus would do well to salvage what they can of their sovereignty, by pursuing a more Byzantine policy of balancing the forces. In this context, increased cooperation with Russia is important.

Atavism is an important human characteristic: just as Britain and France fought the Russians in the Crimean War, so now the same kind of frightened forces are interfering on Russia's doorstep. For better or worse, Greece and Cyprus are connected to this tawdry picture, owing to the irrational and atavistic fear of Russia on the part of Britain and its successor empire, the US. In Italian historian Francesco Guicciardini's words, the same things return with different colors, while in his compatriot political philosopher Giambattista Vico's thinking, we are passing into a state of anarchy. This is what happens when empires are beginning to die.

Notes

1. Here I am not of course referring to the sensible English School of the 1960s and the likes of Hedley Bull and Martin Wight. See Butterfield and Wight (1966).
2. Top Secret Foreign Office Memorandum for Secretary of State, 7 June 1944, BNA FO 371/43646, file R 9092. In Mallinson (2011, 12–14).
3. Report by Joint Planning Staff, 3 December 1945, FCO 371/48288, file R 21028/G.
4. BNA FO 371/67084. File R13462/G. In Mallinson (1999, 41).
5. MOD paper on the defence implications of an early military withdrawal from Cyprus (annex A to COS5/77), BNA DEFE 24/1525, fileD/DS8/24/2, part 36, covering note by Group Captain Bliss (Acting Secretary, Chiefs of Staff Committee), dated 28 January 1977.
6. Foreign Office paper, 13 March 1964, BNA DO 220/170, file 2-MED 193/105/2.

7. "British Interests in the Eastern Mediterranean," paper prepared by Western European Department, FCO, 11 April 1975, BNA FCO 46/1248, file DPI/516/1.
8. Interestingly, at the time of writing Biden's son has just taken up a position in a Ukrainian gas company, Burisma Holdings, which has its headquarters in Cyprus. Most serendipitous!
9. Minute from Fergusson to Foreign Minister's Private Secretary, 8 December 1980, BNA FCO 9/2949, file WSC 023/1, part C.
10. State Department Policy Statement on Cyprus, enclosed with a letter of 6 February 1969 from Folsom (State Department) to Smart (British Embassy, Washington), BNA FCO 9/971, file WSC 3/3 18/2.

References

Bell, Duncan. 2006. "Beware of False Prophets: Biology, Human Nature and the Future of International Relations Theory." International Affairs, 82: 493–510.

Buckle, B. E. 1920. The Life of Benjamin Disraeli, Earl of Beaconsfield. London: John Murray.

Butterfield, Herbert, and Martin Wight (Eds.). 1966. Diplomatic Investigations. London: George Allen and Unwin.

Cyprus Newsletter. 2014. Cyprus Newsletter, 23, May.

de Bertier de Sauvigny, Guillaume. 1962. Metternich and his Times. London: Darton, Longman and Todd.

GR Reporter. 2012. "Burgas-Alexandroupolis Oil Pipeline behind the Plan to Assassinate Kostas Karamanlis." GR Reporter, 15 March.

Hill, Christopher. 2003. The Changing Politics of Foreign Policy. Basingstoke: Palgrave Macmillan.

Kissinger, Henry A. 1957. Nuclear Weapons and Foreign Policy. New York: Harper & Brothers.

Mallinson, William. 1999. "Turkish Invasions, Cyprus and the Treaty of Guarantee." Synthesis – Review of Modern Greek Studies, 3: 39–48.

—. 2011. Britain and Cyprus: Key Themes and Documents since World War Two. London: I. B.Tauris.

Michaletos, Ioannis. 2011. "Transformations in the Greek Natural Gas Market: EU Strategy, Azerbaijan, and a Regional Role for DEPA," Balkanalysis.com, 1 November. http://www.balkanalysis.com/greece/2011/11/01/transformations-in-the-greek-natural-gas-market-eu-strategy-azerbaijan-and-a-regional-role-for-depa/. Accessed November 2014.

—. 2014. "China Eyes Greece Investment as a Staging Post for EU Operations." Balkanalysis.com, 13 November.

http://www.balkanalysis.com/greece/2014/11/13/china-eyes-greece-
investment-as-a-staging-post-for-eu-operations/.
Accessed November 2014.
Noel-Baker, Francis. 1946. Greece: The Whole Story, London:
Hutchinson.
O'Tuthail, Gearóid, Simon Dalby, and Paul Routledge (Eds.). 1998. The
Geopolitics Reader. London: Routledge.
Sked, Alan (Ed.). 1979. Europe's Balance of Power, 1815–1848. London:
Macmillan.
Yutang, Lin. 1976. The Importance of Living. London: Heinemann. (First
published in 1938.)

CHAPTER THREE

NATURAL GAS FUNDAMENTALS, GEOPOLITICS AND THE WAY FORWARD

SOLON KASSINIS

Natural gas fundamentals and characteristics

The word "gas" was proposed by the seventeenth-century Flemish chemist Jan Baptist van Helmont, as a phonetic spelling of his Dutch pronunciation of the Greek word "chaos," which Paracelsus had used for "air" since 1538 (New World Encyclopedia 2013). Natural gas is a gaseous fossil fuel consisting primarily of methane, but with minor quantities of ethane, propane, butane, and pentane-heavy hydrocarbons (Wikipedia 2014a)

Natural gas, as the name suggests, is a naturally occurring hydrocarbon compound, usually found in the earth as a mineral resource. Natural gas is colourless and odorless (an artificial odor is purposely added to help detect leakages during pipeline transport), and is lighter than air (DEPA 2014a).

Natural gas can be commercially produced from conventional, or indeed unconventional, oil fields and natural gas fields. Other types of gas exist, however (see Table 3.1).

Natural gas is mainly composed of methane (see Table 3.2), of the alkanes group, which is the simplest hydrocarbon; yet being a fossil fuel it encompasses very many forms and uses today. Associated gas, non-associated gas, gas hydrates, coal bed methane (CBM), shale gas, and tight sands are some of its source forms known to date, while the use of natural gas has been extended from power generation purposes to petrochemicals production, heating/cooling, cooking, and co-generation of heat and electricity.

Table 3.1: Town gas vs. biogas vs. landfill gas. Source: Adapted from http://en.wikipedia.org/wiki/Natural_gas.

Town gas is a mixture of methane and other gases, mainly the highly toxic carbon monoxide that can be used in a similar way to natural gas and can be produced by treating coal chemically.
Biogas is usually produced from agricultural waste materials, such as otherwise unusable parts of plants and manure. Biogas may also be produced by separating organic materials from waste that otherwise goes to landfill.
Landfill gas is usually produced from waste material buried at landfill sites.

Table 3.2: Typical natural gas components (methane is the primary component). Source: Information from Pierre-René Bauquis, Total Professeurs Associés (2008).

C1	Methane
C2	Ethane
C3	Propane
C4	Butane
C5+	Pentane and heavier hydrocarbons (also known as natural gasoline and condensates)
Impurities	Water Nitrogen Helium Carbon dioxide Hydrogen sulfide Mercury

Gas has been used since the 1820s in the Fredonia City of New York for lighting purposes (DEPA 2014b). In Athens (Greece), the production of gas from coal (mainly lignite) began in the late 1850s, with the construction of gas production facilities in an area known as the "Gas Works." This gas was used for around 60 years for street lighting, while its application then extended to houses and factories (Technopolis 2014).

After the mid-1980s, gas production operations from coal ceased and those from naphtha began (naphtha was obtained from crude oil refineries), followed finally by natural gas imports from external suppliers in the late 1980s (Attica Gas Supply Company 2014). Nowadays, natural gas is also used for cooking and domestic heating in addition to its traditional use for power generation and lighting.

The formation and forms of natural gas

Natural gas was created after millions of years of thermal anaerobic (i.e., in the absence of air) decomposition and compression of organic matter buried deep underneath the Earth's surface (Theodoropoulos 2010, 55–56).

The following five characteristics are essential for a system of hydrocarbons to exist:

- *Source rock* – a deep rock within which hydrocarbons are formed/generated from its original organic matter.
- *Migration* – the movement of hydrocarbons from the source rock to the reservoir rock over time.
- *Reservoir rock* – a porous, permeable, sponge-like rock that retains the hydrocarbons in place.
- *Trap* – the overall geological structure within which hydrocarbons gather.
- *Cap rock* – an impermeable seal that prevents hydrocarbons from escaping.

Hydrocarbon systems involve complex geological functions, as shown in Figure 3.1:

Generation:
- Oil and gas are formed in source rocks.

Migration:
- Oil and gas move over time from the source rock to the reservoir rock.
- Reservoir rocks have the following characteristics:
  o Porosity – to store oil and gas.
  o Permeability – to allow oil and gas to move through the reservoir rock.

Accumulation and entrapment:

- Oil and gas are retained in reservoir rocks (sedimentary rocks such as limestone or sandstone), which are buried deep below the surface.
- A geological trap halts the movement of oil and gas and allows the accumulation of entrapped oil and gas. (Theodoropoulos 2010, 64–66)

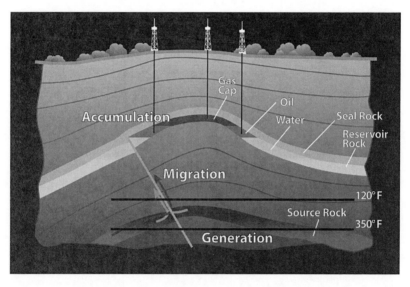

Figure 3.1: The functions of hydrocarbon systems. Source: Adapted from http://doddys.files.wordpress.com/2006/10/petroleum-system.jpg.

Natural gas found deep underneath the Earth's surface can be either biogenic gas or thermogenic gas, depending on the actual mechanism by which the gas in place was originally formed (Wikipedia 2014a). Biogenic gas formation is nearly identical to biogas generation. Biogenic gas usually has very pure methane content, while thermogenic gas formation is an indirect consequence of kerogens generation; kerogens are derived from organic matter under conditions of high heat and pressure (Booth, Rowe, and Fischer 1996). Table 3.3 provides a summary of the main characteristics of each formation mechanism.

Natural gas can exist either as "dry gas," which is pure methane, or "wet gas," which is mainly methane together with heavier hydrocarbons in varying proportions (Wikipedia 2014b). The presence of inert components in natural gas, such as nitrogen and carbon dioxide, tends to reduce the calorific value of the gas. On the other hand, hydrogen sulfide, when present in natural gas, needs to be removed during the initial processing because of its toxicity and corrosiveness. The presence of hydrogen sulfide accounts for the "sourness" of natural gas (natural gas in the absence of hydrogen sulfide is called "sweet" gas). The presence of significant quantities of acidic gases, such as hydrogen sulfide or carbon dioxide, makes the gas "acidic" (Wikipedia 2014c).

Table 3.3: Biogenic gas vs. thermogenic gas. Source: Adapted from Booth, J. S., M. M. Rowe, and K. M. Fischer. 1996. "Offshore Gas Hydrate Sample Database with an Overview and Preliminary Analysis." U.S. Geological Survey Open-File Report 96-272. Reston, VA: USGS.

Biogenic gas   • Contains ≥ 99% methane   • Produced as a direct consequence of anaerobic bacterial activity
Thermogenic gas   • Also known as petrogenic gas   • Usually a mixture of ethane, propane, and other light hydrocarbons including methane   • The hydrocarbon gases are produced under conditions of high temperature and great pressure from kerogens (which are derived from organic matter)

Gas fields with an appreciable proportion of heavier hydrocarbons are known as condensate deposits ("condensates"). While wet natural gas and condensates are found near to or in combination with oil deposits, dry gas is usually found alone in individual gas fields. This is explained by the fact that most of the dry natural gas derives from terrestrial plants.

There is also a distinction between "associated gas," which is natural gas associated with crude oil, and "non-associated gas," which is generated individually (see Figure 3.2).

In the case of "associated gas," natural gas is dissolved in crude oil and released during production due to the pressure relief (from a high pressure inside the underground reservoir to a lower pressure, close to atmospheric pressure, at the surface). If crude oil is supersaturated, then part of the gas

66 Chapter Three

migrates upward and forms a gas dome, which under certain conditions may be exploitable.

The main components of natural gas deposits are often related to crude oil, particularly as to their formation. Oil and gas are often found in the same geological stratum of a region. "Dry gas," which is mainly a product of carbonization, can also be found next to oilfields, considering that the majority of natural gas fields around the world are related to oil deposits.

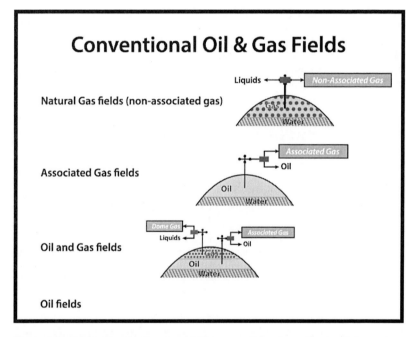

Figure 3.2: Conventional oil and gas fields – configurations. Source: Information provided by Pierre-René Bauquis, Total Professeurs Associés (2008)

The recovery of oil and gas from hydrocarbon fields can be carried out by various mechanisms. In most cases, and for newly producing fields, the reservoir pressure causes the fluid (oil or gas) to rise to the surface when a borehole is drilled down to the reservoir rock. This reservoir pressure diminishes as production expands and at some point other methods (usually physical and chemical) must therefore be used to recover the rest of the hydrocarbons in place (such methods can be fluid injection of water or carbon dioxide, fracking, injection of chemicals, etc.).

The portion of hydrocarbons that can be brought to the surface is called "recoverable." The level of recoverable hydrocarbons depends on the physical properties of the reservoir and the recoverability is categorized by the probability of recovery – 10 percent for possible reserves, 50 percent for probable reserves, and 90 percent for proven reserves.

The trading of natural gas

Natural gas is gaining more ground as the "preferred" conventional fossil fuel for the coming decades due to its characteristically more efficient and cleaner combustion. It has yet to become the most utilized fossil fuel, replacing oil. The complete (integrated) natural gas market value chain is shown in Figure 3.3.

Although being a gas fuel, rather than a liquid fuel (like oil), makes natural gas lighter and therefore of a low energy density, this in turn makes its transportation and storage more costly per energy content when compared to oil. Its distinct characteristics give it many more advantages (in addition to the ones already referred to), mainly versatility and robustness in use, as well as safety and flexibility during transport (this is especially true for liquefied natural gas (LNG), which is contained and transported at atmospheric pressure by special marine tankers).

Crude oil is traded today as a commodity, similarly to gold and other valuable goods, and is available through spot markets on a global basis. Spot prices and trading of natural gas differ between regions and continents, while gas supplies (either in natural form or as LNG) are most usually carried out through long-term sales and purchase agreements (SPA).

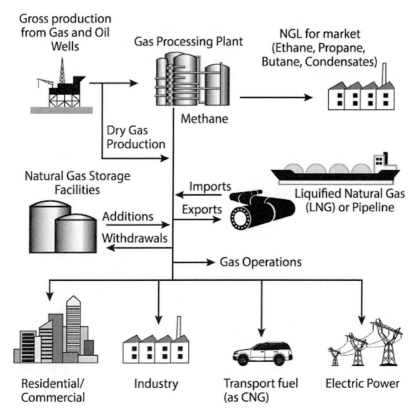

Figure 3.3: The natural gas market value chain. Source: Adapted from http://www.natgas.info/gas-information/what-is-natural-gas/gas-pipelines.

Gas fields in remote areas are utilizable only if the market price makes the processing and export of natural gas economically feasible. A common practice (in the case of large volumes and large distances) is the liquefaction of natural gas to produce LNG and its subsequent export by special marine tankers to consumer countries (Figure 3.4 shows the LNG chain). Likewise, associated gas or "stranded" gas may be used as feedstock for the production of petrochemicals, such as methanol, dimethyl ether (DME), ammonia, urea, ethylene, synthetic gasoline, and so on.

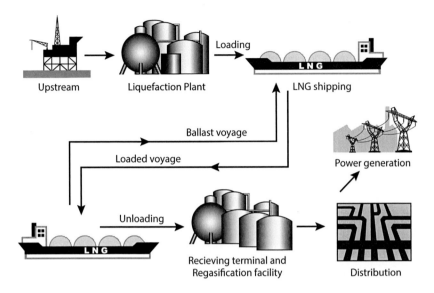

Figure 3.4: The LNG chain. Source: Adapted from http://www.natgas.info/gas-information/what-is-natural-gas/lng.

Ways of utilizing and monetizing natural gas

As already mentioned, natural gas can have many uses – from large-scale power generation and industrial co-generation, to petrochemicals production and even to small-scale domestic heating and cooking. The uses of natural gas by sector are as shown in Table 3.4.

Table 3.4: Uses of natural gas by sector.

Industrial Sector	Commercial Sector
– Power generation – Co-generation of power and heat – Heating – Raw material for the production of petrochemicals (such as methanol, ammonia, etc.)	– Central heating – Heating/cooling – Hot water production
Transport Sector	**Domestic Sector**
– Cars – Trains – Trucks – Buses – Ships	– Mainly for central heating and cooking

The monetization (exportation) of natural gas can take many forms, the main ones being the following:

Liquefied natural gas (LNG)
- Small-scale liquefaction plants (small-scale LNG)
- Large-scale onshore liquefaction plants (LNG plants)
- Floating liquefaction plants (FLNG)

Petrochemicals
- Petrochemical plants (using natural gas as a raw material for the production of petrochemical products)
- Natural gas liquids (NGL) – used in the production of LPG and natural gasoline

Gas-to-liquids (GTL)
- Used for the production of synthetic gasoline

Compressed natural gas (CNG)
- Pipeline CNG
- Marine CNG (this technology is not yet commercially available)

Electricity
- Using natural gas as a fuel for power generation and subsequently exporting the electricity that is produced

Natural gas operations and processes: Purification, liquefaction, regasification, storage, and petrochemicals production

Prior to any further use or processing, raw natural gas produced by the upstream oil/gas fields needs first to be treated and purified. This process occurs at a gas processing plant (or gas plant) and mainly involves the separation of the gas from any water and condensates (i.e., heavy hydrocarbons that condense out of the vapor phase during transport) using a three-phase separator followed by water treatment and condensate stabilization:

- Acidic or corrosive gases are removed by contacting the dry gas with *amine absorbers*.

- Drying using *glycol dehydration towers* to remove any water vapor in solution with the gas.
- Natural gas liquids are removed through cooling/expanding the gas, and *fractionation* of the liquids in a series of distillation columns to purify each NGL and the methane gas.

LNG is natural gas (predominantly methane) that has been converted into liquid form for ease of storage and transport, by cooling it down to -161 °C, through a series of refrigeration cycles. It is an odorless, colorless, non-toxic, and non-corrosive liquid that can float on water (i.e., it is less dense than water). LNG has the great advantage of taking up about 1/600th of the volume of natural gas in the gaseous state, therefore it can be stored and transported over long distances and in large volumes practically and economically (Wikipedia 2014d).

The stages of the natural gas liquefaction process are as follows (see also Figure 3.5):

1a. Pre-treatment – to remove impurities and water.
1b. Pre-cooling – to remove any condensates.
2. Liquefaction – by a series of refrigeration cycles to liquefy the gas.
3. Storage – to maintain the LNG until needed, and then loading it onto LNG carriers to transport/export it.

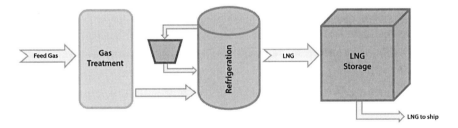

Figure 3.5: The natural gas liquefaction process. Source: http://goldborolng.com/about-lng/what-is-lng

Following regasification at a regas terminal, LNG is converted back to natural gas and fed into the transmission system (for delivery to the power generation plants and other large industrial units), and then into the distribution network (for distribution to the commercial, domestic, and transport sectors). The process at the regas terminal entails the following steps:

1. Storage (keeping LNG until needed).
2. Pumping LNG out of tanks and into the gas send-out system.
3. Passing LNG through a recondenser unit (to liquefy any boil-off gas collected from LNG vaporizing inside the tanks; thus balancing the process).
4. Pumping LNG through a series of heat exchangers (usually open rack vaporizers, ORV, which use seawater as the heating medium) to vaporize it back to gas and heat it up to atmospheric temperature.
5. Compressing the gas and feeding it to the transmission system.

Gas storage is absolutely necessary considering that gas consumption throughout the year is typically uneven and that demand and supply need to be matched. Natural gas can be temporarily stored in its natural form (as an artificial gas deposit) in natural underground reservoirs, such as depleted gas reservoirs, aquifer reservoirs, and salt cavern reservoirs. Alternatively, natural gas can be stored in its liquid form (i.e., as LNG) in full containment tanks; assuming of course that natural gas is liquefied before storage and then regasified before use.

Petrochemicals are produced in petrochemical plants through a series of processes (chemical reactions and purification methods) that turn the feedstock (natural gas) into chemical or fuel products (petrochemicals). Most final products can be produced directly or indirectly from their preceding compounds (see Figure 3.6).

The most important petrochemicals are:

• Lower or lighter alkenes (olefins), e.g., ethylene, propylene, and butadiene.
• Aromatics: benzene, toluene, xylene, DME.
• Ammonia, methanol, synthesis gas (carbon monoxide and hydrogen).

Alternatively, natural gas can be converted into liquid products via a process called gas to liquids (GTL); these liquid products, together with the NGL recovered from the initial processing and liquefaction of the gas, can be used as fuels, mainly for the transportation sector.

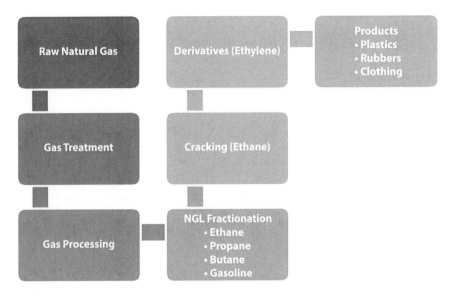

Figure 3.6: The petrochemicals production process. Adapted from
http://www.shell.us/aboutshell/projects-locations/appalachia/about-project.html.

The geopolitics of natural gas in the Eastern Mediterranean region

The Eastern Mediterranean (EM) has been a hydrocarbons producer for many decades. Hydrocarbon production facilities have been in operation for several years, especially in Egypt but also in Israel (although at a much lower level and only for gas).

Palestine has an offshore gas field located 30 km off the coast of the Gaza Strip, pending development. Cyprus joined the energy fraternity recently and is now engaged in many ongoing hydrocarbon exploration activities, while Lebanon has been making attempts toward launching hydrocarbon exploration activities in its exclusive economic zone (EEZ). At the moment Greece, which has been producing oil for some years and recently made significant steps toward launching hydrocarbon exploration activities in its EEZ, seems to have more or less stalled, mainly due to its political and economic situation.

It can be deduced from this discussion that currently the main energy players in the region are Cyprus, Egypt, and Israel. Multilateral regional cooperation between these states (i.e., Cyprus–Egypt and Cyprus–Israel) regarding hydrocarbon development and exploitation will clearly benefit the EM discovery and exploitation process. Cooperation between these three countries can also set the baseline for a future extension toward Greece and Lebanon, and possibly Palestine, which also have an important role to play in the EM. Overall, the EM presents opportunities as well as challenges that can be offset by some common facts (see Table 3.5).

Table 3.5: The Eastern Mediterranean region: Opportunities, challenges, and facts.

Opportunities	Challenges	Facts
• Promising regional geological background • Big hydrocarbon discoveries in the region • Many attractive major "plays" have been identified • Market with large potential for oil and gas trading • Located at the crossroads of international energy routes	• Historical tensions in geopolitical setting • Unstable political scene • Deep and ultra-deep operations	• Hydrocarbon activities can serve as a catalyst toward cooperation and stability in the region • New deep water technologies decrease the risk for the oil companies • Increased gas (and LNG) demand can secure the commercial potential of hydrocarbon discoveries

Some of the new investments and recent major actions recorded in this region include the following:

- Memorandum of understanding for the preparation of a technical study for the export and sale of natural gas from Block 12 to Egypt signed between Cyprus Hydrocarbons Company and Egypt's EGAS.
- Italy's ENI enlarging its investments/activities in Egypt's energy sector.
- UK-based Noble Clean Fuels to supply Egypt with 7 LNG cargoes.
- Memorandum of understanding for cooperation in the field of oil and gas signed between Cyprus and Egypt.

Hydrocarbon prospects in the Eastern Mediterranean region

An assessment from US Geological Survey in 2010 estimated that the Nile Delta Basin had 1.76 billion barrels of undiscovered oil and 223 trillion cubic feet of undiscovered natural gas reserves, while the figures for the Levantine Basin were 1.68 billion barrels and 122 trillion cubic feet, respectively (USGS 2010a, b). The corresponding geological regions are shown in Figure 3.7.

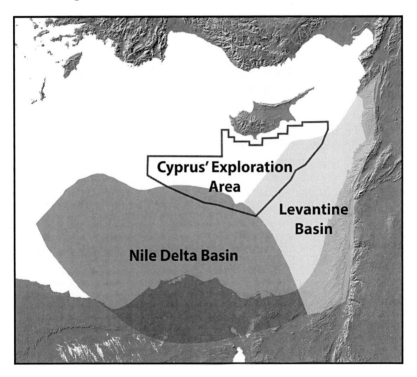

Figure 3.7: The Nile Delta Basin and the Levantine Basin. Source: Adapted from US Geological Survey. 2010. "Assessment of Undiscovered Oil and Gas Resources of the Nile Delta Basin Province, Eastern Mediterranean," Fact Sheet 2010–3027, May, and "Assessment of Undiscovered Oil and Gas Resources of the Levant Basin Province, Eastern Mediterranean," Fact Sheet 2010–3014, March.

These estimates were later updated by US-based Noble Energy following the announcement in the highlights of the 2013 Analyst Conference held in Houston, Texas:

> In the Eastern Mediterranean, discovered gross resources have grown to approximately 40 trillion cubic feet of natural gas … Significant exploration potential remains on the Company's acreage position in the Eastern Mediterranean, with approximately 3 billion barrels of gross unrisked oil potential in the deep Mesozoic play in both Cyprus and Israel and four trillion cubic feet gross of natural gas potential in Cyprus. Current plans are to resume exploration drilling in the Eastern Mediterranean in late 2014 or early 2015. (Noble Energy 2013)

Bilateral projects of common interest between Cyprus and Greece

Cyprus and Greece are both included in the European Southern Corridor for Gas and Electricity (see Figure 3.8), with two jointly proposed projects of common interest. Through these bilateral projects, Greece could become a major transit country for the supply of EM gas to Europe. In addition, Cyprus could assume the role of a central and integrated energy hub for gas exports from the EM.

The two bilateral projects jointly submitted within the context of the Southern Corridor by Cyprus and Greece (see Figure 3.9) are the EuroAsia Interconnector, a submarine cable for the transmission of electricity between Israel, Cyprus, Crete, and Greece (mainland); and the Trans-Med/East-Med Gas Pipeline, a subsea gas transmission pipeline between the Levantine (offshore), Cyprus, Crete, and Greece (mainland). Both projects would provide diversification and additional means for hydrocarbon exploitation. In addition, the EuroAsia Interconnector project could provide an "interim solution" to security of energy supply for Cyprus, Greece, and Israel.

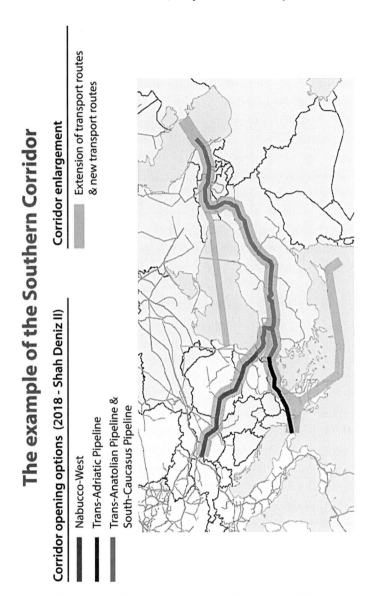

The example of the Southern Corridor

Corridor opening options (2018 - Shah Deniz II)

Nabucco-West

Trans-Adriatic Pipeline

Trans-Anatolian Pipeline &
South-Caucasus Pipeline

Corridor enlargement

Extension of transport routes

& new transport routes

Figure 3.8: The proposed European Southern Corridor. Source: "Energy priorities for Europe." Presentation of J.M. Barroso to the European Council, 22 May 2013. Courtesy of the European Commission.

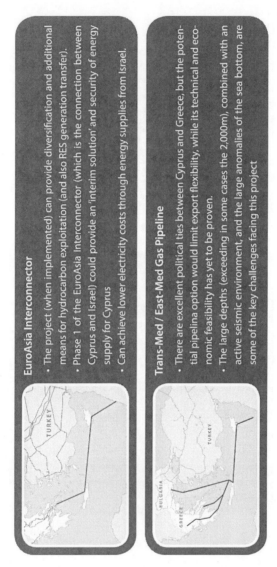

EuroAsia Interconnector

- The project (when implemented) can provide diversification and additional means for hydrocarbon exploitation (and also RES generation transfer).
- Phase 1 of the EuroAsia Interconnector (which is the connection between Cyprus and Israel) could provide an 'interim solution' and security of energy supply for Cyprus
- Can achieve lower electricity costs through energy supplies from Israel.

Trans-Med / East-Med Gas Pipeline

- There are excellent political ties between Cyprus and Greece, but the potential pipelina option would limit export flexibility, while its technical and economic feasibility has yet to be proven.
- The large depths (exceeding in some cases the 2,000m), combined with an active seismic environment, and the large anomalies of the sea bottom, are some of the key challenges facing this project

Figure 3.9: Bilateral projects of common interest between Cyprus and Greece. Source: Top: "Electricity Interconnection – North-South Electricity Interconnections in Central Eastern and South Eastern Europe." Project of Common Interest: 3.10.2, January 2014. Bottom: "Gas Interconnection – Southern Gas Corridor." Project of Common Interest: 7.3.1, January 2014. Both courtesy of the European Commission.

Hydrocarbon exploration in Cyprus

Early onshore hydrocarbon exploration attempts in Cyprus were carried out by different foreign companies. Between 1938 and 1949, a series of onshore geophysical surveys were carried out, while for the rest of the period up to 1970 various onshore exploration wells were drilled at long time intervals. These efforts had no success in terms of finding oil or gas, and were followed in 1975 by an 8,000 km 2-D offshore seismic survey in the EM conducted by Canadian company Sefel Geophysical (in collaboration with Delta Exploration, also Canadian) and in 1985–87 by studies on the seabed bathymetry, stratigraphy, lithology, sediments, and so on, led by the Soviet Academy of Sciences (in collaboration with the Geological Survey Department of Cyprus).

In 1999, UK-based Spectrum Energy and Information Technology carried out a study on the seismic lines and reprocessed the seismic data acquired in 1975 by Sefel Geophysical, while in 2000 the same company conducted an offshore 2-D seismic survey of 12,300 line-km in the greater Southeastern Mediterranean region. (Information in this section obtained from the Cypriot Ministry of Energy, Commerce, Industry and Tourism.)

Exercising its sovereign rights, as derived from the United Nations Convention on the Law of the Sea (UNCLOS '82), in 2003 Cyprus signed its first agreement on the delimitation of the EEZ with Egypt. Likewise, agreements with Lebanon and Israel followed in 2007 and 2010, respectively (Figure 3.10 shows the EEZ median lines).

These actions were vital in attracting oil and gas companies to invest in exploration activities in offshore Cyprus, as well as for strengthening ties of cooperation with countries neighboring Cyprus, particularly Israel, but also Lebanon and Egypt.

Cyprus officially inaugurated its offshore exploration activities in 2006 with the acquisition of 2-D, and some 3-D, seismic data, followed by further 2-D seismic data acquisitions in 2008, and subsequent interpretation of the processed data (see details in Figure 3.11). These seismic surveys were the basis for the preparation of the relevant seismic data interpretation reports that followed each survey and accompany each seismic data set acquired.

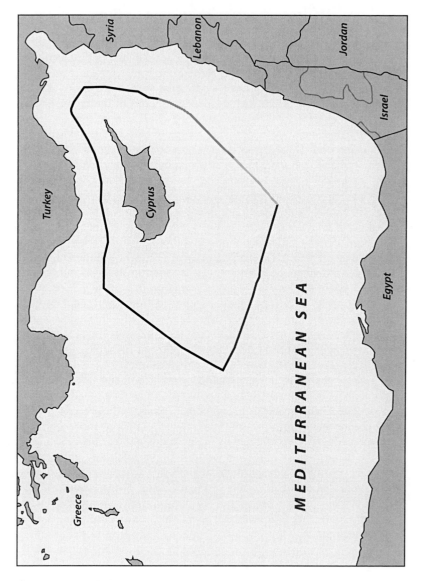

Figure 3.10: Exclusive economic zone median lines between Cyprus and Egypt, Lebanon, and Israel. Source: Information obtained from Cypriot Ministry of Energy, Commerce, Industry and Tourism.

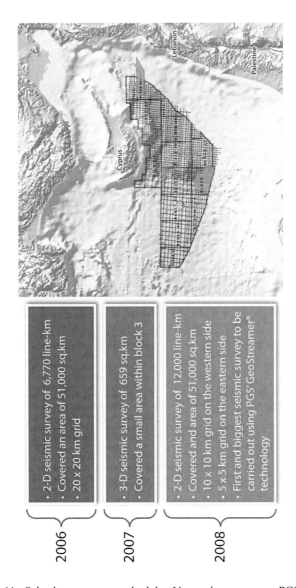

Figure 3.11: Seismic surveys acquired by Norwegian company PGS offshore Cyprus between 2006 and 2008, and relevant grid map showing all seismic surveys. Source: Information obtained from PGS and the Cypriot Ministry of Energy, Commerce, Industry and Tourism; map from http://pgs.com/Data_Library/Middle-East-and-Mediterranean/Cyprus, courtesy of PGS.

In early 2007, Cyprus proceeded with its first hydrocarbon licensing round with a total of 11 offshore blocks on offer, attracting three applications from two applicants. Within this context and following negotiations, one hydrocarbon exploration license was awarded to US-based Noble Energy International in October 2008 for Block 12 (the relevant production sharing contract was also signed on that date). Following all the necessary preparatory work and data assessment, Noble Energy proceeded with drilling its first exploratory well in September 2011.

The breakthrough for Cyprus came in December 2011, when Noble Energy announced, after the first exploration well, the discovery of natural gas (7 trillion cubic feet gross mean estimated resources) in Block 12 within Cyprus's EEZ (the deposit was named "Aphrodite"). The appraisal well of that discovery that followed in 2013 resulted in an updated estimate of approximately 5 trillion cubic feet mean gross resources of natural gas.

The success in Block 12, coupled with a clear regime and a transparent legislative framework that was established in full harmonization with the relevant European Directives, caught the attention of the international oil and gas companies around the globe and created a huge interest in Cyprus's second hydrocarbon licensing round, held in 2012, with 33 applications from 15 companies/consortia. After evaluation of the applications, three different hydrocarbon exploration licenses for Blocks 2, 3, and 9 were granted to ENI/Kogas (Korea Gas Corporation) in January 2013, while the following month two different hydrocarbon exploration licenses were awarded to French company Total for Blocks 10 and 11 (see Figure 3.12 for the map of the licensed blocks).

Relevant exploration and production sharing contracts (EPSC) were also signed with the two licensees for each of the blocks awarded. Through these contracts, the licensees are committed to executing an "aggressive" exploration work program for each block.

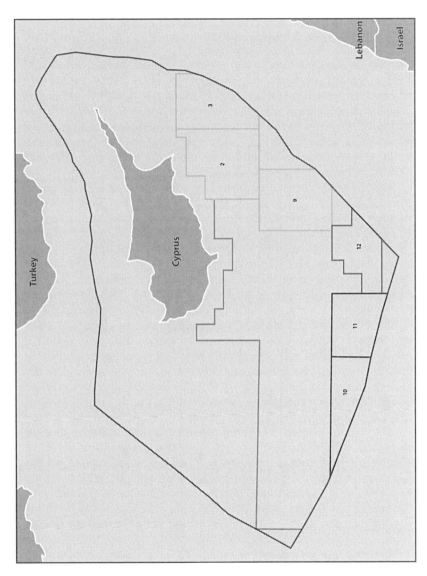

Figure 3.12: Licensed blocks for hydrocarbon exploration offshore Cyprus. Block 12: Noble Energy International – 70% (Delek and Avner were later added with a 15% participation share each). Blocks 2, 3 & 9: ENI (80%)/Kogas (20%). Blocks 10 & 11: Total (100%). Source: Information obtained from the Cypriot Ministry of Energy, Commerce, Industry and Tourism

Latest Eastern Mediterranean oil and gas developments

The Government of Cyprus has recently renewed Total's exploration license for 2 more years, but for Block 11 only (Total has already relinquished the whole of Blocks 10). Based on this, Total will remain and continue its exploration activities within the Cypriot EEZ. Similarly, Eni has been awarded with a 2-year extension of its exploration licenses for Blocks 2, 3 and 9. Currently, following the previously unsuccessful exploration attempts, both Total and Eni are re-evaluating their geological models, before resuming exploration drillings.

Noble Energy declared commerciality and submitted a Development Plan for the exploitation of the 'Aphrodite' gas deposit in Block 12 within the Cypriot EEZ. Currently, the Government is negotiating/discussing this Plan with Noble Energy. Very recently, Noble Energy has agreed with BG International to sell half of its 70% share in Block 12, i.e. 35%.

As far as Israel is concerned, production in the Tamar field is ongoing but regarding Leviathan, Noble Energy is still in discussions with the Israeli Government regarding the development of the field and marketing of the gas.

Regarding Egypt, a Mega Survey tender procedure (for the Western Part offshore Egypt) is being followed by EGAS. This new, extensive offshore exploration will help identify new targets leading potentially to new hydrocarbon discoveries especially in the deeper zones. Eni has recently announced the discovery of "Zohr" in the Shorouk Block offshore Egypt, which has a potential of 30 trillion cubic feet of lean gas in place (5.5 billion barrels of oil equivalent in place).

The current situation in Lebanon remains as before, making it difficult to predict any future progress (following the pre-qualification of 12 companies as "Operators" and 34 as "Non-Operators", out of all the applicant companies, the licensing round stalled with little progress in the past year). The situation remains the same (pending adoption by the Government of the necessary decrees for the licensing round involving Block delineation and the Exploration & Production Agreement), making prediction of any future progress difficult.

Similarly, Greece's plans for the Oil & Gas industry are difficult to predict at this moment and it is unknown at this stage whether matters will go forward or not. The new Government seems to be supporting a different regime for hydrocarbon exploitation where Production Sharing Contracts are favored over Concession Agreements.

The role of Cyprus in the Eastern Mediterranean region

As matters stand, the oil and gas sector could be a promising new industry for Cyprus; the country has already attracted worldwide attention and hopefully this will lead to improved prospects for serious international investment. The discovery of substantial quantities of natural gas, in combination with the potential utilization of other gas deposits and future gas findings in the area, opens up new perspectives and gives new impetus to the role of Cyprus in the global energy map and the European energy market. If Cyprus is to grasp this great opportunity, it needs to proceed swiftly with planning and development of the required energy infrastructure and facilities for the exploitation of natural gas reserves. Cyprus is aware of the urgency of the matter and is now moving in the direction of approving a development plan for at least one of its fields, encompassing the following activities:

- Drilling the production wells.
- Installing an FPSO (floating, production, storage, and offloading) platform over the field to collect the gas, process it to separate out any liquids (condensates + water), and treat it to remove any other impurities potentially present.
- Transporting the gas (gas may be delivered to local and nearby markets) through subsea pipelines, for export/utilization from/at (existing or new) related infrastructures.
- Potential gas export pipelines that could include:
  o Pipeline to Egypt for export through existing LNG production facilities.
  o Pipeline to Cyprus for the local market – gas supply for power generation and petrochemicals production.
  o Pipeline to Jordan for the local market (potential, pending discussions and agreement).

Opportunities exist for serving power generation stations (market volume of 0.5 billion cubic meters per annum for all power stations) and the prospective petrochemicals industry (planned market potential of 1 billion cubic meters per annum for a single methanol production plant). Two main operating power stations exist in Cyprus and these belong to the Electricity Authority of Cyprus (EAC), while other independent power producers (IIP) have filed applications and obtained licenses to operate. "Methanol Plant in Cyprus" is a project involving the installation and operation of a production unit and associated facilities to produce methanol from natural gas. This project is promoted by Dor Chemicals of Israel, which already deals with methanol and other petrochemicals. In addition, some shore-based services for the offshore industry exist in Cyprus (albeit at a quite small scale). Two oil and gas industry services companies (Halliburton and Schlumberger) are established in the country with their own facilities and operations (supported by local marine and engineering companies). There are also plans for a new port with large-scale shore-based facilities to serve the offshore industry.

Such initiatives in such a strategically located EU member as Cyprus could significantly contribute to efforts toward establishing secure natural gas resources and diversified energy corridors for the EU and beyond. Once Cyprus is successful in establishing the necessary infrastructure for hydrocarbons operations and exports, one would then reasonably expect to see additional oil and gas exploration and production activities across the EM, leading to the evolution of the oil and gas industry in the area.

These developments will see by far the largest investments in Cyprus's history and will certainly constitute the key driver for the monetization of its offshore gas resources. No doubt, this energy infrastructure will upgrade the geostrategic role of Cyprus in the EM and will yield great benefits for the local economy and industry by generating a significant number of new jobs, creating new business opportunities and revenue, stimulating rapid technological development within the manufacturing sector, and developing new industries such as the production of petrochemicals. In addition, energy development will open up the possibility of Cyprus becoming a major energy hub, able to handle natural gas from its own fields as well as from the adjacent offshore gas discoveries of neighboring countries.

The importance of human resources in the hydrocarbons sector

The staffing requirements and skill sets that would be required for Cyprus to undertake large oil and gas projects were first recognized in 2006. In response, many activities have taken place since then in the direction of educating and training a potential cadre for this undertaking. Development programs were unveiled covering a broad spectrum of such needs: technical, administrative, managerial, and so on. A timeline of educational and training events appears in Table 3.6.

Table 3.6: Timeline of events related to education and training of human resources for oil and gas. Source: Information obtained from Cypriot Ministry of Energy, Commerce, Industry and Tourism; Cypriot Human Resources Development Authority; and Noble Energy, Inc.

Date	Main developmental events
Mid-2011	Initial training programs (and preparation of related material) offered by the Energy Service (Ministry of Energy, Commerce, Industry and Tourism) covering the oil and gas sector and energy in general.
Late 2012	Cyprus Human Resources Development Authority (HRDA) prepared a study covering the early identification of employment needs and requisite training in the direction of preparing a cadre to manage natural gas effectively.
2012–13	Academic institutions in Cyprus began offering a series of degrees in the oil and gas sector.
Early 2013	Noble Energy completed a study through which it identified local employee/labor requirements for the Cyprus LNG Project (construction phase and operational phase).
Late 2013	A new, two-year Professional Diploma in Oil and Gas was established. This program was specifically designed to educate and train students in professions related to the technology, practices, processes, and operations of the oil and gas sector, thus preparing them to become skilled blue-collar workers, e.g., mechanical engineering technicians, electrical engineering technicians, welders, and drilling engineers.

Although current training programs feature mainly vocational education and some engineering specialization for the oil and gas industry, these programs lack the essential "hands-on" activities that would allow students to blend knowledge and practice, making them effective and productive at work once employed.

More needs to be done in the area of education and training, including the following:

- Advancement of skills and work expertise through more training on location.
- Cooperation between educational institutions and large oil and gas services companies to enable students to work as interns or visiting students.
- Creation of a regional training center for technical training in the oil and gas sector, which would potentially be located in Cyprus.

Global oil and gas market overview

Oil prices have been declining recently (with rare but transient signs of recovery), while historically oil prices used generally to rise. This trend has also affected natural gas prices to a certain degree, even though demand seems to remain basically unchanged. These new trends have had a major impact on the commerciality of hydrocarbon discoveries:

- Major oil companies are cutting down their upstream (exploration and production) business.
- Operations and jobs in the oil and gas sector have been reduced.
- All shallow, deep, and ultra-deep water exploration activities have been affected.

Declining oil prices have affected LNG export projects as well as LNG prices:

- LNG prices are falling due to their link with oil prices and the price renegotiation/reopening clauses in sale and purchase agreements. Spot LNG prices, however, remain fairly stable, despite reduced global output from some LNG export plants.
- The commerciality of LNG export projects has been affected, although most major plans in Canada and the US seem to be going forward.
- According to the Gas Union president, "destination clauses on LNG will soon fade away," since unlike piped natural gas a cargo of LNG can be diverted en route. This particular feature gives consumer nations flexibility in the management of their supplies and at the same time enables producers to optimize the monetization of their assets.

Demand for natural gas is expected to continue rising, although at a slightly slower pace than before considering the global economic turmoil and international oil prices. Stronger economic growth, lower oil and gas prices, and the growing need for reduction of emissions are the main causes of increasing global natural gas demand.

The world is now experiencing significant trends, including a rise in local gas production in the US (mainly from shale), a "reboot" in Japan's nuclear energy industry, a drop in internationally traded oil prices, and, most importantly, new players (producers) entering the scene and novel technologies coming online.

Conclusion

Energy matters in Cyprus are interrelated with economic, political/geo-political, national security, strategic/geostrategic, historical, social/cultural, EEZ, and other issues. These make energy considerations more complex than they already are. Cyprus is at a relatively early stage in its energy experience and as such it needs to be particularly careful in managing every step. The country should therefore concentrate on taking rational decisions and managing major hydrocarbon exploitation prospects professionally. Rational decision making and wise management will prove to be absolutely vital if the country is to meet successfully the many technical, geopolitical, and economic challenges that will certainly arise in the future.

Cyprus will need to establish strong alliances with its neighbors in the region, but also with Russia. At the same time, it should develop its hydrocarbon exploration activities and its oil and gas businesses, keeping in mind the interests and plans of the superpowers (and their meddling). If Cyprus manages to deal successfully with its significant energy issues, the country can then hope to reap benefits across all major areas of interest: political (the Turkish occupation), economic (recession), demographics (falling birth rate with falling optimism), unemployment, GDP levels, productivity, financial (liquidity), and so on. In the process Cyprus needs to remember that the road ahead will be bumpy, decisions will be complex, and superpower involvement will not go away, while new alliances will certainly prove necessary.

For many years the economy of Cyprus was dominated by financial services (which are now in intensive care) and the tourism sector (where much needs to be done). The exploitation of natural gas reserves (without excluding the possibility of oil discoveries) offers the country a path out of the economic vicious circle in which it now finds itself. However, it first needs to navigate through all sorts of obstacles, which are complicated by the historical geopolitical tensions of the EM. Cyprus thus has to brace itself for some difficult decision making, the outcome of which could make the difference to its economic and maybe political future.

Cyprus remains to this day an isolated "energy island," since it has no interconnections with the trans-European electricity or gas networks, nor does it have the necessary infrastructure to be able to take part in the single European energy market. This puts an additional burden on the competiveness of local enterprises, as well as affecting economic prospects and the cost of life in general.

Added to this, the world economy has been in turmoil for the last five years and this has had a strong negative impact on the economies of some European countries in particular, most of which are now planning their economic recovery. However, the austerity measures remain in effect and suppress the full and true recovery of the economy of Cyprus. The country urgently needs long-term growth and development. To this end, oil and gas could play a major positive role. The large investments in infrastructure and installations for the production and export of oil and gas could be instrumental in rejuvenating the economy. The substantial natural gas deposits that were discovered in the Southeastern Mediterranean region in the last few years justify the investments in large infrastructure and interconnection projects.

In the meantime, many major geopolitical, exploration, and production challenges will need to be managed before benefits can materialize. These include, among others, bilateral or trilateral (or even multilateral) cooperation between countries in the region, pipelines versus marine transport, risks and returns, technical issues, and many more. In addition, the market outlook – that is, demand and supply trends, oil and gas and LNG prices, LPG–LNG–CNG, shale gas, sustainability, energy alternatives, energy prices, finance and investments, and innovations/new technologies – all need to be considered carefully and weighed against probable future outcomes.

Therefore, the situation as it is today renders the energy sector key to the achievement of Cyprus's economic restart and growth. Nevertheless, some critical issues need to be dealt with first:

- Transforming hydrocarbon wealth into sustainable, equitable, and people-centered development.
- Building broad consensus on the efficient management of the wealth resulting from hydrocarbons.
- Developing appropriate proactive measures to safeguard the security and environmental integrity of the island.

A number of other outstanding issues (all significant) need to be addressed and resolved through taking specific steps. The main among these are:

- Conclusion of the development plan for the "Aphrodite" field in Block 12 and the subsequent granting of an exploitation license.
- Decision over Cyprus's involvement in natural gas exploitation. Given the current difficult economic environment, the state's involvement would need to be limited to infrastructure and services

that would support the oil and gas industry, but could generate significant revenues for the state.

- Creation of bilateral frameworks of cooperation with Israel, Egypt, and Greece, for natural gas exports through a common infrastructure.
- Conclusion and signature of the relevant agreements with Israel and Lebanon for the joint exploitation of hydrocarbon deposits extending across the median line.
- Establishment of a National Hydrocarbons Fund through drafting the relevant legislation.
- Creation of a more favorable business environment for the implementation of projects in the field of services/supplies for the oil and gas industry, aiming to serve both the domestic market as well as those of the EM.

A pipeline to Egypt seems to be what Noble Energy is now planning in Block 12 as far as infrastructure is concerned. However, this pipeline should be complemented with a gas supply pipeline to Cyprus's shore, to serve the local Cypriot market (a large potential exists, in particular for a petrochemicals industry); geopolitical reasons dictate the need to supply Cyprus with its own gas.

Clearly, the outcome of the recent exploration plans by Total and ENI was not as expected. Despite this, the initial plans for the hydrocarbons sector in Cyprus should remain firm, as the future is expected to be more prosperous with successful exploration and new hydrocarbon findings. These actions should be complemented by efforts directed at implementing prospective projects that could serve exports from Cyprus to the EU market, possibly in cooperation with Russia. One needs to remember, however, that a fresh slump in oil prices could create further problems for scheduled gas export projects and plans for hydrocarbon exploration and production. In conclusion, the economic potential of Cyprus and other countries in the region would be much enhanced if energy wealth were managed smartly and unflinchingly and with geopolitics in mind.

References

Attica Gas Supply Company. 2014. "Historical Review." http://www.aerioattikis.gr/Default.aspx?pid=6&la=1. Accessed July 2014.

Booth, J. S., M. M. Rowe, and K. M. Fischer. 1996. "Offshore Gas Hydrate Sample Database with an Overview and Preliminary

Analysis." U.S. Geological Survey Open-File Report 96-272.
http://pubs.usgs.gov/of/1996/of96-272/ch03s07.html. Accessed July
2014.
DEPA. 2014a. "Natural Gas Composition."
http://www.depa.gr/content/article/002002001002/65.html. Accessed
July 2014.
—. 2014b. "The History of Natural Gas."
http://www.depa.gr/content/article/002002001001/12.html. Accessed
July 2014.
New World Encyclopedia. 2013. "Gas."
http://www.newworldencyclopedia.org/entry/Gas. Accessed July 2014.
Noble Energy. 2013. "Noble Energy Announces Highlights of 2013
Analyst Conference." December. Houston, TX: Noble Energy.
Technopolis. 2014. "The History of the Gas Production Factory."
http://www.technopolis-athens.com/web/guest/museum/history.
Accessed July 2014.
Theodoropoulos, Theodore E. 2010. The Secret World of Energy: Oil, Gas
and Petrochemicals. Nicosia: Caye Global Investments.
USGS. 2010a. "Assessment of Undiscovered Oil and Gas Resources of the
Levant Basin Province, Eastern Mediterranean." U.S. Geological
Survey Fact Sheet 2010–3014, March. Reston, VA: USGS.
—. 2010b. "Assessment of Undiscovered Oil and Gas Resources of the
Nile Delta Basin Province, Eastern Mediterranean." U.S. Geological
Survey Fact Sheet 2010–3027, May. Reston, VA: USGS.
Wikipedia. 2014a. "Natural Gas."
http://en.wikipedia.org/wiki/Natural_gas. Accessed July 2014.
—. 2014b. "Wet Gas." http://en.wikipedia.org/wiki/Wet_gas. Accessed
July 2014.
—. 2014c. "Acid Gas." http://en.wikipedia.org/wiki/Acid_gas. Accessed
July 2014.
—. 2014d. "Liquefied Natural Gas."
http://en.wikipedia.org/wiki/Liquefied_natural_gas. Accessed July
2014.

CHAPTER FOUR

EASTERN MEDITERRANEAN ENERGY AND THE PIVOTAL ROLE OF ISRAEL

GEORGE GEORGIOU

The 2013 banking-cum-sovereign debt crisis will undoubtedly stay etched in the memory of Cypriots for many years to come as this small European Union (EU) island economy continues to struggle to maintain both its financial solvency and its membership in the Eurozone. In fact this economic drama continues to unfold, with Cyprus desperately casting around for a lifeline to save it from a recession and an uncertain economic future. Not only is the financial crisis affecting Cyprus and its people, it will remain as a constant reminder of the potential threats to the Eurozone banking system and the nascent European Monetary Union. The potential lifeline for the Cypriot economy lies in the hydrocarbon (primarily natural gas but also petroleum) deposits located within the country's exclusive economic zone (EEZ) and off its southern coast, in the Levantine Basin between Cyprus, Lebanon, Israel, the Gaza Strip, and Egypt. While Cyprus has negotiated and delineated its EEZ with both Egypt (2003) and Israel (2010), as well as with Lebanon (2007; although that treaty has yet to be ratified by the Lebanese legislature), it is its energy partnership with Israel that could make or break this economic reprieve for Cyprus. As will be seen, this potential partnership is both complicated and fraught with difficulties of Byzantine proportions. The focus of this chapter is the energy partnership between two unequal partners in what is obviously a very complicated and dangerous region of the world.

The Cyprus problem

Cyprus has been a potential flashpoint from the very beginning of its existence as an independent (of sorts) nation in 1960. The economic problems of this small island in the Eastern Mediterranean have at the same time paralleled its roller-coaster political problems. At the time of

Independence in 1960, the Cypriot economy, although battered by the effects of the anti-colonial liberation struggle against British rule from 1955 to 1959, was in relatively good shape thanks to British outlays in Cyprus, both in terms of civilian infrastructure and military build-up. In that period Britain continued to withdraw from more far-flung imperial outposts and to adopt a more limited global posture, including its withdrawal from Palestine, Aden, and the Suez Canal. These expenditures were further bolstered by its efforts to suppress EOKA's (National Organization of Cypriot Fighters) struggle for independence from Britain and union with Greece (James 1994).

The early years following Independence saw remarkable economic progress in spite of inter-communal clashes during 1963–64 and 1967. The economy moved from a primarily import-substitution manufacturing strategy to a more export- and service-oriented strategy focusing on tourism and banking (Georgiou 1981). This brief post-Independence economic miracle came to an abrupt halt in July 1974 when Turkey invaded the island, purportedly to restore constitutional order following the coup carried out by the military junta then ruling Greece, with the collusion of Greek Cypriot collaborators on the island. As it turned out, the real purpose of Turkey's invasion was the dismantling of the constitution and the division of the island, taking a part for itself through a proxy regime in the north. The human and economic consequences of the Turkish invasion and subsequent occupation of approximately one-third of the island were catastrophic, resulting in the displacement of one-third of the population, the contraction of the economy by two-thirds, and the forcible separation of the historically intermingled Greek and Turkish Cypriot ethnic communities into two separate geographic entities (Georgiou 1979).

In 1983 the Turkish-occupied northern area attempted secession through a declaration of unilateral independence of the "Turkish Republic of Northern Cyprus" (TRNC), since recognized only by Turkey, which was behind the whole affair all along. The Greek-dominated and internationally recognized Republic of Cyprus (RoC) in the south has since managed to restructure its economy after the loss of the most productive and resource-rich northern areas, investing heavily in tourism, banking, shipping, and financial services. The per capita GDP of the RoC had reached $23,735 in 2004 when it became a full member of the EU, while the "North" lagged behind, internationally isolated and subsidized heavily by Turkey, managing at best a per capita GDP one-third that of the more dynamic and prosperous "South" (Index Mundi 2013). The 2004 Treaty of Accession to the EU encompasses the RoC with provision for the suspension of the application of the acquis in the northern, Turkish-occupied part, to be lifted when the island is reunited (Miltiadou 2012).

In 2008, Cyprus became the 14th member state of the EU to join the Eurozone, adopting the euro as its currency and abandoning the Cypriot pound. It appeared at the time that the economic success story of the RoC together with its accession to the EU was a palatable alternative, if not full compensation, for the political and social cost (often inflicted from outside) of the "Cyprus problem" that had plagued Cyprus since its creation in 1960. By 2008 the per capita GDP had risen to $29,400, while in the Turkish-occupied North the figure continued to remain at approximately one-third that of the "South" (World Bank 2013). Unfortunately, the jubilation of the Greek-dominated RoC resulting from its accession to the EU and the adoption of the euro would be short-lived, as the Cypriot economy subsequently imploded on account of the fallout of the Greek debt crisis. Cypriot banks had invested heavily in Greek government bonds, which were subject to a 70 percent write-down "hair-cut" as part of the Eurozone's bailout of the Greek economy. This virtually wiped out the equity of Cyprus's two largest banks (Bank of Cyprus and Cyprus Popular Bank "Laiki"), which were the backbone of the economy.

Enter Israel

Israel for the most part has treated Cyprus, its much smaller and only non-Muslim neighbor, with indifference and on occasion disdain over the past 50 years. One could argue that this originated with newly independent Cyprus's association with and founding membership of the Non-Aligned Movement (NAM), made up of nations of the world that sought to stay out of the Cold War confrontation that was at its most intense at the time of Cyprus's Independence in 1960 (Ministry of Foreign Affairs 2013). Under the leadership of its first president, Archbishop Makarios, Cyprus developed close ideological ties with the likes of Egypt, under Gamal Abdel Nasser; with India, under Jawaharlal Nehru; and with what was then Yugoslavia, under Josip Broz Tito. It is therefore not surprising that Cyprus has traditionally been a firm supporter of Palestinian rights for self-determination and statehood; Israel eyed its posture with suspicion.

In the 1980s and increasingly in the 1990s when Israeli–Turkish relations grew ever closer militarily, politically, and economically, it was not surprising that Israeli–Cypriot relations were at best "proper" if not "frosty," as they were when two alleged Israeli spies were expelled from Cyprus in 1998 (Charalambous 1998), or in 2002 when Androulla Vassiliou, the wife of a former Cypriot president, was declared persona non grata in Israel because a parliamentary delegation she was leading tried to meet with Palestinian leader Yasser Arafat, who was then under house arrest (Pseka 2002).

Israeli–Cypriot relations thawed almost overnight in the aftermath of the Gaza flotilla raid by Israeli commandos, which led to the death of nine Turkish nationals. This was a military operation by Israel against six ships of the "Gaza Freedom Flotilla" on May 31, 2010 in international waters. The flotilla, organized by the Free Gaza Movement and the Turkish Foundation for Human Rights and Freedoms and Humanitarian Relief (IHH), was carrying humanitarian aid and construction materials, with the intention of breaking the Israeli–Egyptian blockade of the Gaza Strip (Kershner 2012). Turkey's Prime Minister then, and now president, Recep Tayyip Erdoğan, has since adopted a decidedly anti-Israeli position in Turkey's policy toward Israel. This has earned him admiration across the Muslim world, but it has left the Israeli–Turkish relationship in a shambles, much to the dismay of the United States (US), a key ally of Israel and Turkey, since it sees both countries playing key, but different roles in its strategic policy for the region as a whole.

While 2010 marked a low point in Israeli–Turkish relations, it also marked a high point for Israeli energy independence when Israel discovered the Leviathan natural gas field, the world's biggest offshore gas find of 2010, estimated at 17–18 trillion cubic feet, in the Levantine Basin between Cyprus, Lebanon, Israel, the Gaza Strip, and Egypt (Offshore Technology 2013a). This came on the heels of another discovery, the Tamar field in 2009, with estimated natural gas reserves of 8–9 trillion cubic feet (Offshore Technology 2013b).

When in 2011 Cyprus also discovered natural gas in an adjoining area to Israel's Leviathan find, known as the Aphrodite field and since estimated at 3–6 trillion cubic feet, the prospect of a joint exploration for oil and gas in the Levantine Basin, now totaling an estimated 30–35 trillion cubic feet, brought the two countries closer together (Glain 2012). The US Geological Survey estimated the natural gas reserves of the whole Levantine Basin at 122 trillion cubic feet, enough to supply the world at the present rate of consumption for one year (Robertson and Schenk 2010). The recent rapprochement of Cyprus and Israel now includes very close collaboration on military, cultural, and political matters. Given the inherent dangers of alliances of smaller and weaker nations with more powerful nations that inevitably have broader national interests, one wonders whether it is prudent for Cyprus to enter into such a relationship with no holds barred. However, given the recent and ongoing financial and debt problems that it is facing, as well as the deepening economic recession accompanied by historically high levels of unemployment, not to mention the increasing pressure on the RoC to reach an overall settlement of the broader "Cyprus problem," it might no longer be a matter of choice for Cyprus but a national and economic necessity.

The Cyprus banking-cum-debt crisis

Just as the Cyprus problem had begun to take on the status of a perennial issue, to the point of being abandoned by the international community as one of those intractable conflicts that had no plausible resolution, the picture began to change quickly, taking many astute international observers by surprise. The surprise did not come from the political arena – namely, a possible breakthrough in the interminable inter-communal discussions that have been held on and off for decades – but from the economic arena.

The economy of Cyprus is small, open, and dynamic, with services constituting its "engine of growth." For the most part, since the country's Independence in 1960 the economy has been what would be considered in the economic literature a success story. For a number of years, Cyprus had been experiencing rising living standards, as shown by the high level of real convergence with the EU, with per capita GDP standing at around 92 percent of the average for the EU27 in 2011 (CIA 2013).

The services sector of the economy was the fastest growing and accounted for about 80.5 percent of GDP in 2011. This reflects the gradual restructuring of the Cypriot economy from being an exporter of minerals and agricultural products in the period 1960–74, to an exporter of light manufactured goods through the early part of the 1980s, and to a tourist, banking, shipping, and financial services provider since then. The manufacturing sector accounted for about 17.1 percent of GDP in 2011, while the primary sector (agriculture and fishing) continued to shrink, reaching only 2.4 percent of GDP in 2011. The economy of Cyprus is open, with a share of total imports and exports to GDP of over 90 percent (Ministry of Finance 2013).

Serious problems surfaced in the Cypriot banking and financial sector in early 2011 as the Greek fiscal crisis and Eurozone debt crisis deepened. Cyprus's borrowing costs had risen steadily because of its exposure to Greek debt. Two of its biggest banks (Bank of Cyprus and Cyprus Popular Bank "Laiki") were among the largest holders of Greek bonds in Europe and had a substantial presence in Greece through bank branches and subsidiaries. In July 2012, Cyprus became the fifth Eurozone government to request an economic bailout program from the Euro group – European

Commission, European Central Bank (ECB), and International Monetary Fund (IMF); collectively also known as the "Troika" (Georgiou 2013).

Without an international bailout there is no doubt that the Cypriot banking sector would have collapsed, and with bank balance sheet assets approximately seven to eight times the size of the economy, Cyprus itself would inevitably have defaulted. The apparent lack of urgency on the part of the Troika leading up to the March 16, 2013 initial bailout agreement was more political than economic, with most of the hesitancy coming from national governments such as Germany, France, Austria, the Netherlands, and Finland. German officials in particular had questioned the necessity of bailing out a small island economy that represents no more than 0.2 percent of Eurozone output, arguing that such a "small-scale" sovereign default would not present a systemic risk to the Eurozone. According to this argument, Cyprus was not eligible for aid unless it threatened contagion and hence the stability of the entire Euro region.

In stark contrast, the ECB's position was that the approximately €10 billion cost of a Cyprus bailout was a small amount to pay for the peace of mind it would bring to a Eurozone still recovering from the much larger bailouts of Ireland, Portugal, Spain, and especially Greece (Pop 2013). After all, what ultimately led to the Cypriot banking crisis were the facts that its banks were out of proportion to the country's economy; the banks were overloaded with Greek debt; and the Greek debt suffered a 70 percent haircut. Unlike Greece, which experienced a true sovereign debt crisis, the Cypriot crisis is primarily a banking problem. However, since the Cypriot banking sector is such a large multiple of the nation's GDP, any bailout of the state would be a bailout of the private banking sector and vice versa.

Thus, the main reason for the reluctance of German and other north European governments to be more forthcoming with aid for a fellow Eurozone member, as had been the case with Greece, was a desire not to be seen as using German taxpayers' money to aid private banks that had grown too big for their own good, and whose main depositors are foreign, non-EU nationals, and primarily Russian to boot. The fact that the German media was full of allegations that many of these Russian bank deposits are the product of money laundering, or of tax avoidance, if not outright tax evasion, did not help matters either. Consequently, it had been made clear to Cyprus that the memorandum for assistance would include a section on money laundering that would set out measures that it must examine on the issue, and that progress would be monitored.

On the other hand, it is also known that these primarily northern Eurozone nations want taxes in all member nations of the EU to be brought into line upward, so that those tax rates are closer to their own levels. They are afraid that lower taxes in places such as Cyprus, Luxembourg, and Ireland attract foreign capital flows and act as a source of tax evasion. Consequently, they are seeking closer EU cooperation on tax evasion, and they saw an opportunity to squeeze countries such as Cyprus to reduce legal loopholes for tax evasion and to force them to raise their tax rates. Unfortunately, no clear distinction is made between tax avoidance and tax evasion, and by extension money laundering allegations (Apostolides 2013).

Lastly, it was simply not acceptable to the well-balanced and diversified northern economies that the financial or banking sector of a tiny member nation of the EU could possibly be seven to eight times the size of its economy. Such an overweight sector needed to be cut down to size: namely, to the weighted size of the EU average, which is at most three times that of the national economy.

Although all this was common knowledge, the decision of March 16, 2013 and the actual terms came as a shock not only to Cyprus, but also to the financial markets and to many international observers. Cyprus had officially requested €17 billion in June 2012, but the Eurozone finance ministers reached a deal to provide only €10 billion in bailout funds, with an additional €5.8 billion to be generated by a bank deposit tax, or a "haircut" in current jargon. Unlike other Euro bailouts, Cyprus would not be given a "debt haircut" but a "deposit haircut" instead (Spiegel Online 2013).

What was most striking and a first in modern banking times is that according to the terms of the bailout agreement, all bank deposits would bear the brunt of the haircut, given that Cypriot banks had relatively few bondholders. These banks at the time held close to €70 billion in deposits, almost half of which were believed to be from non-resident Russian citizens, with Russian banks having $12 billion and Russian corporations about $19 billion at the end of 2012, according to ratings agency Moody's (Hope and Spiegel 2013). According to the agreement Cyprus also contracted to raise its nominal corporate tax rate, the lowest in Europe, from 10 percent to 12.5 percent.

Faced with an ultimatum from the ECB that emergency funding to Cypriot banks would be terminated, and a "take it or leave it" attitude from the Euro group, Cyprus agreed to the terms of a "revised" bailout in the early hours of March 25, 2013. Unlike the initial deal, it ended up agreeing to guarantee all bank deposits less than €100,000, but also to "shut down" its second largest bank (Cyprus Popular Bank "Laiki"), consolidate if not dismantle its largest bank (Bank of Cyprus) by ceding the operations of all its branches in Greece to Greek banks, as well as accept a one-time levy (haircut) on bank deposits exceeding €100,000 at a rate of at least 40–60 percent as needed. This of course would be coupled with short-term capital controls and other administrative regulations as required.

It was clear from the bailout agreement that the Cypriot economy would contract severely. However, it was not long before another bombshell fell when the terms of the agreement were "updated" at a meeting of the 17 finance ministers of the Eurozone in Dublin on April 12, 2013, to reflect a more detailed "debt sustainability analysis" showing that the economy was actually in worse shape than initially assumed. In order to keep its debt and deficit from spinning out of control and to meet the terms of the €10 billion bailout secured just two weeks earlier, Cyprus would now need a total of €23 billion of financing, of which it would have to contribute €13 billion, more than twice what was originally expected. In so doing, Cyprus also agreed to sell €400 million of its gold reserves, or an estimated 10 tonnes from its 13-tonne reserve, renegotiate the terms of its €2.5 billion loan with Russia, and impose further losses on Bank of Cyprus depositors and creditors. It was also suggested that holders of Cypriot government bonds could be urged to agree to a debt swap (another haircut; Alderman 2013). Dutch finance minister Jeroen Dijsselbloem and German finance minister Wolfgang Schäuble made it crystal clear that the extent of aid from the Euro group would remain at €10 billion, with €9 billion coming from the ECB and the remaining €1 billion from the IMF (Riegert 2013).

No doubt the repercussions of the terms of this bailout agreement will be far-reaching, as this is the first time bank depositors have been asked to shoulder any of the losses from bank failures. European officials have been quick to claim that Cyprus is a unique case and that depositors' money is safe, no matter what the circumstances. Realizing the loss of faith that Cyprus's haircut caused, ECB officials went all out to reassure financial markets and depositors that the European banking system is sound and that depositors have no safer place to keep their money than EU banks. Cyprus may be small in just about all respects from a global perspective, but it is once again living up to its reputation as a potential flashpoint of regional if not global significance, especially as global integration makes contagion more the norm than the aberration. It remains to be seen if a Eurozone-wide unified banking system is feasible, considering that there is a double standard as far as the integrity of bank deposits is concerned as a euro in Cyprus is not the same as a euro in

Germany. This will not help alleviate the perception that there is a growing north–south rift in the Eurozone.

An energy solution for Cyprus

The day after the terms of the initial bailout were made public, the newly elected president of Cyprus, Nicos Anastasiades, appealed to Cypriots to accept the levy on bank deposits as the "least painful solution." He went on to say that depositors would be offered bank shares covering the full amount of their losses, while those who left their savings in banks for another two years would be rewarded with bonds backed by future income from exploiting Cyprus's natural gas deposits. It was not clear at the time whether these were the off-the-cuff remarks of a recently elected politician or actual policy prescriptions. What is clear is that no one expected the backlash that ensued, not only from Cypriot bank depositors but also in European financial markets and beyond. It was highly unlikely that Cyprus would survive as a regional financial services provider considering that the sector had been downsized. In fact, the whole purpose of the exercise was to put an end to the "Cyprus banking model" once and for all. The subsequent lifting of capital restrictions did not change matters much and the Cypriot banking sector continues in the doldrums.

The fallout from the whole financial crisis in combination with the onerous terms of the bailout agreement have resulted in a predicted recession, deeper than anything that Cyprus had experienced since the Turkish invasion and occupation of 1974. Thus, all hope for the Cypriot economy now appears to lie with the future development of its oil and natural gas resources; a scenario that is by no means a foregone conclusion.

The potential future revenue flows from the exploitation of offshore natural gas reserves again came into play when the Cypriot finance minister was in Moscow a few days after the Cypriot House of Representatives unanimously rejected the Euro group's initial bailout offer, suggesting a role for Russia in Cyprus's energy development in return for Russian aid with the bailout efforts. The initial Russian response was unexpectedly negative, even though Russian nationals represent at least a third of bank deposits in Cypriot banks. For decades Russia has coveted a foothold on the island, both militarily (possibly a naval and air base, especially now that Russia's role in Syria is expanding) and more recently for the exploitation of Cypriot natural gas reserves. Russia is Europe's largest supplier of natural gas, and has as its key energy objective to stay in that position. Russia's recurring and most recent troubles with Ukraine and its annexation of Crimea only reinforce its interest in Cyprus and Levantine Basin energy reserves in general.

However, any substantial revenues from natural gas are likely to be five to eight years away at the earliest, and the development of energy resources will now be much more difficult to orchestrate given the stark financial situation in which the Cypriot authorities presently find themselves. Furthermore, following its recent major financial crisis, Cyprus is now negotiating the future of its energy sector from a greatly weakened position. This situation is further undermined by the political pressure that is put on Cyprus to reach an unfavorable political settlement of the "Cyprus problem," considering the many economic links between the West and Turkey. Cyprus's weak economy has given outside interested parties an opportunity to press for a compromise in the reunification talks presently taking place between the RoC and the self-declared TRNC. To outside (Western) parties, any solution is better than no solution, given the long-term nature of the Cyprus problem and the constant threat of flare-ups that could draw in Greece and Turkey (fellow NATO member nations), as well as the UK (former colonial ruler) and the EU (now that Cyprus is a member state). Under the 1960 Treaty of Guarantee, Britain, Greece, and Turkey pledged to ensure the independence and territorial integrity of Cyprus as well as respect its Constitution. One can add to this chorus the US and the United Nations (UN), both of which were involved in the Cyprus problem for decades and probably for different reasons. The strategy employed by outsiders is once again the classic carrot-and-stick approach, with the potential windfall from natural gas revenues smoothing away the many obstacles to an overall settlement. The current dire economic straits of the Cypriot economy make the potential cost of another failed round of negotiations for an overall settlement even greater than before. Cyprus is likely to be blamed for the failure of negotiations, even if it rejects a proposed solution that is patently unfair and unworkable.

It goes without saying that the weakened economic and political position of Cyprus accentuates the importance of a close energy partnership with its neighbor Israel. What might have been before a matter of strategic decision making is now possibly the only trump card Cyprus has to play. This trump card, however, is precarious, as its value is primarily dependent on Israel's willingness to play its energy hand in partnership with Cyprus. In this regard, Israel has yet to declare its true intentions. The reason for this could be that Israel has yet to map out for itself its long-term energy path. A true energy partnership between Israel and Cyprus, however, is increasingly doubtful given that an inevitable

Turkey–Israel rapprochement inches ever closer, egged along by Israel's national interest in restoring its strained relationship with its erstwhile only non-Arab ally in the region, combined with heavy prodding from America, which is anxious to see its two main allies in the region restore their former military partnership. However, even if the Turkish–Israeli relationship is not restored in the not too distant future, Turkey will always present an obstacle to the RoC's exploitation of any oil and gas reserves in its EEZ, as Turkey continues to occupy militarily the northern third of the island and purports to speak on behalf of and as a defender of the interests of the Turkish Cypriot minority. The role of Turkey as an obstacle to Cyprus's energy development and as an energetic spoiler in the Cypriot–Israeli energy relationship will be addressed later in this chapter.

More recently, Israel's potential energy partnership with Cyprus received a setback from the former's commitment to supply both Jordan and the Palestinian Authority with natural gas. These developments reduce the pressure on Israel to commit itself to an energy partnership with Cyprus. For a number of reasons, Egypt is also positioning itself to become a strategic energy partner for Israel in the potentially lucrative energy market. These latest developments have resulted in Israel placing its erstwhile energy partnership with Cyprus on the back burner pending further developments, including the possible discovery of additional natural gas deposits in Cyprus's EEZ.

Israel: A nascent energy power

The potential for a mutually beneficial energy partnership between Cyprus and Israel is predicated on a combination of natural and man-made circumstances. Geography is a paramount reality of nature. In terms of energy, both Cyprus and Israel border Lebanon, the Gaza Strip, and Egypt. All these countries form the Levantine Basin, which is estimated to hold up to 122 trillion cubic feet of natural gas. However, until recently this area had been neglected by major oil and gas corporations in favor of more abundant and already known sources of hydrocarbon deposits in the Persian Gulf and North Africa. All this changed in January 2009 when Israel, working through a Houston, Texas-based firm, Noble Energy, discovered natural gas in the Tamar field, located roughly 80 km off Israel's northern coast. The Tamar field is estimated to hold 8.4 trillion cubic feet of gas (Offshore Technology 2013b).

Gas began flowing to Israel from the Tamar field on March 30, 2013, with the Israeli Energy and Water Resources Ministry estimating that Tamar could meet between 50 percent and 80 percent of the country's natural gas needs over the next decade. The Tamar project was not intended to become a primary source of natural gas for Israel, but rather to bolster the country's energy security by making it less dependent on natural gas imports from Egypt. In fact, natural gas provided by the Arish–Ashkelon pipeline from Egypt (brokered in 2005 through the East Mediterranean Gas Company, an Egyptian–Israeli natural gas consortium) was officially shut down in April 2012, when Egypt's state-owned natural gas company announced that it would pull out of the agreement and the Israel Electric Corporation formally followed suit. This was not an unexpected development, as Israel's energy partnership with Egypt had been beset with problems from the start. Egypt, a net exporter of gas, was facing its own problems with rising domestic demand and had renegotiated a price increase in 2008, when it became known that the initial price agreed to was significantly below the world market price. Furthermore, strains on Israeli–Egyptian relations resulted from the onset of the Arab Spring in 2011, which further curtailed Israeli imports from Egypt. Significantly, militants in the Sinai Peninsula had frequently targeted the natural gas pipeline after Egypt's former president Hosni Mubarak was deposed, shutting down flows for weeks at a time until the gas supply came to a complete stop (Stratfor Global Intelligence 2013).

The fact that natural gas flows from Egypt ceased and domestic reserves of natural gas from the Mari B reservoir in the Yam Tethys field located off the coast of Ashdod had been depleted much faster than expected led to stopgap measures, including the building in 2012 of a floating liquefied natural gas (LNG) import terminal by the state-owned Israel Natural Gas Lines. This floating natural gas terminal was built in record time and actually received its first shipment of LNG from petroleum conglomerate BP in January 2013. This floating import terminal was never intended to become a primary source of natural gas for Israel, but rather to bolster its energy security by making the country less dependent on its pipeline with Egypt. In fact, imported LNG costs three to four times as much as domestic natural gas. Consequently, production of Tamar natural gas serves as a stable source of energy that is fully under Israeli control and in this way promotes Israeli energy security (Stratfor Global Intelligence 2013).

The Tamar gas proved to be of great importance for Israel's economy. As a result of gas flowing from this field, as well as other more significant offshore gas fields in the future, Israel will achieve energy independence for the first time in its history. The price of electricity is expected to decline, after rising significantly following the termination of gas supplies from Egypt. State coffers are expected to overflow with money that if directed into a special fund (i.e., a sovereign wealth fund) and managed properly will contribute to the wellbeing of future generations. More specifically, Israel's trade balance is likely to improve significantly, its currency will appreciate, and its economy could easily grow by an additional 1 percent a year going forward (Grinbaum 2013).

While the long-run energy picture for Israel looks bright, numerous short-run issues remain to be considered before achieving energy security, even as the Tamar gas continues to flow. First, as in the case of the Arish–Ashkelon pipeline, we are talking about one single pipeline. It reaches Israel's coast in the vicinity of the city of Ashdod and from there supplies gas to all consumers. No matter how well guarded it is, all it would take is a single accident or deliberate sabotage and the gas supply could be disrupted, certainly for days and possibly for weeks. Moreover, while a second pipeline was ruled out, the construction of an additional intake terminal for offshore gas is still a possibility; but again, due to cost considerations, opposition by local residents, and opposition from defense authorities to specific locales, no additional terminal has yet been built.

When gas was discovered in the Tamar field in 2009, Israel had no clear vision for exporting any of its future Tamar field gas flows considering its dire need for energy to satisfy its domestic market. However, matters began to change with the discovery in 2010 of an even larger offshore gas reserve estimated at 16–18 trillion cubic feet, the Leviathan natural gas field, located also in the Levantine Basin, approximately 90 miles west of Haifa. Thus far, energy companies operating in Israel have discovered a total of seven offshore gas fields with a confirmed combined reserve of about 32 trillion cubic feet (Khadduri 2014).

While there is an obvious constituency for putting domestic interests first, it is also clear that energy companies would only be willing to commit to developing Israel's gas industry if they could be assured of a gas export market that would be sufficiently profitable to justify the necessary investment. In 2011, the Tzemach Committee (headed by the director-general of the ministry of energy, Shaul Tzemach) was convened to study the issue. Its initial recommendation in 2012 was to set aside 450 billion cubic meters, or 47 percent of a presumed resource base of 950 billion cubic meters of gas for Israeli domestic needs. A cabinet decision subsequently changed this to 540 billion cubic meters or a 60 percent retention. This was interpreted by the Israeli media as a 40 percent cap on gas exports (Roberts 2013). Little attention was paid to the fact that the size of the resource base itself was constantly changing, as with the discovery of the Karish gas field in July 2013, as well as Israel's domestic requirements, which at best were estimates. The Tzemach Committee assumed Israeli gas demand averaging 18 billion cubic meters per year over the next 25 years, yet at present Israel consumes only around 6.5 billion cubic meters a year. Presumably this provides sufficient political wiggle room for all the parties involved going forward.

Israel is presently ahead of neighboring countries in terms of natural gas exploration and drilling operations, although Egypt, recently beset by various difficulties both political and economic, had a head start. As indicated, Israel started production in the Tamar field for internal consumption in March 2013. More recently, it signed gas export agreements with neighboring countries and regions, such as the West Bank and Jordan, in an attempt to assume the main role in the regional gas industry in the EM. As of 2016, Israel will export to Jordan about 66 billion cubic feet of gas from the Tamar field for a period of 15 years. Exportation is expected to start on completion of the construction of a short pipeline south of the Dead Sea.

In January 2014, US-based Noble Energy signed a $1.2 billion contract with the Palestinian Electric Company to supply the power station in Jenin on the northern West Bank with natural gas from the Leviathan gas field for the next 25 years. It must be noted that the gas to be exported to the West Bank was considered part of Israel's 60 percent domestic consumption share, which is not intended for export. The Palestinian Authority accepted this agreement, despite the fact that Israel is still objecting to the development of the Gaza Marine field off the coast of the Gaza Strip (Khadduri 2014). According to the British company BG Group, this field, which was discovered in 2000, has reserves of about 1 trillion cubic feet and could supply Palestinian power stations with gas for the next few years, thus eliminating the need to import gas from Israel. However, Israel shut down that operation in 2001, after a new Palestinian uprising began. When Hamas took over in Gaza in 2007, Israel imposed an economic boycott, causing BG to pull out of negotiations with the Israeli government and finally shutting down its office in Israel in 2008. The whole operation has been on hold since then (Dickey 2014).

As noted, this last agreement was deemed to fall under Israeli "domestic" gas consumption, leaving more for export under the "40 percent gas export cap" agreement. In the meantime, Israel is also promulgating the laws required for the next phase of its energy industry development, which is related to internal gas distribution through the construction of a national pipeline network. This still leaves open the last and most difficult phase of Israeli gas industry development: the size, method, and direction of its gas exports. In this regard negotiations are ongoing, with the final outcome uncertain and unpredictable. The list of issues that need to be addressed is long: taxes to be imposed on energy companies operating on its territory, quantities of gas to be exported, required domestic gas reserve ratio that must be kept for Israel's own energy security, delineation of an Israeli EEZ with its maritime neighbors (including both Lebanon and the Palestinian Authority/Gaza Strip), whether gas exports will use fixed pipelines and if so the route(s) such pipelines will follow, and whether gas exports are to be in the form of LNG via LNG terminals on Israeli territory or on neighboring Cyprus territory or from a floating LNG platform.

Will Israel go it alone or in cooperation with Cyprus?

A significant decision for Israel is whether to engage in its new role as an energy exporter alone, or in cooperation with its much smaller and only non-Muslim neighbor Cyprus. While this is a strategic decision for Israel as a regional power, it is of significant national importance to Cyprus with an economy that is still reeling from the after-effects of its recent financial crisis and is presently in the midst of recession. Furthermore, without the protection of Israel's defense umbrella, it is doubtful whether any energy company would brave Turkish threats against Cyprus's energy wealth.

Given Cyprus's present weak economic situation and the constant threats coming from Turkey, Cyprus's erstwhile allies within the EU, with the full support of the US and the UN, have all seized the opportunity to push for a settlement of the Cyprus problem that would remove an international headache for the West and the international community in general that has been intractable for the past 60 years. The proposed solution amounts to the resurrection of a version of the 2004 Annan Plan that was soundly defeated by the Greek Cypriots (76 percent against), although accepted by the Turkish Cypriots and illegal settler voters (65 percent in favor) in separate referenda. That plan would have legitimized Turkish gains from its invasion and occupation of northern Cyprus and would have de facto partitioned the island. The plan envisions a bizonal, bicommunal, politically equal federal state with a single national identity with veto powers on practically every single major future decision. As is usual with these proposed settlements, the devil of an unworkable and grossly unjust arrangement is in the details (Georgiou 2009, 2010).

In reality, Israel could develop its natural gas energy export sector single-handedly (i.e., without Cyprus), given that Israeli proven gas reserves now stand at 32 trillion cubic feet, dwarfing those of Cyprus at approximately 5 trillion cubic feet. Of course, thus far only one sector

(Block 12) of Cyprus's EEZ has been fully surveyed and expectations are high that much larger deposits could be found, if not in that sector, then in adjoining sectors of its EEZ. However, talk of potential, as yet not discovered, reserves constitutes mere speculation at this stage.

On the other hand, collaboration with Cyprus could prove to be quite rewarding for Israel. First, the more proven gas reserves that can be pooled for development and export, the greater the economies of scale and the lower the cost of production and processing would be. Second, an Israeli partnership with Cyprus that would be willing to provide a location for the construction of an LNG processing site and export terminal would relieve Israel from the domestic debate over the issue of locating the facility within Israeli borders. Third, an offshore terminal located in Cyprus would greatly reduce the environmental impact on Israel proper. This option would, however, add to Israel's already large security burden, considering that the offshore facility would be on the territory of another nation. Furthermore, it would be difficult to defend the position that Israel's independence and energy security would be enhanced given that the facility would be located in another country.

Fourth, as an EU member Cyprus would grant Israel direct political and geographic links to the vast, highly lucrative, and growing European energy market. It could thus be argued that natural gas exports from Cyprus/Israel to the EU would benefit from EU financial and political support, as this would further diversify EU energy supplies and increase its energy security. It would also strengthen further EU support for Israel in the Israeli–Palestinian question, as well as in the overall Israeli–Arab conflict. Fifth, a direct energy link between Cyprus/Israel and the EU via Greece, another EU member, would enable the EU to further its energy security and energy independence by bypassing Russia and Turkey, both questionable long-term sources of secure energy for Europe. Reliance on Russia as a secure source of energy is clearly under question in the EU because of the Ukrainian issue and more specifically Russia's annexation of Crimea.

Finally, recent developments in Turkey are unsettling Israel, as the current Turkish leadership under Erdoğan is turning the country steadily into a more Islamic and authoritarian state. As already mentioned, Erdoğan singled Israel out for harsh criticism for its treatment of Palestinians. Following the 2010 Gaza flotilla raid, relations between the two countries, once warm and cordial, have turned cold, despite Israel's formal apology (with US encouragement). These events and the Turkish stance should give Israeli policy makers reason to question the reliability of Turkey as a secure energy market or as a conduit for its gas exports to

Europe. If anything, Israel should aim for diversity of energy export outlets, given its focus on security. Furthermore, it might be a good long-term strategy for Israel to look for export markets both east (Asia) as well as west (Europe).

What form should gas exports take: Pipeline or LNG?

Maybe one of the first decisions that Israel (and Cyprus for that matter) has to make is whether to rely on pipelines or LNG (or possibly compressed natural gas, CNG) for its gas exports. If initial cost is the number one consideration, clearly pipelines are a more cost-effective option. In that regard, and up until very recently, a pipeline to Turkey was considered the major contender. Turkey is relatively close to Israel, its economy is growing, and the country is expected to see domestic demand increase from 43.5 billion cubic meters in 2012, to as much as 60 billion cubic meters by 2020. Furthermore, Turkey has only secured 6 billion cubic meters (of the additional 16–17 billion cubic meters of gas that it will need to import) from Azerbaijan, and that will not start until 2018–19 (Roberts 2013). Over the past three years, Turkey has experienced some of the fastest growth in energy demand among countries in the Organization for Economic Cooperation and Development (OECD). Unlike a number of other OECD countries in Europe, its economy avoided the prolonged stagnation that characterized much of the continent in the past few years. Its energy use is still relatively low, although it is increasing fast. According to the International Energy Agency (IEA), energy use will continue to grow at an annual rate of around 4.5 percent from 2015 to 2030, approximately doubling over the next decade (Maritime Executive 2014).

However, a pipeline to Turkey could prove to be a political nightmare for Israel, even if at first sight this option looks worthy. The Israeli foreign ministry probably likes the idea because it would help improve ties with an important neighbor, and the defense ministry may well appreciate the notion of improving security ties with a former military ally. However, it is not clear whether a pipeline to Turkey is possible without first settling important maritime boundary issues between Israel and Lebanon; or even solving the Cyprus problem, considering that Turkey holds the key. One thing is certain: a land pipeline through (or along shallow seabed) Lebanon and Syria would reduce both operating as well as construction costs. However, such a route would entail unacceptable political and security risks for Israel; not to mention open hostility to such an option coming from both Lebanon and Syria, which are formally in a state of war with Israel.

A pipeline east of Cyprus would have to run through waters that are Cypriot, unless Lebanon and Syria acquiesce to a path through their waters. Cyprus and Israel have delineated their EEZ boundaries (2010), as have Cyprus and Lebanon (2007), although Lebanese legislators have yet to ratify that agreement. Cyprus had already delineated its maritime boundary with Egypt in 2003. All three are model agreements based on the application of the median line and with a third-party dispute-settlement provision between an island state and its continental neighbors in accordance with the Regime of Islands, Article 121 of the 1982 UN Convention on the Law of the Sea (UNCLOS III). The UN defined the land border between Lebanon and Syria in 2000, but not the delineation of their maritime zones (territorial sea, contiguous zone, exclusive economic zone, and continental shelf; Jacovides 2012, 2013a, b).

As it turns out, the respective claims of Israel and Lebanon overlap by about 860 sq km in a potentially rich portion of the Levant Basin close to already proven Israeli and Cypriot gas fields (Dickey 2014). Although the potential path of any pipeline east of Cyprus may be in Cypriot waters (according to UNCLOS and international law), in reality any route taken by a pipeline from Israel to Turkey to the east of Cyprus would also have to pass through waters controlled not by the RoC, but by Turkey through its TRNC proxy regime.

Nonetheless, veteran observers of the region were not surprised when the Israeli media announced on March 23, 2014 that more than 10 companies had submitted bids for the tender of a proposed undersea pipeline that would export natural gas from Israel's offshore Leviathan field to the Turkish port of Ceyhan, a distance of 450 km. What is also interesting is that the pipeline would run from a floating production, storage, and offloading (FPSO) ship, avoiding for the time being the decision on a land terminal either on Israeli or Cypriot territory. However, the proposed pipeline would lie totally in Cyprus's EEZ, averaging a depth of 2,000 meters and costing in the vicinity of $2.25 billion, thus bypassing both Lebanon and Syria as well as avoiding the disputed maritime boundary between Israel and Lebanon. Of course, a pipeline of such depth would require significant engineering and technical expertise, rivaling other pipeline initiatives such as the Baltic Sea's North Stream and the Black Sea's South Stream (Stratfor Global Intelligence 2014).

The technical obstacles of course pale in comparison to the political obstacles that the Cypriot coastline route presents. Such a route would require the consent of the RoC, which, based on long-standing positions held by the Cypriot government, would be out of the question without a political solution to the de facto division of the island. The recognized Greek-dominated RoC in the south cannot for the time being exercise control over the northern part of the island, which is held under occupation through more than 40,000 Turkish troops, thousands of tanks, and other military equipment.

An alternate route that would avoid the Lebanon/Syria problem altogether would be a pipeline overland in Cyprus and from there to Turkey. If distance, engineering, and cost were the only considerations, this might be the best option. It would entail a subsea line from the Israeli and Cypriot gas fields to Vassiliko, on the southern coast of Cyprus, then an overland pipeline to the northern coast, followed by a subsea pipeline to Turkey. At the moment this remains a pipedream, because the RoC would not allow the laying of a pipeline from the southern government-controlled coast of Cyprus to the Turkish-occupied northern coast.

A third option would be to lay a pipeline west of Cyprus to Crete and from there to mainland Greece and on to Europe. This would skirt the Israeli–Lebanon–Syria and Cyprus–Turkey problems, but would need to pass through waters that are diplomatically murky. Equally, the pipeline would need to be laid 3000 meters deep, calling for very difficult engineering feats, not to mention the much greater distance to be covered (1040 km versus 450 km) and of course the much greater cost, estimated at approximately $15–20 billion (Mitsos and Economides 2011). The problem with this option is that Greece, Turkey, and Cyprus have yet to declare what their respective EEZs are in this area, let alone reach an agreement on the delineation of their maritime borders. However, the west-of-Cyprus option generates two important consequences: first, the pipeline would bypass Turkey altogether, both as export route to the European market and as an export market; and secondly, an Israeli partnership with Cyprus and Greece would provide Israel with a direct geographic and political link to the very important EU energy market, since both Cyprus and Greece are EU member nations.

A straightforward interpretation of the Regime of Islands would give Cyprus a common boundary with Greece's EEZ, thanks to the Greek island of Kastelorizos off the coast of Turkey (Jacovides 2013b). While rightfully much is been made of the importance of EEZ boundaries, it must be remembered that UNCLOS does not give nations the right to prevent third parties from laying pipelines, phone lines, and so on through their respective EEZs, but it does require the approval of the host nation, which effectively gives the host nation veto power over pipelines through its own EEZ. More than likely in this case is that Turkey would want to claim a common boundary with Egypt's EEZ by discounting (wishing away!) the existence of the Greek island of Kastelorizos. This was shaping up to be a difficult problem for Cyprus and Greece because Egypt's former Islamist president Morsi was a great friend of Islamist Erdoğan, which made Egypt's position dubious. Matters changed quickly, however, when Morsi was deposed in a military coup. The present Egyptian regime headed by Abdel Fattah el-Sisi cannot be pleased with the support that Erdoğan's Turkey gave the Morsi government. Therefore, one would expect the Sisi government to side with Cyprus and Greece on this matter, since this political alignment might provide future access to the vast EU market for Egyptian gas. However, it appears that in the short run Egypt is more likely to be an importer of Israeli natural gas rather than an exporter of natural gas to Europe, or anywhere else for that matter, due to Egypt's growing domestic demand and serious Egyptian gas production and distribution problems following poor investment under the regimes of both Mubarak and Morsi. Access to Levantine Basin natural gas that would alleviate the current energy shortage in Egypt would also reduce the political pressure, both domestic and international, on a less than fully democratic Egyptian military regime that is still trying to suppress opposition from the Muslim Brotherhood and establish its legitimacy.

For the time being, neither Athens nor Ankara seems to wish to deal with this very hot EEZ issue, because it involves Cyprus and because the two countries have yet to delineate their maritime boundaries in the sensitive Aegean sea. Of course, there is the possibility, albeit slight, that this problem might be avoided altogether if a pipeline route to Crete and mainland Greece could be found through Egypt's EEZ. Either way, a pipeline to Greece for Israeli and Cypriot gas (and maybe even Egyptian gas) would be more technologically complex than even the route east of Cyprus to Turkey. It would require state-of-the-art technology to lay pipes at depths of 3000 meters or greater, and at a cost estimated to be in the region of $15–20 billion (Pope 2013; Tsanis, Gkanoutas-Leventis, and Andriosopoulos 2014). Thus, cost alone might rule out such a project, unless Greece finds gas in the vicinity of Crete or some other convenient intermediate location, or Cyprus discovers significantly larger gas deposits in its remaining EEZ.

Unfortunately for Cyprus, recent developments have made any pipeline plans for its natural gas exports even more remote, as Israel is looking for an intermediate solution to its energy future. In this regard Israel is developing its regional energy market further by adding Egypt to its list of neighborhood clients, which already includes Jordan and the Palestinian Authority. This reduces transportation costs due to proximity.

Equally, such short distances can easily be traversed with relatively inexpensive pipelines, and in the case of Egypt connected to the existing Egyptian pipeline network.

While this development might appear surprising to outsiders, it might in the end prove to be both a politically wise and economically sound energy option for Israel. First, Egypt is facing a domestic natural gas shortage that makes Israeli natural gas a good option. Second, decreased Egyptian natural gas production resulted in under-utilized existing LNG plants, which in turn reduced the need for new investment in energy infrastructure. Third, the existence of LNG plants and a pipeline network in Egypt opens up the possibility of Israeli natural gas reaching the Asian market, where LNG fetches twice the price that the EU pays. Fourth, the close proximity of Egypt together with the existing Egyptian pipeline network would reduce the transportation cost of Israeli natural gas to a fraction of the cost of constructing any pipeline to Turkey. To make matters even more difficult for Cyprus's energy future, a pipeline from the Levantine Basin to Turkey would cost a fraction (estimated at $2.2 billion) of any such pipeline linking Israel and Europe by way of Cyprus and Greece, the so-called southeast corridor, estimated to cost $15–20 billion (Vukmanovic and Bousso 2014).

The liquefied natural gas option

Given the political problems that all pipeline routes face and the significant cost of an Israel–Cyprus–Greece pipeline, it would appear that the LNG option makes sense for Cyprus and also provides Israel with an option that it can pursue in tandem with its pipeline plans. While LNG is clearly Cyprus's preference, Israel has yet to commit to it. In theory, the LNG route could proceed irrespective of whether an overall solution to the Cyprus problem is found soon, or whether the relationship between Israel and Turkey is normalized. It would not require the declaration of EEZs and delimitation of the maritime boundaries of Cyprus and Greece, Cyprus and Turkey, or Greece and Turkey. It would also avoid any conflict with Turkey (or possibly Egypt) that the pipeline option might create. It would furthermore strengthen and cement Cyprus's position as a regional energy hub, especially if the LNG plant/terminal is located as planned at Vasilikos on the southern coast of Cyprus. This plant would be connected by subsea pipelines to the Israeli Leviathan gas field and the Cyprus Aphrodite gas field, as well as to any future gas fields yet to be discovered.

In this way Israel would avoid any domestic opposition to situating the LNG terminal on its territory, given the potential environmental threats and the heightened risk of sabotage that such a target would present if located in Israel proper. Given Cyprus's dire economic situation and precarious political circumstances, as well as the ever-present Turkish military threat, fears of sabotage are likely to fall on deaf ears in Cyprus. Of course, Israel would have to extend its naval presence and defense umbrella to encompass the southern coast of Cyprus, but this probably falls within Israeli defense planning in any case. However, the cost of building a new LNG facility would also be high, although less than the projected cost of a pipeline to Greece. Building costs are estimated at $10 billion for the initial terminal and one liquefaction unit, with the cost increasing by an additional $8 billion and $6 billion if in the future a second and third unit were added, respectively (Tsanis, Gkanoutas-Leventis, and Andriosopoulos 2014).

For both Israel and Cyprus there are other long-term benefits favoring LNG rather than pipelines: namely, reliability and the security of their export markets. Much has been made of the possibility of Israel–Cyprus–Greece providing a southeastern energy corridor for Europe, which would diversify its energy supplies and contribute to its energy security. It is said that this option would provide Europe with an alternative to Russian energy sources and supply lines (mainly bypassing Ukraine), as well as an alternative to a Turkey–Greece–Bulgaria energy corridor (thus bypassing Turkey). However, with rapidly increasing world natural gas energy supplies and the diversification of natural gas energy sources, including the growing availability of US LNG directed to export, it behooves Israel (and Cyprus) to look both east and west for their natural gas exports. The demand for natural gas in Asia is growing at 3.3 percent a year, versus 0.7 percent a year for Europe (US Energy Information Administration 2013), with the price being 50 percent higher (BP 2013). Unless Israel is prepared to construct a pipeline to the Red Sea, a highly unlikely proposition given the experience with the Egyptian pipeline, the export of natural gas through the Suez Canal to markets in Asia would have to be in the form of LNG. Of course, any Israeli–Egyptian energy partnership would preempt a Cyprus LNG option in the short run, but it is doubtful that the Israeli defense establishment would agree to an export strategy that relied solely on Egypt, even if backed by the current Egyptian leadership under Sisi.

In fact, LNG is exactly the intent of the memorandum of understanding signed on June 26, 2013 by the government of Cyprus with the Delek Group and Noble Energy (the companies currently developing the major offshore gas fields discovered so far in both Israeli and Cypriot waters).

This aims to put in place the basic terms of a formal agreement to develop a joint two-train LNG plant at Vasilikos on the southern coast of Cyprus, with operations to start in 2018–19. However, it is not clear what the intentions of Israel are at present, given that in March 2014 it proceeded to accepted bids for a pipeline to take gas to Turkey east of Cyprus. It is more than likely that Israel will keep all its options open and will not reveal its true or final intentions till it chooses.

However, no nation has as yet approved the construction of an LNG plant in another country that would be primarily designed to serve its own resources. This would certainly raise security questions and inevitably increase the cost of providing de facto military security for such an installation and the naval region stretching from the coast of Israel to the southern coast of Cyprus where the Israeli and Cypriot gas fields lie. Not only are there logistical and technical concerns around such a prototype arrangement, but undoubtedly a significant financial commitment would be necessary on the part of Israel, as the cost of such an LNG processing plant and terminal would be in the range of $10–15 billion or more. A project of such proportions is clearly beyond the means of Cyprus to manage on its own, even if the country were not beset by financial woes. At any rate, even if finance were not an issue, Cyprus's proven natural gas reserves thus far cannot justify the cost of an LNG processing plant and terminal plus additional supporting infrastructure. Without Israeli gas and Israeli financial participation, Cyprus's energy future would be uncertain. It would also require international energy companies to weigh their commitment to such a Cyprus project, considering that Turkey has threatened to use force against Cyprus and to deny energy companies access to Turkish investment projects if they participate in one involving Cyprus. Given the size and rate of growth of the Turkish "emerging" market and the non-existent economic clout of the Cypriot economy, Turkish economic threats will no doubt be studied closely by all concerned.

Of course, there is still the option of Israel going it alone, but that would require building an LNG plant in Israel itself (and here we are reminded of the country's limited Mediterranean coastline), which would most likely trigger serious environmental protests. The option of an LNG plant in Israel proper becomes more probable the longer an agreement between Cyprus and Israel fails to materialize. Another option would be to develop floating LNG terminals or FPSO ships, which again are not free of environmental dangers. Either option would of course constitute an obvious target for missile attack and sabotage. These domestic options undoubtedly would come at no less cost to Israel than the Cyprus LNG option (Roberts 2013). A decision on the part of Israel to go it alone with its energy development would constitute a severe blow to Cyprus's energy future and to the resuscitation of the Cypriot economy.

Conclusion

Partnerships between disparate parties are never easy and the potentially mutually beneficial energy relationship between Cyprus and Israel is a case in point. While there are many benefits to such a partnership, it remains precarious and elusive for the time being. Israel is clearly the dominant partner in the relationship. While attempting to appear decisive and bold in its declarations, Cyprus is in fact treading water, awaiting decisions taken in Jerusalem and not in Nicosia. However, as time does not stand still, both Cyprus and Israel are likely to take action in the short run that in the end may prove detrimental to the long-term partnership. Cyprus feels more threatened and vulnerable than at any time since the Turkish invasion of 1974 because of its financial and economic crisis and pressure from the US and the EU to compromise on the Cyprus problem, even at the expense of its very future. Israel, on the other hand, is emboldened by its new-found energy position, its fast-growing economy, the weakening Palestinian opposition, the ongoing Syrian civil war, the dysfunctional Iraqi state, and more broadly the unraveling of the Arab Spring revolution, particularly in Egypt.

References

Alderman, Liz. 2013. "Future Looks Bleaker Than Anticipated in Cyprus, Its Creditors Claim." New York Times, April 11.
   http://www.nytimes.com/2013/04/12/business/global/cyprus-bailout-to-cost-more-than-predicted-creditors-say.html?_r=0. Accessed April 2013.
Apostolides, Costa. 2013. "Not-So Hidden Agenda behind Money-Laundering Claims." Cyprus Mail, January 27. http://www.cyprus-mail.com/opinions/not-so-hidden-agenda-behind-money-laundering-claims/20130127. Accessed January 2013.
BP. 2013. "Natural Gas Prices."
   http://www.bp.com/en/global/corporate/energy-economics/statistical-review-of-world-energy/natural-gas-review-by-energy-type/natural-gas-prices.html. Accessed May 2014.
Charalambous, Charlie. 1998. "Israel Tries to Mend Fences." Cyprus Mail, November 12. http://www.hri.org/news/cyprus/cmnews/1998/98-11-12.cmnews.html. Accessed January 2013.

CIA. 2013. "The World Factbook: Cyprus."
https://www.cia.gov/library/publications/the-world-
factbook/geos/cy.html. Accessed February 2013.

Dickey, Christopher. 2014. "Are These Gas Fields Israel's Next
Warzone?" Daily Beast, February 6.
http://www.thedailybeast.com/articles/2014/02/06/are-these-gas-fields-
israel-s-next-warzone.html. Accessed March 2014.

—. 1979. "Alternate Trade Strategies and Employment in Cyprus."
Doctoral dissertation. Washington, DC: George Washington
University.

Georgiou, George C. 1981. "Alternative Trade Strategies and Employment
in Cyprus." Journal of Economic Development, 6: 113–131.

—. 2009. "Cyprus: Economic Consequences of Reunification." Mediterranean Quarterly, 20: 51–62.

—. 2010. "Cyprus: Economic Consequences of the Christofias-Talat/Eroglu
Plan." Journal of Southeast European and Black Sea Studies, 10: 411–
424.

Georgiou, George C. 2013. "Cyprus Financial Crisis and the Threat to the
Euro." Mediterranean Quarterly. 24: 56–73.

Index Mundi. 2013. "Cyprus GDP – per capita (PPP)."
http://www.indexmundi.com/cyprus/gdp_per_capita_(ppp).html.
Accessed January 2013.

Glain, Stephen. 2012. "Gas Field off of Cyprus Stokes Tensions with
Turkey." New York Times, December 12.
http://www.nytimes.com/2012/12/13/world/middleeast/gas-field-off-
of-cyprus. Accessed February 2013.

Grinbaum, Idan. 2013. "Israel's Natural Gas Brings Opportunity,
Choices." Israel Pulse – Al-Monitor, April 3. http://www.al-
monitor.com/pulse/originals/2013/04/israels-natural-gas-is-
flowing.html. Accessed March 2014.

Hope, Kerin, and Peter Spiegel. 2013. "Cypriot Authorities in Revised
Deal Talks." Financial Times, March 18.
http://www.ft.com/intl/cms/s/0/a2eac7d0-8f11-11e2-a39b-
00144feabdc0.html#axzz3mm7zS0Yr. Accessed March 2013.

Jacovides, Andreas. 2012. "Recent Delimitation Practice in the Eastern
Mediterranean." European Rim Policy and Invertment Council, July
25. http://erpic.org/wp-content/uploads/2014/05/delimitation-practice-
in-the-eastern-mediterranean.pdf. Accessed April 2014.

—. 2013a. "Disputes and the Regime of Islands and Rocks, under the
United Nations Convention on the Law of the Sea." New York:
American Bar International Law Association (ABILA).

—. 2013b. "Regime of Islands: Article 121 of the 1982 United Nations Convention on the Law of the Sea, UNCLOS III." European Rim Policy and Investment Council, July 5. http://erpic.org/wp-content/uploads/2014/05/regime-of-islands-2013.pdf. Accessed April 2014.

James, Lawrence. 1994. The Rise and Fall of the British Empire. New York: St. Martin's Griffin.

Kershner, Isabel. 2012. "Israeli Watchdog Criticizes Government over Gaza Flotilla Raid." New York Times, June 13.
http://www.nytimes.com/2012/06/14/world/middleeast/israeli-watchdog-criticizes-government-over-gaza-flotilla-raid.html?_r=0.
Accessed January 2013.

Khadduri, Walid. 2014. "Israel Looks to Develop Its Oil Industry." Al-Hayat (Pan Arab), March 4.
http://www.al-monitor.com/pulse/business/2014/03/israel-develop-oil-industry-export-turkey.html. Accessed March 2014.

Maritime Executive. 2014. "Turkey Ponders Role as Oil Hub." Maritime Executive, April 22.
http://www.maritime-executive.com/article/Turkey-Ponders-Role-as-Oil-Hub-2014-04-22. Accessed April 2014.

Miltiadou, M. 2012. The Republic of Cyprus: An Overview. Nicosia: Cyprus Government Press and Information Office.

Ministry of Finance, Republic of Cyprus. 2013. www.mof.gov.cy. Accessed February 2013.

Ministry of Foreign Affairs, Republic of Cyprus. 2013. "Cyprus and the Non – Aligned Movement."
http://www.mfa.gov.cy/mfa/mfa2006.nsf/0/11E2EC1C0EE098C6C225727C002A04A8?OpenDocument. Accessed March 2013.

Mitsos, Nicolas, and Michael J. Economides. 2011. "Israel's Options for Monetizing Its Vast Reserves of Offshore Natural Gas in the Mediterranean Predicament." Sea NG, January 1. Sea NG.
http://www.coselle.com/resources/news/israel%E2%80%99s-options-monetizing-its-vast-reserves-offshore-natural-gas-mediterranean-predicament. Accessed April 2014.

Offshore Technology. 2013a. "Leviathan Gas Field, Levantine Basin, Mediterranean Sea, Israel."
http://www.offshore-technology.com/projects/leviathan-gas-field-levantine. Accessed February 2013.

—. 2013b. "Tamar Natural Gas Field, Israel." http://www.offshore-technology.com/projects/tamar-field. Accessed February 2013.

Pop, Valentina. 2013. "German Musings: Is Cyprus Too Small for a Bailout?" EU Observer, January 30.
https://euobserver.com/economic/118893. Accessed January 2013.

Pope, Hugh. 2013. "The Cost of Frozen Conflict for Cyprus, Greece and Turkey". Kathimerini, March 25.
http://www.ekathimerini.com/149678/article/ekathimerini/comment/th e-cost-of-frozen-conflict-for-cyprus-greece-and-turkey. Accessed April 2013.

PSEKA, 2002. "Israel Justifies Decision to Deny Entry to Cypriot Deputies." International Coordinating Committee.
http://news.pseka.net/index.php?module=article&id=704.   Accessed January 2013.

Riegert, B. 2013. "532 Billion Euros to Rescue Five Countries." Deutsche Welle, http://www.dw.com/en/532-billion-euros-to-rescue-five-countries/a-16800256. Accessed April 2013.

Roberts, John. 2013. "A Nice Problem to Have… But Vexing: How Much Natural Gas Should Israel Export?" The Barrel, August 8.
http://blogs.platts.com/2013/08/08/east-med/. Accessed August 2013.

Robertson, Jessica, and Chris Schenk. 2010. "Natural-Gas Potential Assessed in Eastern Mediterranean." United States Geological Survey, May. http://soundwaves.usgs.gov/2010/05/research3.html.
Accessed February 2013.

Spiegel Online. 2013. "Euro Zone Reaches Deal on Cyprus Bailout." Spiegel Online, March 16.
http://www.spiegel.de/international/europe/savers-will-be-hit-as-part-of-deal-to-bail-out-cyprus-a-889252.html. Accessed March 2013.

Stratfor Global Intelligence. 2013. "The Limited Geopolitical Clout of Israeli Natural Gas." Stratfor Global Intelligence, April 2.
https://www.stratfor.com/sample/analysis/limited-geopolitical-clout-israeli-natural-gas. Accessed April 2013.

—. 2014. "A Potential Turkey-Israel Pipeline Project." Stratfor Global Intelligence, April 2. https://www.stratfor.com/sample/image/potential-turkey-israel-pipeline-project. Accessed April 2014.

Tsanis, Konstantinos Ilias, Angelos Gkanoutas-Leventis, and Kostas Andriosopoulos. 2014. "Cyprus and Greece: Dilemmas in Energy Infrastructure." Natural Gas Europe, February 15.

US Energy Information Administration. 2013. "International Energy Outlook 2013." Eia.gov.
http://www.eia.gov/forecasts/ieo/pdf/0484(2013).pdf. Accessed May 2014.

Vukmanovic, Oleg, and Ron Bousso. 2014. "Insight: Israeli Gas Holds Promise of Better Ties with Neighbors." Thomson Reuters, April 14. http://www.reuters.com/article/2014/04/14/us-israel-egypt-gas-insight-idUSBREA3D07720140414. Accessed April 2014.

World Bank. 2013. "GNI per capita, Atlas Method (Current US$)." Worldbank.org. http://data.worldbank.org/indicator/NY.GNP.PCAP.CD. Accessed January 2013.

CHAPTER FIVE

EASTERN MEDITERRANEAN ECONOMIES

ARIS PETASIS

The Eastern Mediterranean: Challenge and promise

In the last hundred years the Eastern Mediterranean (EM) has seen more than its fair share of tumultuous events. During this period the region (Greece, Cyprus, Egypt, Lebanon, Syria, Jordan, Israel, and Turkey) experienced multiple wars (four wars between Arabs and Israelis alone), plenty of coup d'états (Egypt, Turkey, Greece, Cyprus), occupation by one neighbor of another (Turkey occupies 37 percent of Cyprus's territory to this day), civil wars (Greece, Lebanon, Syria), numerous near-bankruptcies (Greece, Egypt), serious economic calamities (Egypt, Cyprus), banking failures (Cyprus, Greece) and one bail-in of depositors that was meant "to save the banks" (Cyprus).

The region managed in an amazing manner to balance tumult with promise. Despite the many conflicts and troubles, the area managed to stay open for business. Its proven energy reserves are now offering new promise as well as fresh challenges and risks. The potential of gas and oil has already brought with it the threat of violence by one country against its neighbors: Turkey threatens to stop Cyprus militarily from exercising its legal right to exploit its energy reserves. Turkey also threatens Greece's energy reserves. A high-ranking Turkish government official served notice recently that no country in the region can come into any agreement with another country in the region without Turkey's consent. It is therefore clear that the EM continues to suffer from volatility and instability and in the process is making investors wary. Instability heightens investor risk and increases the probability of revolution, civil strife, war, expropriation, economic turmoil, and other catastrophic outcomes that can ruin economies and people's lives.

The entire EM region is suffering from varying degrees of instability that thwart the drive toward economic development. Investors with long-term plans are particularly sensitive to country instability because of worries that their investment may get trapped in a conflict. Past bad experiences with a particular country tend to exacerbate investor fears. For example, a few years after the Egyptian government was overthrown in a military coup (1952), investors in the country saw their properties expropriated literally overnight. Not surprisingly, this event lingers in the minds of potential investors to this day. Worse still, most of those who lost their investment had been in Egypt for many generations and had a long-term commitment to the country and its economy; they were proud of Egypt. Investors in energy are especially sensitive to instability as energy-focused investments are typically long term. Not surprisingly, when Turkey sends warships to threaten Cyprus's exclusive economic zone (EEZ), investors begin to worry about Cyprus's energy potential. Militarization is perhaps the fastest way to frighten off investors from a country or region, no matter how lucrative the project might look.

Economic instability and foreign investment

The amount of foreign direct investment (FDI) is a good measure of the stability of a host country. Assuming that other things are equal, a foreign investor is likely to prefer investing in a politically stable country than in less stable one. The Organization for Economic Cooperation and Development (OECD 2014) defines FDI as follows:

> Foreign Direct Investment (FDI) is a category of investment that reflects the objective of establishing a lasting interest by a resident enterprise in one economy (direct investor) in an enterprise (direct investment enterprise) that is resident in an economy other than that of the direct investor. The lasting interest implies the existence of a long-term relationship between the direct investor and the direct investment enterprise and a significant degree of influence (not necessarily control) on the management of the enterprise. The direct or indirect ownership of 10% or more of the voting power of an enterprise resident in one economy by an investor resident in another economy is evidence of such a relationship.

Let us consider each country in turn.

Egypt

Egypt has been experiencing its own set of political problems in the last six or more years. Tourism was the first victim of uncertainty, which in part led to the country's foreign currency reserves all but disappearing at some point. Egypt's major current risks are mostly internal, because it is not really threatened by outside forces. Not surprisingly and in an effort to reduce long-term risk, a considerable number of investors in Egypt prefer to rent premises rather than acquire them freehold. This option gives them flexibility in case trouble erupts. Although far-fetched, the nationalization of private firms and businesses in 1956 and the political turmoil of a few years back resonate in today's business thinking. Successive Egyptian governments tried repeatedly to privatize many state enterprises, but this effort failed to attract serious money for the government, as would-be investors worried about the country's economic environment. Uncertainty about the future of the economy and the notorious Egyptian bureaucracy held the privatization process back and limited FDI. Indicatively, in the period 2002–14 Egypt managed to attract on average a meager $2,263.99 million in FDI (Trading Economics 2015a).

Greece

The instability that affects Greece's economy comes from many sources, chief of which is the depressed mood that has engulfed the country and frightens investors away. The absence of confidence in its long-term future has hit Greece with devastating effect. The government is trying to change matters, but progress remains elusive and it is unlikely that much will alter in the near future. The Greek people are economically hard-pressed and many are on their knees financially and without end in sight, considering that Greece's creditors want their money back and are pressing for budget surpluses. As things stand, and given the lack of economic growth and the unwillingness to restructure, Greece will find it very difficult to create and maintain surpluses, as these would largely have to come from taxes that in the end would make people poorer still. A vicious circle has taken hold of its economy and its political system. In September 2015, Greece went through its fifth election in six years. Although the current government coalition now enjoys a majority in parliament, its longevity will depend on how well the economy does and how people respond to continuous austerity, which is one of the hallmarks of Greece's reform program. Clearly, the current state of affairs is not sustainable and something will surely have to give. The country is suffering from massive unemployment, a low birth rate (much below replacement), an unsustainable pension system that requires about €10 billion yearly to be spent on pensions for people below 65 and in some cases below 55, general poverty and hopelessness, and low investment. The demographic problem that Greece (and Cyprus) are now facing is overwhelming and puts the future of these countries and their economies at risk. Regrettably, in neither country is demographics at the top of the political agenda.

Greece has a long tradition of largely irresponsible labor unions that in the past put forward unreasonable demands and encouraged work stoppages, particularly in the public sector. Foreign investors were aghast to see the universities taken over by student activists who at one point invaded the office of a vice chancellor and showered him with rubbish brought in from the street in bins. Now, Greece is experiencing much destructive social tension between the haves and the have-nots and between those who label themselves "leftists" and those who claim to be "rightists." Such phenomena exacerbate the situation, cause investors to stay away, and reduce FDI prospects (Trading Economics 2015b). The promotion of limited reforms in the last three or so years and the subsequent cost reduction in some of the factors of production created encouraging investment opportunities that regrettably were not fully realized. If the government now manages to develop some of Greece's public property commercially, then this would be a positive sign. The potential exploration of its energy resources (oil and gas) will certainly buttress the country's economy, although a threatening Turkey continues to be a thorn in the side of Greece's oil and gas potential.

Lebanon

Lebanon has been suffering from intractable internal political problems for decades, which continue to this day, resulting in perpetual instability and keeping foreign businesses away. Internal political and factional problems can be as bad as or even worse than external problems; internal tumult pits neighbor against neighbor and spreads suspicion and distrust among citizens. This awful spiral ultimately permeates the whole of society and stealthily paralyzes the nation and economic activity. Lebanon's problems are having a detrimental effect on the economy and particularly on FDI levels (Trading Economics 2015c). FDI to Lebanon dropped sharply in 2013 on account of reduced capital inflows from the Gulf countries into the Lebanese real estate sector. Political instability and security issues, arising from the Syrian crisis just across the Lebanese border, frightened wealthy Gulf investors away from Lebanon's real estate sector. The country's paucity of structural economic reforms is also taking its toll and affecting FDI negatively.

Israel

FDI in Israel averaged $4,070.62 million from 1995 to 2014 (Trading Economics 2015d). Israel is now in fourth place internationally in FDI relative to the size of the economy. It attracts FDI equivalent to 4 percent of GDP (vs. an average of 1.4 percent for OECD countries). Inflows come primarily from the United States (US), China, Japan, and Russia. Growth of the Israeli economy in the second quarter of 2014 (before the fighting in and around Gaza) dropped to 1.7 percent. For the first time in a long while, the shekel showed signs of weakening, although it is a very stubborn currency. All these go to show the potent effects of stability on a country's economy.

Turkey

Turkey's FDI averaged $12,415.09 million from 2003 to 2013 (Trading Economics 2015e). The energy sector emerged as the largest recipient of foreign capital, with $2.55 billion. The European Union (EU) was the main source of money flowing into Turkey, with 52 percent of the capital coming from members of the 28-nation bloc. During 2013 a total of 2,960 new foreign-funded companies were established in Turkey, a figure down from the 3,703 of 2012. As at December 2013, a total of 37,000 companies operating in Turkey received their capital from abroad. Istanbul, the economic capital and largest population center, got the lion's share of the foreign-funded businesses, with nearly 22,000 operating in the city. Neighboring Greece's trade with Turkey is increasing fast even if Turkey continuous to occupy militarily 37 percent of Cyprus's territory, turning a quarter of a million Greek Cypriots into internal refugees. Trade between Turkey and Greece doubled between 2010 (€2.2 billion) and 2013 (€4.3 billion) and a total of 500 Greek companies are reckoned to be active in Turkey.

Cyprus

In the main, Cyprus's cumulative FDI stock was invested in three key service sectors: financial, real estate, and wholesale trade. Greece, the United Kingdom (UK), and Russia have traditionally been Cyprus's largest foreign direct investors. Central Bank of Cyprus (CBC) statistics show that FDI peaked in 2009 (just as the signs of recession began to show), and then fell as the global financial crisis started to take its toll.

The financial and insurance sectors traditionally attracted more than their fair share of FDI.

In terms of FDI, the countries in the EM can be slotted into three groups: Israel with FDI far exceeding the OECD average of 1.4 percent of GDP; Turkey roughly on a par with the OECD average; and Greece, Egypt, Cyprus, and Lebanon with FDI rates below the OECD average. The World Bank reports FDI figures for the six countries for each of the four years 2010–13 (Table 5.1).

Table 5.1: FDI (in $ billion) in the Eastern Mediterranean region, 2010–13. Source: World Bank. 2015. "Foreign direct investment, net (BoP, current US$)." http://data.worldbank.org/indicator/BN.KLT.DINV.CD.

Country	2010	2011	2012	2013
Cyprus	0.0706	2.0	1.2	0.607
Egypt	6.3	-0.482	2.8	5.5
Greece	0.533	1.0	1.6	2.9
Israel	5.5	9	8	11
Lebanon	4.2	3.5	3.5	3.0
Turkey	9.0	16	13.2	12.8

Energy and militarism

Cyprus and Greece are classic examples of energy-rich countries that failed to exploit their energy resources to cushion their economies against downturns. Both countries were (and maybe still are) champions of public-sector employment, rampant unionization, and destructive party politics; not that the other countries in the region do any better. Most critically, both countries were unable and/or unwilling to reverse the bad decisions of the past once these proved to be detrimental to their economies. As a result, both are now under the control of their creditors, who currently dictate what needs to be done in their economies. These creditors are unelected and have no economic mandate from the people. Equally, both countries, but especially Greece, failed to show tenacity at the right moment in the area of energy exploration. Both are victims of Turkey's militarism, which threatens them with violence if they refuse to obey

Turkey's wishes over their EEZs. This is badly affecting their chances of economic recovery and prosperity.

If properly and fairly managed, the energy factor can make a huge difference to the economies of all countries in the region. In Chapter 3 of this book, Solon Kassinis discusses the proven energy reserves in the region and makes optimistic assessments of its energy potential. Recognizing the serious geopolitical impediments that lie ahead, he sounds the following words of warning:

> In the meantime, many major geopolitical, exploration, and production challenges will need to be managed before benefits can materialize. These include, among others, bilateral or trilateral (or even multilateral) cooperation between countries in the region, pipelines versus marine transport, risks and returns, technical issues, and many more.

Energy may be a defining factor in the fortunes of countries in the region. Nevertheless, huge challenges lie ahead, prime among which are the Palestinian–Israeli conflict and the occupation of 37 percent of Cyprus's territory by Turkish troops. Both these issues need to be resolved fairly and in strict compliance with the rule of international law and human rights. The Turkish occupation does not look like coming to an end soon. Turkey is not ready to respect international law and continues to aggravate the situation by keeping down both Cyprus and Greece.

While the latter countries are basically bereft of serious capacity to manufacture armaments, Turkey manufactures and even exports arms, at the same time importing large amounts of weaponry, largely from the US (some in the form of military aid). Angelo Young (2014) writes that Turkey is rising in the arms export area and notes, "The country is trying to boost exports by $1.6 billion [in 2014] by focusing on markets that can't afford the premium-grade offers from the world's top defence companies."

The Turkish defense industry is now looking into the South American and African markets for contracts. Turkey's two defense companies – Turkish Aerospace Industries and Aselan – will benefit most from its efforts to sell weapons systems and vehicles to these countries. It is determined to push hard for arms exports and hopes to export armaments worth $25 billion by 2023. Turkey is not content with what it has and has already put in place an ambitious plan to produce its own fighter jet locally. Hurriyet Daily News (2015) reports the words of the national defense minister: "We manufacture our own ships and all of our land vehicles, including tanks. We also manufacture our own helicopter and training jets. Another thing we are planning is producing a fighter jet ...

Turkey's main target is being able to produce its ground, naval and air defence arms domestically." The minister continued ominously, "We will hopefully be … fully powerful when we accomplish this." Turkey already manufactures land vehicles and tanks, helicopters, and training jets.

Unless real peace reigns in the region and unless disputes are resolved amicably and within the bounds of international law, the EM will most likely experience an increased military build-up (typical of countries with energy reserves). In such an event, resources will be diverted from other sectors of the economy to fund the purchase of military hardware (which will speedily become obsolete). This cannot be good for the long-term potential of these economies. Post-World War II Germany and Japan demonstrate how economies can thrive when military expenditures remain at minimum levels.

The Stockholm International Peace Research Institute (SIPRI 2015) reports that in the ten years between 2004 and 2013, defense expenditure across the world increased by 25 percent, in North America by 12 percent, in Europe by 8–9 percent, in Africa by 65 percent, and in the Middle East by a thundering 155 percent. Clearly, the Mediterranean region is becoming militarized fast. In 2013, the biggest spender of all was Algeria (with probable oil reserves of 18.1 billion barrels). It spent $10 billion, largely to defend its energy reserves. Energy-rich Angola was Africa's largest spender with $6 billion, and has now overtaken South Africa as the biggest defense spender in sub-Saharan Africa. Cyprus, the smallest country of the six in the EM region and also energy rich, is entertaining offers from Israel and Greece to buy two offshore patrol vessels (OPV). It was also reported that Cyprus signed an agreement with France to buy two large vessels based on the Gowind corvette design. A recent agreement between Russia and Cyprus provides docking facilities in Cypriot ports to the Russian navy, giving some hope to Cyprus and improving people's morale and confidence. Russia and Cyprus have had close relationships for centuries and are traditional friends.

Competitiveness

Competitiveness is discussed here with reference to the performance of each country in the EM as assessed by the World Economic Forum (WEF) report on global competitiveness (Schwab 2014), and the specific but vital performance factors that it highlights. For further information consult the report itself.

One factor in the Global Competitiveness Index (GCI) is *general government debt as a percentage of GDP*. The six countries of the EM region score as follows out of 144 countries (the lower the number the better):

- Cyprus 136
- Egypt 125
- Greece 142
- Israel 111
- Lebanon 141
- Turkey 53

So all six are doing badly on government debt, with Turkey's unimpressive 53rd position being the best score. All have worryingly high levels of debt, which undoubtedly puts pressure on their finances through payment of interest and loan installments.

High government debt is a known precursor of bad things to come. Greece and Cyprus (both members of the EU) are now in economic trouble, mostly on account of high debt levels. Egypt too is under pressure to stop subsidies on a large assortment of goods in an effort to reduce government expenditure, even if this hurts the country's poor. It has been fighting this battle for a very long time, but with few results. The dust has yet to settle from the recent economic turmoil caused by the government's decision to lift energy subsidies. This led to price increases of up to 78 percent on gasoline and 175 percent on natural gas. As Egypt continued to witness a public backlash against actual or envisaged price hikes, the International Monetary Fund (IMF) issued a report in which it makes recommendations on how best to implement energy subsidy reforms in the region, basically aiming to control public outcry and reduce unwanted economic effects (Sdralevich et al. 2014).

The IMF acknowledges that reforming energy subsidies is a difficult task, both technically and politically. Therefore, it recommends that the timing and duration of reforms should be carefully planned in advance of rolling out subsidy reductions. Cutting benefits is always fraught with risks for any government, as Greece, Egypt, and Cyprus (and other countries in the region) know from experience. Media campaigns to spread awareness regarding the cost of subsidies and the benefits of reform are in most cases an absolute necessity. All are vital in rallying the largest possible political and public support for reforms. As subsidies typically go to the poor, attempts to reduce such expenditures often meet with great resistance from this fragile and luckless group.

The 2014 budget deficit in Lebanon reached $5.1 billion, registering an increase of 20.6 percent over the year before; thus, little restraint on spending and not much reform either (Al Monitor 2014). As almost everything in Lebanon is judged from a sectarian viewpoint, cutting down the budget deficit or taking benefits away from any class becomes a Herculean task.

The Troika's response to high debt levels (accumulated budget deficits over time) in Greece and Cyprus has been simple and three-pronged: reduce government operating expenses; reduce social benefits (to the poor); and collect more taxes. Admittedly, some of these measures were long overdue, but they were put off largely because the two governments irresponsibly skirted expenditure reduction for fear of voter backlash and loss of voter support. Petty party politics have been a central feature of the political life of both these countries; not that the other governments in the region are doing any better on populism. As regards the impact of voter loss, the reader is reminded that in two former presidential elections in tiny Cyprus, the difference between winner and loser was a swing of less than 1,000 votes.

Vested interests and party politics are major problems with which governments have to contend in their attempt to reduce expenditures. The unions are always a factor because of their power to create chaos, particularly in the state sector. Ill-understood (in the minds of beneficiaries) "acquired rights" sometimes make organized groups fight those who try to take away from them what they see as an entitlement. For example, in Cyprus public-sector employees receive on retirement a lump-sum payment from their employer (the government) plus a monthly pension. This lump sum is a defined end-of-service, tax-free benefit that in most cases exceeds €100,000, even for middle-level employees. In addition, on retirement public-sector employees are entitled to a monthly pension roughly equal to 50 percent of their last salary, index linked (growing annually in line with inflation). The lump sum and the pension come from contributions that the employer made, save for a minute contribution by the employee. Thus, retiring civil servants are covered from both sides: a lump sum (in case they die early) and a monthly pension for as long as they live. This arrangement may sound unusual to average public-sector employees in other countries, who are paid salaries and benefits at or below the national median and who typically make an equal contribution to their retirement plan. These Cypriot arrangements changed (slightly though) after the arrival of the Troika, but the bets are on that it will not be long before things slide back to what they were before the financial crisis.

Naturally, the Cypriot taxpayer feels annoyed with such arrangements, knowing that the average pension for private-sector employees is only a fraction of that in the public sector. Ludicrous and annoying as this practice may be, when the government attempted to tax the lump-sum benefit, public-sector unions threatened fire and brimstone. Fearing a shutdown of services that would have brought the country to a grinding halt, the government speedily recanted, telling the furious employees, to the mirth of the independent observer, that it was all a misunderstanding and that no tax would be levied.

In most countries in the region, public-sector employees do not mind flexing their muscles and going on strike to have their demands met, because of their disproportionately high voter power. Sometimes they even strike preemptively to continue browbeating their employers. Indicatively, Lebanese public-sector employees recently went on a week-long strike over parliament's unwillingness to pass a bill that would have increased their salaries by a whopping 121 percent.

In the countries of the EM the *current account balance* (trade balance plus the net amount received from factors of production used abroad; an indicator of competitiveness) does not look good, except for Israel. Cyprus's current account balance stood at -1.6 percent of GDP at December 2014 (it was -1.9 percent in 2013 and -6.8 percent in 2012). The improvement is largely accounted for by reduced imports rather than by improved exports. Greece's current account balance at December 2014 stood at +0.7 percent of GDP, largely on account of an exceedingly strong tourist season. For many years it registered large current account deficits, often reaching 8 percent of GDP. As at December 2014 the remaining countries in the region registered these current account balances (Trading Economics 2015f):

- Egypt: -0.4 percent; -2.4 percent in 2013
- Israel: +1.9 percent; +2.4% in 2013
- Lebanon: -12.7 percent; -16.18 percent in 2013
- Turkey: -5.2 percent (unofficial); -7.9 percent in 2013

On the factor of *imports as a percentage of GDP*, the GCI gives the six countries the following positions (out of 144 countries):

- Cyprus 78
- Egypt 124
- Greece 113
- Israel 108
- Lebanon 23
- Turkey 106

Lebanon performs relatively well, while the remaining countries leave much to be desired. On overall *competitiveness* (which is basically the overarching, and difficult to change in the short-run, index of how a country's economy is performing), the countries in the region hold these positions on the GCI:

- Cyprus 58
- Egypt 119
- Greece 81
- Israel 27
- Lebanon 113
- Turkey 45

This means that with the exception of Israel (and to some extent Turkey), the region suffers from weak competitiveness. The factor of competitiveness thus summarizes the strengths and weaknesses of the region's economies.

Productivity in relation to pay is a problem for all six countries, because wages in the region grew faster than justified by productivity and consequently reduced the countries' ability to compete on cost. The GCI reports these ratings:

- Cyprus 59
- Egypt 131
- Greece 121
- Israel 76
- Lebanon 60
- Turkey 81

Having dealt with labor issues in the region for many years, I can offer three generalized explanations as to why productivity lags behind salaries in the six countries:

- Strong unionization in organizations with high headcounts tends to give employees the feeling that the union is there to push for higher salaries irrespective of output and of the economic realities. Importantly, unchecked unionization brings with it other ailments such as a lack of ability to determine wages flexibly, which hits employers hard. On the factor of *wage determination flexibility*, the GCI positions Greece and Cyprus in the depressing positions of

118th and 108th, respectively. The ratings of the remaining four countries are:

- o Egypt 67
- o Lebanon 51
- o Israel 78
- o Turkey 49

- There is low public-sector productivity, largely because of poor accountability in the sector; not many public-sector employees are truly held personally accountable for their actions in any of the six countries.
- Access to technology is also insufficient. In some countries in the region (but not all) technology is at times kept back for a while, because of either administrative inertia, union pressures, or political considerations, particularly when technology threatens jobs. Interestingly, at the time of writing railway employees in the UK are threatening to go on strike because the employer planned to bring more modern and efficient trains into use. In some cases the application of technology is delayed in the EM because the country's stage of development is such that it fails to support the speedy adoption of the new technology. As a general rule, the lower a country's stage of development, the slower the technological absorption. The GCI classifies the stage of development of each of the economies in the region as follows (the higher the grade the better): Greece and Cyprus (both EU members) get a rating of 3 ("innovation driven"). Israel (with a high degree of innovation) is also a level 3 country. Lebanon and Turkey earn a 2–3 rating, classifying both as "transitional" (from stage 2 to stage 3 economies). Egypt only manages to earn a level 2 rating, putting it in the "efficiency driven" category.

Using Cyprus as an example, I will attempt to demonstrate how disproportionate (to productivity) wage increases can with time create massive problems for the economy. For the last 30 years, Cyprus's average net annual productivity stood at roughly 2 percent, while average net annual salary growth was 3.6 percent (Cyprus Department of Statistics). Union pressures, politics, inefficient bureaucracy, and a host of other problems kept the country uncompetitive. The current recession has worsened its productivity, because it reduced investment in machines and technology, thus hitting hard an already low level of innovation. Understandably, Cyprus's firms are now reluctant to take borrowing risks to invest in plant, equipment, technology, and intellectual property. Reluctance to borrow can be explained largely by three factors:

- Cypriot banks make lending difficult by charging prohibitive interest rates plus additional exorbitant "other" charges. Some of the more discredited banks in the country have been known to act arbitrarily (amounting almost to piracy) in an effort to cover the bad decisions and inefficiency that devastated their capital base. In effect, good clients are punished for the infractions of bad clients who fail to pay their debts, which in turn become non-performing loans.
- The poor development of the financial market (Cyprus is in 83rd position on the GCI on this factor) and the small size of businesses make it difficult to secure money from the financial market (except possibly from banks). It appears that the economies of other countries in the region are also held back by poorly developed financial markets (with Israel an exception). The GCI positions the remaining five countries as follows out of 144 countries:
  o Egypt 125
  o Greece 130
  o Israel 20
  o Lebanon 102
  o Turkey 58
- Businesses have little confidence in the economy (and even less in banks) and are thus loath to take medium- or long-term risks that would entail payback periods of, say, 5–10 years. Unsavory practices such as the haircut of bank deposits convinced businesspeople to adopt short-termism in their investment strategies.

With the exception of Israel, countries in the region are not doing particularly well on the GCI factors of *innovation* and *capacity for innovation*, which are crucial to productivity. On the factor of innovation Israel earns a remarkable 3rd position. The other ranks are:

- Cyprus 36
- Egypt 124
- Greece 79
- Lebanon 119
- Turkey 56

On the factor of capacity for innovation, the picture looks disappointing for all except for Israel, which again has a distinguished 3rd position. Of the other five countries, some score lamentably low:

- Cyprus 63
- Egypt 132
- Greece 109
- Lebanon 54
- Turkey 77

On *production process sophistication*, which tells us about a country's capacity to operate efficiently and competitively in manufacturing and related functions, Israel takes 21st position and again ranks ahead of all other countries in the region:

- Cyprus 45
- Egypt 120
- Greece 76
- Lebanon 84
- Turkey 36

On the factor of *FDI and technology transfer*, which reflects the degree to which FDI helps enhance technology, Israel earns impressive marks followed by Turkey (11th and 28th positions, respectively). The other four countries earn worrisome scores:

- Cyprus 78
- Egypt 85
- Greece 105
- Lebanon 139

As regards the vital factor of *quality of infrastructure* (ports, airports, roads), which can be crucial to productivity and economic performance, Cyprus and Turkey come out better than the other four. The positions of all these countries on the GCI is as follows:

- Cyprus: ports: 45; airports: 43; roads: 24; overall: 30
- Egypt: ports: 66; airports: 60; roads: 118; overall: 125
- Greece: ports: 49; airports: 40; roads: 55; overall: 57
- Israel: ports: 86; airports: 50; roads: 45; overall: 63

- Lebanon: ports: 73; airports: 65; roads: 120; overall: 140
- Turkey: ports: 57; airports: 34; roads: 40; overall: 33

In relation to *quality of management schools*, so crucial in today's business environment, Lebanon earns an astonishing 17th position; a considerable achievement for a small country, despite its perennially unsettled political situation. Cyprus and Israel also earn decent rankings. More specifically, the six countries have these positions:

- Cyprus 30
- Egypt 114
- Greece 89
- Israel 32
- Lebanon 17
- Turkey 100

A complementary factor is *availability of research and training services*, on which Israel earns a surprisingly undistinguished 38th position, four ranks lower than Cyprus in 34th. The other countries score as follows:

- Egypt 124
- Greece 90
- Lebanon 67
- Turkey 57

A particular point to note from this discussion is that Cyprus lies in a lowly 63rd position on GCI's capacity for innovation. This is disappointing for a country that is relatively rich in talent and claims a large pool of academically qualified people, whom one would have expected to push strongly for innovation. The country's notorious public service bureaucracy is of course a huge impediment to innovation, as is the destructive involvement of political parties in every facet of life, but this cannot fully explain this low rank. Importantly, Cyprus suffers from low connectivity between industry and local institutions of tertiary education.

In fact, most countries in the region appear to have a problem with accepting and disseminating innovation fast enough. Rogers (2003) asserts that ideas will spread if innovation exists in the first place; thereafter, one needs to deal with the many and sundry issues (many of which are outside the control of the innovator) that relate to implementation, such as communication channels that will get the innovation known and accepted; time to allow the innovation to be adopted and speed to achieve early results; and a social system that is willing to work toward the common objective of accepting, adopting, and applying the innovation. Many of these countries failed to produce an adequate number of noteworthy innovative products and as such stalled the subsequent stages of the process.

It seems that the availability of research institutions and well-qualified individuals does not guarantee ongoing innovation and high rates of adoption. What countries need most is an innovation culture that encourages people and institutions to invest the needed energy, commitment, and resources to lift the country to new heights. Innovation requires infrastructure at country and institutional levels. Most importantly, it requires an efficient public sector that believes in innovation, can support private initiative, and is able to team up with institutions and people to create an innovation culture. The bureaucracies of most countries in the EM tend to work poorly and disappointingly. Departments and ministries more often than not create fiefdoms that isolate staff and ideas and harm the cooperation, communication, and teamwork that are so important to innovation. Expecting the private sector to develop innovation alone is not enough; innovation is the business of a multitude of players. The countries in this region can learn much from Israel and its innovation-driven culture.

Cost of energy and competitiveness

The cost of energy is crucial to the competitiveness of the energy-importing countries of the EM region. Expensive energy adds to the cost of doing business and hurts the export sector in particular. Prolonged high energy prices damage the general economy: agriculture, tourism, manufacturing, and practically every other economic activity. Although energy rich, the region has yet to find a way to use its own cheaper energy sources, which, if properly managed, would help catapult its economies to new levels. While recently per-barrel oil costs dropped dramatically (in some cases to half the price of a year ago), this has not had a proportional impact on cost structures. No one knows how oil prices will develop in the future, as these are often manipulated for political and other reasons. The problem of high energy prices worsens when a government index links taxes to energy prices (rather than actual consumption) and as such has little interest in helping alleviate the problem.

Indicatively, in Cyprus more than half the cost of petrol at the pump goes to the tax collector. Cyprus generates over 4.5 billion kilowatt hours of electricity, relying primarily on imported fuel. Prior to the current (and probably transient) drop in energy prices, Cypriot consumers paid some of the highest electricity prices in the EU. At €0.17 per kWh, Cyprus led the list of most expensive suppliers of electricity among EU members. The five most expensive countries in the EU in terms of electricity before the recent drop in the price of oil, in order, were Cyprus, Ireland, Malta, Spain, and Belgium. The least expensive electricity was in Estonia (at €0.07 per kWh), Latvia, Greece, France, and Lithuania (Economics Research Centre 2014).

When the countries in the region manage to extract their own oil and gas, their economies will use cheaper domestic energy. Israel even passed a law limiting its own energy exports to ensure that enough gas goes to cover domestic needs. Domestic energy will certainly improve competitiveness and advance the export sector. Transport expenses will also reduce. Low oil and gas costs will benefit power generation, considering that many countries in the EM rely heavily on imported oil and gas, and make possible the production of petrochemicals and the setting up of ancillary gas-based industries. Hitherto uncompetitive because of high energy costs, such industries could then become economically viable.

Integrity as an economic factor

The global corruption index (Transparency International 2014) rates 175 countries/territories around the world on *perceived levels of public-sector corruption*. Denmark takes first position as the least corrupt country. Those in the EM score as follows:

- Cyprus 31
- Egypt 94
- Greece 69
- Israel 37
- Lebanon 136
- Turkey 64

At the time of writing, a spate of arrests had taken place in Cyprus – the country with the best relative rating on corruption in the region – involving people working in the broader public sector and politicians accused of receiving kickbacks from construction deals, building permits, and the like. Some are already in prison. The Attorney General's office is also examining a massive file of other cases, many of which involve senior personnel in the collapsed and discredited banking sector. It is not known whether this will improve Cyprus's position on the corruption index (on account of trying to bring suspects to book), or whether it will worsen its rating with the surfacing of more and more corruption.

Corruption of all sorts tends to take a heavy toll on economies. In fact, it can be a fast route to an economic morass. Here is what Paul Krugman (2013, 86–87) has to say:

> There's plenty of raw corruption. ... But in many, perhaps most cases, the corruption is softer and less identifiable. ... At a still more amorphous level, wealth brings access, and access brings personal influence.

So, it appears that political and economic corruption is well entrenched in many societies around the world, with political parties often reported as among the institutions most affected by corruption; an ominous sign considering their power.

Transparency International (n.d.) defines corruption as "the abuse of entrusted power for private gain. It hurts everyone who depends on the integrity of people in a position of authority." Although corruption is typically associated with countries that experience violence and poverty and operate under weak political structures, the Transparency International report leads us to understand that corruption is much more widespread and engulfs most nations. Corruption typically entails money laundering, lobbying with a view to twisting decisions in favor of the lobbyist's client, big company opaqueness, bribery, kickbacks, the deliberate taking of wrong decisions aimed at favoring the government or its allies, secrecy on how decisions are taken, favoritism and use of political connections for gain, unacceptable judicial decisions, and so on. Corrupt practices and hushing up of corrupt practices have a heavy impact on an economy and reduce trust in institutions whose proper functioning is critical to the welfare of the people.

In Egypt, a number of decisions concerning corruption have not gone down well with the public, including recent court decisions concerning corruption allegations against former members of the political elite. In Turkey, while a parliamentary investigation dealt with corruption allegations against a number of ex-ministers, the media were banned from reporting on the issue. The imprisonment of journalists in Turkey goes on unabated and justifiably puts the country at the top of the list of violators of freedom of speech. Trumped-up charges of coup plots and "betrayal" have seen many people go to gaol; Turkey now has more incarcerated journalists than any other country in the developed (and developing) world. In Greece a former minister of defense is now serving a long sentence for receiving kickbacks over defense contracts; a former Cypriot minister has also been jailed in Athens for the same crime. On a brighter note, Israel's pillars of integrity (e.g., the Central Elections Committee, the Judicial Branch, and the State Comptroller) are holding up well. However, the same cannot be said of its Civil Service, Executive Branch, and Political Parties, which are held in relatively low esteem by the Israeli public.

High integrity leads to more trusting relationships, which are essential to the building of a strong economy. Loss of trust rates as one of the most serious impediments to economic growth. The late management guru Peter Drucker is said to have opined that it takes 21 years before a cheated bank customer can forgive and forget. Trust in banks, the political system, institutions, a country's leadership, and so on is absolutely crucial to economic growth. Yet trust is a fickle thing that does not obey diktats. Leadership in all sectors of activity (political, civil service, schools, business, and so on) needs to operate at high levels of integrity if the economy is to have any hope. To gain respectability, businesses need to appreciate that integrity and social responsibility are not luxuries but essential parts of good business practice, just as shareholder value is. Integrity covers all areas of activity and is not limited to business and public-sector activities. Schools, for example, need to be run on integrity if they are to achieve their mission of delivering value to students. Countries that stress integrity are typically at the top of the list for potential investors.

Banking

One of the countries in the EM, and a Eurozone member at that, Cyprus became the first guinea-pig to suffer a bail-in of depositors ostensibly to save its ailing banking system. That banking system is still in tatters two and a half years later. This resulted in the devastation of depositor money and all but wrecked confidence in the country. In terms of soundness, Cypriot banks now rank just one notch above the bottom (143rd) on the *soundness of banks* factor of the GCI. The same applies to Greece's banks (141st position). Egyptian banks also earn a lowly 110th place, but Lebanon, with its many small but relatively well-monitored private banks, does remarkably well with a ranking of 27th. Remember that in order to maintain the credibility of its banking system as open and well functioning, Lebanon's banking authorities steered away from imposing exchange controls during the long and bloody civil war of 1975–90, which ravaged the country. The Central Bank of Lebanon is known to be doing a good job in keeping a tight but reasonable rein on the banking system. Israel, which not long ago sold numerous state-owned banks to private investors, does much better than all the other countries in the region and finds itself in an enviable 18th position. Turkey's banks rank 38th.

Recent banking affairs seriously tarnished the name of Cyprus and all but ruined the country's ability to attract foreign investors, in the immediate future at least. Cyprus is a victim of what the ancient Greeks called hubris: the arrogance that ultimately brings destruction through nemesis and retribution. Put simply, the banking elite of Cyprus (and particularly the ineptitude of some of the officials of the CBC) pushed the country into a financial abyss. They tried to play a role that was far beyond their capabilities as parochial players. Small countries that wish to punch above their weight, but do not have the wherewithal to do so, need to be wary of the consequences of their actions. The Cypriot banking disaster is a story of incompetence, greed, over-estimation of capabilities, and failure to understand how far a small country with a ubiquitous political problem is allowed to go. Lebanon, on the other hand, is a good example of how to hold together a banking system under very exacting political conditions.

The other countries in the region could learn much from Cyprus's banking failure. For a start, the Cypriot banking sector was dangerously over-sized and with a balance sheet seven to eight times the country's GDP, far beyond the government's ability to protect in case of failure; it is surprising that the authorities could not see this most obvious anomaly. Cyprus's banking sector was also grossly mismanaged:

- The CBC worked less than proficiently and committed the monumental error of allowing a massive banking sector to build up. As such, it helped create some of the preconditions for the catastrophe. It was as if the CBC allowed the planting of incendiary devices in the foundations of the sector that was under its supervision and protection.
- Successive government administrations knew full well that the cumulative amount of secured bank deposits (up to €100,000 per depositor per bank is "guaranteed" by the government) was beyond the ability of Cyprus to handle in the event of a major bank collapse or bank run. Yet no steps were taken to allow the government to keep its promise to depositors.
- The ineptitude of some senior members of the banking fraternity had reached farcical levels. Board members exercised little control over management and allowed senior officers with only a parochial understanding of international banking to play big and operate unchecked. Boards allowed managers who obviously suffered from delusions of grandeur to take ruinous decisions. These delusions

led them to get involved and trade in high-risk financial instruments that were complicated, toxic, and dangerous. In the end the two major, and disproportionately large, banks in the country had basically collapsed: one went into liquidation and the other was crippled.

The many businesses that have since shut down and the thousands of unemployed are now paying heavily. As Timothy Geithner (2014, 94) aptly comments, "The greater the concentration in the financial system means the systemic consequences of the failure of a major firm could be more acute.". While the Cypriot economy is beset by crippling interest rates and exorbitant banking fees, some EU countries are moving in the opposite direction in an effort to revitalize the economy. Indicatively, the deputy governor of the Bank of England was predicting that the official UK interest rate could reach an average of 3 percent in 2017–19; UK rates were at a historic low of 0.5 percent in 2009 as the recession began to bite (BBC News 2014).

One of the reasons for some of the economies of the EM lagging behind is the difficulty of accessing bank loans at affordable rates. On the GCI factor of *ease of access to loans* Cyprus holds a dismal 109th position, with the other countries in the region also having less than commendable positions:

- Egypt 129
- Greece 136
- Israel 51
- Lebanon 76
- Turkey 64

Even Israel's ranking, though the highest in the region, is not good enough. The difficulty of accessing loans plus the high indebtedness of businesses and individuals in some of these countries (e.g., Greece and Cyprus) worsens the situation by some margin. So, in both Greece and Cyprus we are now seeing the Minsky effect in practice, as insolvent debt pushes the economy into recession or stalemate (Minsky 1992).

Lebanon and its love affair with the property market should take note of what happened to Cyprus, and less so to Greece, where the unchecked land/property values of the past caused great harm to their economies. Speculation in land created what are commonly known as Ponzi schemes. As is typical of such schemes, people borrowed on over-priced land but were unable to service the debt. They survived by refinancing these loans on the strength of yet higher land values, which allowed some property dealers to stay in business for a while. The Cypriot banks were ever ready to advance risky loans and to offload their ever-growing deposits. Speculative borrowing was on the rise as people borrowed to pay later. Banks even promoted schemes that required the borrower to cover only interest payments for a period (say, 3–5 years), thus literally trapping the borrower in an illusionary process. These schemes let many borrowers see the repayment of principal as a non-threatening, far-distant event. Other borrowers were under the illusion that if the banks pressed for repayment of the loan, all they had to do was sell the asset at an appreciated value and they would even make a profit. For an interesting analysis of this theory, read Wolfson (2002).

The banks of Greece and Cyprus suffer heavily from non-performing loans (NPLs) that simply refuse to go away. The World Bank defines an NPL as when "the gross value of the loan as recorded on the balance sheet, not just the amount that is overdue." Thankfully, the remaining countries in the region find themselves in good standing in this regards. At the time of writing, NPLs in Israel, Turkey, and Lebanon were below 4 percent and in Egypt were at 9.5 percent (World Bank 2015a).

Inflation rates in Greece and Cyprus are at all-time lows and interest rates are at all-time highs. While both these events serve the banks well, they have a punishing effect on the economies of both countries. It is said that bankers hate low interest rates and high inflation. The corollary would be that they love high interest rates and low inflation. Now the banks of Greece and Cyprus are enjoying both these windfalls, except that they are going nowhere.

Banks call a debt haircut a "moral hazard," as it encourages other borrowers to default on their loans. They already know that they will simply not recover fully what is owed to them, even if they bankrupt their customers (and in some cases their guarantors). So it would be better for them to consider a debt haircut than to sell people's properties at forced-sale prices and then spend money and time in court trying to bankrupt borrowers and guarantors and ending up back at square one by collecting only a fraction of what is owed. Both options lead to the same result in the case of some customers: banks lose money in both cases, except that a debt haircut is more rational, less expensive, less harmful to the economy, and less detrimental than other options. In practice, it could work as follows: the banks tell distressed borrowers (banks know which borrowers are distressed and which ones are simply bad payers) that as long as they meet revised repayment terms, the balance of the loan will be written off once they repay an agreed level of debt (say, 60 percent of the loan) plus interest. Nevertheless, bankers in Greece and Cyprus are unlikely to accept this recommendation, no matter how rational it may be. It all goes back to psychology and the sin of greed and fear. The banks in both countries call their obsession with acting pitilessly with borrowers "sound business practice," carefully avoiding use of the word "greed."

Employment

The World Bank (2015b) reports the following percentage average unemployment rates in the EM region for the period 2010–14, with 2013 figures in brackets:

- Cyprus 11.8 (15.8)
- Egypt 11.9 (12.7)
- Greece 24.2 (27.3)
- Israel 6.9 (6.3)
- Lebanon 8.9 (6.5)
- Turkey 9.2 (10.0)

This means that all these countries are suffering from unemployment, albeit to varying degrees. Typically unemployment hits the young hard; 40 percent of the 15–24 age group were unemployed in Greece and Cyprus at the time of writing.

Published unemployment figures often under-estimate the problem, because governments are prone to exaggerate downward for obvious reasons. That is why official figures do not typically take into account those who are unemployed but not registered as such. Equally, they do not account for the under-employed who do not report to labor offices (8 people who work for 2 hours a day each and sit around for the remaining 6 hours a day in effect make up 2 employed and 6 unemployed persons). Also, an unspecified number of young men and women with potential and with a high competitiveness index emigrate, giving the false impression to bureaucrats that unemployment is reducing. To make matters worse, the young professionals who emigrate are typically those with high scores in competitive examinations, and who succeed in competitions against strong and gifted international candidates. The first to emigrate are typically those who maintain an international focus, are highly numerate and verbal, and have a command of foreign languages.

Unemployment: The economic scourge

Unemployment is thought to be the worst manifestation of economic malaise because it hits people economically and psychologically at the same time. To be considered as unemployed a person needs to:

- declare that he or she is not working;
- want to work;
- have been actively seeking employment in the last 4 weeks;
- be willing to work or waiting to start work in the next 4 weeks.

The International Labour Organization (ILO) also adds the proviso that the person should be 16 years or older. It defines the rate of unemployment as the ratio of economically active people who are unemployed (unemployed/economically active). People who are retired, are pursuing education, or have stopped looking for a job because they have come to the conclusion that there are no job prospects are excluded from the labor force.

Creating unemployment

Employers often refuse to hire new staff because they consider the going wage rates too high; this is known as "classical or "real wage" unemployment. At one point sector unions (e.g., agriculture unions) in Cyprus pushed wages to prohibitive levels and in the process drove some companies into the ground.

Here is an example from my experience of how real wage unemployment can be created. While the free market was paying €850 per month for the services of an unskilled potato packer, the unions forced some packing companies (by threatening a strike, which would have ruined perishable products in a matter of days) to pay two or three times the going rate, ostensibly to compensate long service. In the end an employee with ten years of service was paid one and a half times the wage of an employee with one year of service, with the latter working twice as efficiently as the former in some cases. This happened with the tacit support of the bureaucrats of Cyprus's ministry of labor mediation service, which failed to see any linkage between performance and reward; after all, the same happens in the bureaucrat's place of work, where salary movement depends on years of service and performance plays little or no role.

Even the most vibrant economies have some unemployment, because people who lose their job need time before they can locate a promising vacancy, go through the application and selection processes, and ultimately start work; this is known as "frictional" or "search" unemployment. In times of great economic change, including recessions, the unemployed need to adapt to the new realities quickly. This may entail upgrading and acquiring new skills that may enhance employment prospects. A prolonged skills mismatch unavoidably increases one's period of unemployment, a situation known as "structural" unemployment. Greece and Cyprus have been hit badly by recessional or cyclical unemployment on account of shrinking economic activity that forced many employers to shut down their operations or retrench, and falling aggregate demand (demand-deficient Keynesian unemployment). Getting the unemployed back to work will require more than "normal" growth rates in the economy; Okun's law tells us that there is a direct relationship between an economy's unemployment rate and its gross national product. For the moment, sustainable growth is elusive in both countries.

Although there is little data on voluntary unemployment, one would suspect that there is no major problem on this issue in the EM region. The limits on the right to receive unemployment benefits (six months in some countries) discourage people from willingly staying out of a job for long. Strict guidelines typically apply in countries that offer the needy guaranteed benefits. These guidelines help keep away those who refuse to work and choose instead to live off government benefits.

The problems of unemployment

That unemployment is a major and intractable problem in the countries of the EM causes various economic difficulties:

- The unemployed do not produce even if they wish to, thus restraining economic growth.
- Governments are forced to provide relief funding, which often comes from reduced spending on health, education, and so on.
- High unemployment among the young and the educated means that the costs that parents and society incurred to educate them are not providing a return to justify the expenditure.
- The inflow of direct and indirect taxes to the government purse reduces because the unemployed pay hardly any taxes (except for minimum indirect taxes on food), not to mention the cost of the increased physical and mental health problems that often hit the unemployed.

- In times of prolonged unemployment the surreptitious negatives of diminished skills start to creep into the system, despite attempts to retrain the unemployed. Young technology graduates who stay unemployed for, say, two to three years can hardly remain competitive in the job market in their area of specialization. Equally, an unemployed waiter would need to train for a long time to become a nurse.

Unemployment has the nasty habit of persisting. If Okun's theory of a direct relationship between output and unemployment is to be trusted, then it will take a miracle to put the unemployed of Greece and Cyprus (and Turkey and Egypt) back to work. To make a dent on unemployment the economy needs to grow by more than the "natural" rate, because the labor force has a natural rate of increase that holds the unemployment rate in a steady state. Equally, in the short term unemployment could even grow because of increased productivity and the use of more effective technology (i.e., the introduction of robotics typically reduces the need for labor in a manufacturing enterprise). Therefore, to reduce unemployment the economy needs to grow above its potential (say, by 2 percent in countries in the EM region and by between 2.3 percent and 2.6 percent in the US).

On the basis of Okun's useful prediction technique (and assuming no unforeseen shocks to the region's economies), to achieve a drop of 1 percent in unemployment the economies of the six countries would need to grow by 2 percent above potential/natural growth. This means that it would take 4 percent growth in GDP to reduce unemployment by 1 percent (see Knotek 2007). Davide Furceri and Prakash Loungani report that

> among advanced economies on average, unemployment falls by a third of a percentage point for each additional percentage point of real GDP growth. The relationship between jobs and growth is almost as strong among emerging market economies, on average: an additional percentage point of output growth lowers the unemployment rate by ¼ of a percentage point. (Furceri and Loungani 2014)

In discussing future unemployment in countries like Egypt and Turkey that typically suffer from high inflation, one would need to remember that high inflation and unemployment make terrible twins. Friedman (1968) sheds more light by differentiating between "rising" and "high" rates of inflation, warning that "[a] rising rate of inflation may reduce unemployment, a high rate will not."

Theoretically, reduced salaries and benefits should cause unemployment to fall because, one would think, companies would be encouraged to hire more staff at reduced rates. However, will employers hire more staff if they know there is little demand for their products and services due to falling consumption? Moreover, labor markets often fall victim to "hysteresis" as the unemployed lose their skills and also their will to work. Under conditions of hysteresis unemployment remains higher than expected because of the damage that prolonged economic recession causes and the shocks that this phenomenon creates. Interestingly, those who stay in employment during a recession do not take kindly to having their wages fall. This prevents labor market forces from creating a new equilibrium. Typically, an increased labor supply should lead to a new and lower wage equilibrium. When this does not happen, businesses shy away from hiring additional staff (see Cross 1988).

Unemployment reduction presupposes that serious strategies exist to deal with the problem. The short-term subsidization of the cost of employment hardly ever leads to serious additional long-term hiring. Such schemes naively assume that employers will create new jobs simply because for a while they would enjoy access to cheap labor. In reality, however, what really determines the employment levels of a business is its ability to provide customers with goods and services of value. Wage subsidization has little effect. Cheap labor works up to a point (mostly for businesses employing unskilled labor), but even here the subsidized labor approach does not make much sense. For example, would a hotel that works optimally with a complement of 200 employees (at an average monthly cost of employment of, say, €2,000 per employee) hire 10 additional staff simply because for six months 30 percent of the cost of their employment would be subsidized by the government?

To varying degrees, all countries in the EM have problems with unemployment and all wish to see this problem solved; if anything to preempt social upheaval and problems for politicians. Most countries are comfortable with a 3 percent unemployment rate (e.g., transient unemployment). Unemployment in excess of that usually requires robust growth rates in the economy to create enough new jobs. Economies with high growth rates and high unemployment, such as Turkey, find it exceedingly difficult to reduce unemployment because of fear of overheating the economy.

The public sector

The public sector's general inefficiency (persistent in the EM region) should be a top priority for all six countries. The verdict on the functioning of their civil services is not complimentary. The same applies to the wastefulness of government spending, which exacerbates the problem. Greece, Egypt, and Lebanon are experiencing particularly severe public-sector problems. In the EM one often sees the civil service degenerate into a complex web of unnecessary bureaucratic hubbub that literally throttles progress at business and individual level. It is not unusual to find managers who build absurd but impregnable empires that are of little use to the tax-paying citizen and business. Unnecessary tiers of management often stall efficiency and cause decision making to come to a near standstill.

Lack of accountability and punishment is probably the single most important barrier to the proper functioning of the civil service. Thousands of telephone calls from the public sometimes go unanswered and letters are not necessarily answered in a timely manner, if at all in some cases. In a recent interview, a taxpayer said to me that on a business visit to a government department, he was told that the computers were down and he would have to return later. He left his mobile phone number with the attending clerk, politely asking her to call him once the computers were up and running so that he could return. Her response was rude and difficult to explain: "I am under no obligation to call you. You call as many times as necessary to find out whether the computers are working or not." This attitude would never have been tolerated in any well-functioning organization. Worse, this particular taxpayer had no recourse, knowing that his complaint would go unanswered and that there would be no disciplinary action against the clerk. The problem is that no economy can truly prosper without an efficient bureaucracy.

The public sector in most (or maybe all) of these countries is over-staffed, but rarely do administrations take the step of laying off supernumerary employees, largely because of the political cost that such an action entails. Any reduction in headcount typically follows the attrition route; that is, more people retire than are recruited, but in some unexplained manner in the end net numbers grow. Headcount-reduction projects in the public sector are often long-winded and almost doomed from the start: unavoidably frustration sets in, causing the effort to fizzle out.

Because of their voting power, public-sector employees in the EM are in many ways "untouchable" when it comes to cost reduction (reducing salaries) and downsizing. Powerful union representatives are often befriended by politicians and their support is much sought after at election time. Not that politicians in most other countries behave much differently. Interestingly, the unions are now on the back foot in some countries on account of the economic crisis, although they are fighting back (for an interesting assessment see Naughton, Doan, and Green 2015).

On the GCI factor of *inefficient government bureaucracy*, the countries in the EM find themselves on the inefficient side of the scale. Bureaucracy continuous to be one of the most problematic barriers to doing business and is a great impediment to efficiency and economic growth. These governments are cognizant of the problem, but despite repeated attempts at redressing it little progress has been made. It is as if civil services have in-built mechanisms that block attempts at improving them.

In terms of public-sector headcount, Greece is in a similar position to Cyprus; except that in Greece civil servants' pay is more or less in balance with that of private enterprise. It has been struggling with civil service headcount for the last five years, but with little progress and in the process angering lenders. Egypt is in an even worse position in terms of public-sector headcount and civil service reform. As regards Israel, Nehemia Shtrasler (2013) reports:

> Israel's public sector is getting fatter ... According to the Bank of Israel, in the past year and a half the number of jobs has only increased in the public sector. In the private sector, the number hired has been equal to the number fired.

In 2013 alone, Turkey hired no fewer than 100,000 new government employees. Jobs in the Turkish public sector are known to be cushy, secure, and without many worries; just as public-sector jobs are in most countries in the region.

It is almost comforting to know that the problem of a hydrocephalous civil service afflicts most countries in the world and is not limited to the EM. In a drive to reduce big government, US president Ronald Reagan reduced headcount massively when he first started his term. By the time he left, the public-sector headcount of the federal government was higher than when he took office.

The need to restructure

Restructuring of the economy has been an ongoing problem for the countries in the EM. Turkey's attempts over the last 30 years to turn state capitalism to private capitalism were marked with some success, even if the country's drive for EU membership stalled. It is now faced with the problem of cartels and corruption among the new rich and powerful that keeps the country behind (note Turkey's 64th position in the 2014–15 GCI).

Israel is moving in the direction of restructuring, although government involvement in the economy is still high and taxes account for 40 percent of GDP, much higher than one would expect. Its infrastructure is in better shape and this is good for the economy. Security needs dictate Israel's policy, as it measures every action against the test of national security. The country is geographically tiny and is surrounded by many adversaries. At its narrowest point, Israel can be traversed by a fighter jet in about 4 minutes.

Egypt has been trying hard to restructure for the last 25 years, but at a discouragingly low pace. It is now speeding up a little largely on account of IMF pressure. The problems that lie in the path of its restructuring process have strong social undertones. Structural changes are typically challenged (opposed) by the disenfranchised, and a large portion of Egypt's population lives either just above the poverty line or below and has a heavy dependence on government subsidies for its existence.

Both Greece and Cyprus are struggling to restructure under pressure from the Troika. Both are making some progress, but both are coming up against political opposition from those who stand to lose from restructuring. Just to give an example, a bankrupt airline was kept alive for over five years using taxpayers' money because the government feared the reaction of unions, opposition parties, and others. Fortuitously, the airline closed down through an EU ruling that obliged it to return millions of euros in subsidies (taxpayers' money) that it had received improperly from the government of Cyprus just to stay afloat for a little longer. Cyprus's restructuring plan touches on a wide area of activities, but is fundamentally concentrated on privatizing three organizations that are owned by the government and also shutting down other state entities that have no function to perform but still burden the state purse.

The way things were handled in the period leading up to the economic recession and the way they have been managed since the coming of the Troika have made most people in Greece and Cyprus suspicious all round. They suspect politicians, business leaders, government officials, EU institutions, and so on. People in both countries do not trust foreign ownership either and this may partly explain why Cyprus takes 84th position on the GCI on the factor of *prevalence of foreign ownership.*

Incidentally, all countries in the region earn a failing grade on this factor,
with Israel doing marginally better than the others:

- Egypt 126
- Greece 77
- Israel 52
- Lebanon 113
- Turkey 102

People in most of these countries distrust government as much as they do
private enterprise and its management practices.

When "iconic" state-owned organizations fall into the hands of
outsiders, voters become jittery and this frightens politicians. People fear
cartels and monopolies as much as they fear government inefficiency and
crippling bureaucracy. Many in all six countries are aware that
privatization will change the current take-it-easy approach to work in
publicly owned organizations. Many state employees fear that their current
cozy working conditions will be eroded and the work ethic that is modeled
on the civil service paradigm disturbed. Although by exception some of
these organizations do a reasonably good job, they are usually over-staffed
with over-paid, party-dependent staff prone to frequent work stoppages
with little reason. This makes people wary. Undoubtedly, with
privatization many of those employed in these organizations stand to lose
their jobs as more competent boards and professional executive teams take
over and start streamlining and rightsizing to enhance productivity and
competitiveness.

Some of these state-owned organizations in the region have seen more
than a few former officials charged with corruption. The same applies to
private enterprises as well though. Selling off some of the defunct state-
owned organizations will not be easy, as many of them have no net worth
to speak of; others are in a state of hibernation while staff continue to draw
high salaries. Still others are kept out of bankruptcy by all sorts of comical
funding vehicles. Politicians in the region typically speak with a forked
tongue regarding privatization.

Selling off a publicly owned going concern may not be as easy as it
looks because of the decay in the softer aspects of the business, including
the poor work ethic, what-can-you-do-for-me attitude, and so on, which
worry potential buyers. The most important restructuring requirement lies
in the public sector's work attitudes and behavior, which in most countries
in the region need to improve appreciably.

The GCI ratings on *pay and productivity* show the way forward in terms of the need for structural improvement. The countries in the region tend to fall into two distinct categories. The first includes those that require major change: Egypt in 131st position and Greece in 121st. The others are in the second category:

- Cyprus 59
- Israel 76
- Lebanon 60
- Turkey 81

Egypt has a large population of around 85 million and growing. Its change attempts are seriously hampered by the pressures of a growing population that outpaces GDP growth. Modest GDP growth is not sufficient to satisfy the ever-growing need for new jobs for those entering the market for the first time. Egypt is also suffering from very low GDP per capita (less than $4,000).

Lebanon's GDP per capita hovers around the $10,000 mark and though it exceeds that of Egypt by more than 2.5 times, it still lags behind the standards of developed economies. For different reasons both countries find it difficult to restructure. Israel, with a small population of less than 8 million, boasts an impressive GDP per capita that exceeds $36,000. To the extent that per capita income is an indicator of how urgently a country needs to restructure, it finds itself in a more comfortable position than others in the region. Turkey has a population of more than 75 million, a large land mass, and consistently high GDP growth rates in the last few years. Yet its per capita income is unimpressive by the standards of developed economies (GDP per capita of roughly $11,000). With proper restructuring and continued new investment, the country could stand a good chance of joining the ranks of the more developed economies. Yet all is not well with Turkey, as its economy is showing signs of weakness and its government is becoming more and more autocratic (World Bank 2015c). The eastern region of Turkey that is populated by Kurds is poor and under-developed, with little attention paid to the poverty of the local population; this in turn causes friction and instability.

Greece and Cyprus, both EU members, are under the strictures and censure of their lenders. Cyprus has a population of less than a million and a GDP per capita of more than $25,000, which was reduced by 15.8 percent in the period 2008–13 on account of the financial crisis that hit the country. In 2013 Cyprus's per capita GDP in real terms was 89 percent of the median per capita income of the 28 EU member countries and 83 percent of the median of the Eurozone countries. Greece, with a population of 11 million, boasts GDP per capita of just above $21,965. In 2013 its per capita GDP in real terms stood at 73 percent of the median of the 28 EU member countries and 67 percent of that of the Eurozone. Between 2008 and 2013, it lost 28.9 percent of its per capita GDP in real terms. In comparison, during the same period the financially troubled countries of Portugal and Ireland experienced losses of 6.5 percent and 11 percent, respectively (Eurostat 2015).

Troika high-handedness

Lenders are forcing Greece and Cyprus to restructure and bring changes to some long-overdue structural problems – but at a price. The Troika's high-handedness and its role in degrading the democratic processes of the two countries helped cause mass anti-Troika feelings among large segments of society, particularly in Greece (whose debt stands at about 170 percent of GDP). In both countries the Troika forced through laws without adhering strictly to due democratic process and with little debate. By covertly side-stepping parliament, in its own way the Troika gnawed away at a fundamental pillar of democracy. Worse still, it often exhibited a blatant disregard for the feelings of the general population. I was originally a strong supporter of the Troika, but with time I became disenchanted with the manner in which it behaved in its dealings with these two countries and with its highly condescending attitude.

The Troika seems to have a fixation with austerity, which in the short and medium term at least diminishes the meager chances of economic recovery. Attempts to restart the economies of both Greece and Cyprus in the last two years have failed; public declarations of impending investments proved hollow. No wonder many people in those countries see the Troika as an agent of austerity and a harbinger of poverty rather than an inducer of economic growth. It failed to take short-term growth into account, which partly discouraged foreign investors from putting their money in countries that were "harassed" by the Troika bureaucrats.

Quick fixes

Major structural problems need more than quick fixes. First-aid packages do not work because they are typically bereft of sound planning and fail to take into account the fact that business activity requires sound infrastructure and long-term planning. More importantly, change requires trust and a sound mindset, which will be discussed in more detail later in the chapter. Quick fixes look attractive, but are dangerous because while they plug holes temporarily, at the same time they lull planners into falsely believing that such steps are sustainable and beneficial to the economy in the long term. What countries such as Greece and Cyprus are doing now by selling visas and citizenships is a perfect example of short-term quick fixes that frequently lead to unsavory behavior and cheating that in the end work against the economy's good standing.

Many economic purists look askance at such practices, which are reminiscent of subsidies and are often suspect. The EU is not happy either, because it worries about the impact these activities have on member countries. Recently Malta was criticized by the EU for this reason. Under the fitting title "Where is the cheapest place to buy citizenship?" Kim Gittleson, the BBC's New York correspondent, reported:

> The tiny nation of Malta recently came under fire when it announced plans to allow wealthy foreigners to obtain a passport for a 650,000 euro investment with no residency requirement, which would have made it the cheapest European Union (EU) nation in which to purchase citizenship. Prime Minister Joseph Muscat estimated about 45 people would apply in the first year, resulting in 30m euro (£24m; $41m) in revenues. (Gittleson 2014)

The Economist blog (2014b) noted: "The entire concept of trading residence permits for cash, albeit in the form of property investment has long been under attack."

Sound restructuring entails sound planning. If successful, this in turn leads to the creation of healthy businesses, which in their turn create sustainable jobs and business activity. Doubtful practices that are simply meant to alleviate short-term cash-flow problems but in effect create little in terms of sustainable business simply hide the problem, delay restructuring, and often cause more harm than good.

Economic potential and respect for international law

The economic attractiveness of the region

When put in an international context, the economies of the EM are just a tiny proportion of world economic activity: a mere 2.8 percent (with Turkey accounting for half of this). The region is only a $1.7 trillion economy; comparatively, China's economy is now more than $17 trillion at ppp values (in simple terms, ppp or purchasing power parity measures the size of economies using only one price and the same currency). The same applies to the population of the EM countries, which at less than 200 million is only a tiny portion of the more than 7 billion people now living on the planet; a mere 2.8 percent of the world's population. The energy finds in the region plus its proximity to the surrounding oil and gas reserves of the Middle East – Saudi Arabia, the Persian Gulf, Iran, and so on – give it a geopolitical importance that far exceeds its intrinsic significance. The nexus of this is energy, thus the region's current importance is programmed to reduce once the energy reserves are exhausted. It is therefore critical for these countries to exploit their energy resources optimally as long as they last and to invest the proceeds in projects that will provide benefits long after the energy reserves are exhausted.

Countries in the EM need to rely on good planning and on their own potential to ensure the strengthening of their economies and the inflow of foreign investment. The region clearly needs more FDI. However, outsiders do not invest unless they are sure that, among other factors, the crippling bureaucracy and the stifling regulations have been lifted. Attracting foreign investment is a competitive business and requires countries to introduce changes that attract and encourage investors. The legal framework, and in particular property rights, is critical. The position of Israel, Turkey, and Cyprus on the GCI factor of *property rights* is relatively respectable (2nd quartile), but that of Greece, Egypt, and Lebanon in the 3rd and 4th quartiles is not at all encouraging. The position of the region on the GCI factor of *efficacy of legal system in settling disputes* is more or less the same. Israel, Cyprus, and Turkey have respectable positions, but Greece is 126th, Egypt 105th, and Lebanon 132nd, which are gross under-achievements. Taxation is a vital incentive for foreign investors planning business ventures in the region. On the GCI factor of *efficacy of taxation on incentive to invest*, Cyprus outshines the pack in 20th place, followed by Lebanon and Israel in the 2nd quartile. Greece, Egypt, and Turkey have disappointingly low rankings. Equally, foreign investors like to know that government decisions are objective and not tinted with favoritism. On GCI's *favoritism in decisions of government officials* the performance of the region is checkered, with Egypt scoring well, Lebanon scoring very badly, and the rest in the 3rd and 4th quartiles.

The rule of law

With proven energy reserves in the EM, all countries in the region now have a golden opportunity to work together toward their economic potential. They can do so as owners, users, and exporters of oil and gas (Greece,

Cyprus, Egypt, Lebanon, and Israel) or as users and maybe providers of transit facilities (Turkey). To ensure that all goes well, it is imperative that everyone abide strictly by the rule of international law. The history of the region, however, casts doubt on whether all six countries will in the end cooperate fully for their own good, and whether Turkey in particular will come to respect international covenants and law.

For the last 20 or more years, Greece has failed to exploit its proven energy reserves on account of threats emanating from neighboring Turkey. The latter has a *casus belli* in place that threatens Greece with war if it exercises its legal right to delineate its territorial waters to 12 nautical miles, as permitted under the provisions of the UN Convention on the Law of the Sea, which came into force in 1994. As of 2015, 166 countries and the EU had signed this Convention, which defines the standard width of the territorial waters of a country at 12 nautical miles (22 km). Turkey refused to sign and does not honor its provisions unless they are in its favor. Simply, it does not consider itself bound by the convention; it considers the treaty to apply to others but not to itself. The US has not signed the convention either, although it was instrumental in shaping the agreement. However, it indicated in 1983 that it would respect a country's claim for territorial waters of up to 12 nautical miles. This limit is therefore now established in international law.

Turkey is also threatening Cyprus militarily on account of energy. Not long ago a Turkish seismic frigate accompanied by two naval vessels of the Turkish fleet was traversing Cyprus's EEZ without the latter's permission. For good measure, Turkey also issued a marine advisory for seismic surveys in international waters that include Cyprus's FIR (flight information region) and EEZ. Cyprus claimed its EEZ in 2004 based on the Convention on the Law of the Sea of 1982, which it ratified.

Turkey invaded Cyprus militarily in 1974 and through violent ethnic cleansing removed all the Greek population from their ancestral homes (dating back 3,500 years) in the occupied northern 37 percent of Cyprus. Equally, the Turkish army used threats to move to the north all the Turkish Cypriots who were resident in the southern part of Cyprus. In this way it created de facto two ethnically based zones. Unilaterally, Turkey recognized the illegal regime that is its creation and that now administers de facto the occupied areas under the pseudo name of the Turkish Republic of Northern Cyprus (TRNC). In the eyes of the EU, the UN, and the international community at large, the government of Cyprus holds sovereignty over *all* the territory of the island (free southern side and occupied north). The internationally recognized government of Cyprus de jure governs throughout the island and is the legitimate authority in all of

Cyprus's EEZ. Via its proxy pseudo-state and its military machine, Turkey controls de facto (and illegally) the northern and eastern shores of Cyprus, which are for the time being out of bounds for the legitimate government.

Turkey's "reasoning" for invading Cyprus's EEZ rests on the fact that it does not recognize the state (the Republic of Cyprus, RoC) that exercises sovereign power and grants explorative and drilling rights there; in effect, Turkey does not recognize the RoC and as such does not recognize its actions. In the eyes of Turkey, the RoC (a member of the UN and the EU) is defunct and therefore its decisions are null and void; and as such it should not engage in any activities in the EEZ. Extrapolating from Turkey's "logic," all a country needs to do to gain the right to invade the EEZ of another country is simply to stop recognizing that country. Using a bogus "agreement" that Turkey signed with its own creation, the TRNC, Turkey invaded Cyprus's EEZ ostensibly to "carry out exploratory drilling in retaliation for the activities of the Republic of Cyprus." In Turkey's eyes, the RoC needs to wait until the Cyprus problem is solved (i.e., until Turkey decides to lift its own military occupation of Cyprus) before it can exercise its legitimate right to drill in its EEZ (Rıza 2011). This means that Cyprus's energy reserves will remain hostage to Turkey, which effectively controls the island militarily, and for the time being holds all the cards as regards a final settlement. Turkey has made it known repeatedly that the only solution it would accept is one that abolishes the RoC and creates a new toothless entity (under Turkish suzerainty). At the time of writing, it was threatening everyone in the EM, serving notice that all agreements between countries in the region would first need to have Turkey's approval.

Turkey threatens Greece and Cyprus with relative impunity, relying on its vast military and, most importantly, on its economic and geopolitical importance to the US and to a lesser degree to the EU. The US sees Turkey as a bulwark supporter of its policies in the Middle East and with the oil-rich countries of Iraq, Iran, and so on. The US routinely turns a blind eye to Turkey's aggressive behavior against its two neighbors and takes a "middle" position between aggressor and victim. Whenever Turkey initiates an act of aggression against Greece or Cyprus, the US unfailingly calls on all sides to exercise restraint, in a way insinuating that the Greeks are paranoid.

In many ways, the energy potential of the EM is greatly dependent on the network of relationships between countries in the region, which is not without problems. There is the following interesting set of relationships:

- Greece and Cyprus have trouble-free relations with all the countries in the region except Turkey.
- Turkey has bad relations with everyone in the region, even with Lebanon, as Turkey takes sides in the sectarian divide of the country. Equally, Turkey has the habit of bullying its weaker neighbors, but sits quiet when it comes to conflict with powerful Israel.
- Israel has problematic relations with its Arab neighbors and Turkey and good relations with the Greeks.
- Egypt maintains reasonable relationships with Israel, and good relations with the Greeks and other countries in the region except Turkey.
- Lebanon is in a tense relationship with Israel on account of the instability on its southern border, but has good relationships with the Greeks and Egypt.

Economic potential

If the countries in the EM fail to take full advantage of its energy resources, they will fail to reach their economic potential, with immense consequences for their people and their living standards. The repercussions could even resemble those precipitated by a recession, as in both cases economies fail to perform according to their potential.

In an interesting article under the title "Counting the long-term costs of the financial crisis," *The Economist* (2014a) highlights the issue of wasted economic potential. It refers to the work of Laurence Ball of Johns Hopkins University, Robert Hall of Stanford University (see Hall 2014), and the findings of the OECD, and asserts that based on the OECD Economic Outlook (December 2007 and May 2014), Greece lost about 30 percent of its *potential* economic output in the period 2007–13. Spain lost 18 percent, the US nearly 5 percent, and Sweden about 8 percent. The essence of the article is that in these six or so years of economic crisis, rich economies performed below pre-crisis expectations and below what it seemed possible to achieve. One cannot but wonder what the lost potential will be if the economies of the EM fail to take full advantage of their oil and gas resources.

Potential economic output figures measure what economies actually lose when in recession (or when experiencing slow GDP growth), plus what they lose in terms of what was once thought possible for them to achieve. "Potential economic output" is defined as the "highest level of production each economy could feasibly sustain without igniting inflation." *The Economist* notes that "[b]y 2015 the weighted average loss among rich countries as a whole is projected to reach 8.4% – as if the entire German economy had evaporated." It is to be hoped that this depressing conclusion will galvanize the countries in the EM to work together closely and within the rule of law to exploit jointly the full potential of their energy reserves.

Economic potential can fail to materialize for a variety of reasons. In an inter-related global economy, one country may suffer financially because the economy of a partner country is doing badly. For example, if Europe, as an importer of Chinese manufactures, does badly economically, this will unavoidably hurt the Chinese economy, certainly in the short term and until the Chinese readjust by finding alternative markets. A fall of the Russian ruble unavoidably leads to a drop in tourist numbers to the UK, but also to Egypt and other EM countries. As regards the energy-rich countries of the EM, economic potential could be lost for reasons that include delays in energy exploration due to poor management, lack of organization, or sheer incompetence; procrastination and ambivalence; and external political and/or military pressure that leads to panic and ultimate abandonment of the exploration plan.

Change, trust, and leadership

Poor leadership and the inability of those in power to reverse a bad course can thwart a country's economic progress and potential. Change does not come easily, as people often get trapped in their own bad habits and fail to see the need for change. In essence change entails the following:

- An honest and accurate identification of root causes. Good diagnosis requires skills, judgment, and clarity of mind, with self-interest playing no role in the process. Recently, together with a group of mostly university students, I attended a lecture by one of the central protagonists of Cyprus's banking catastrophe. By all accounts the speaker had previously shown criminal dereliction of duty and unfathomable incompetence (in the period leading up to the crisis as well as in that following the financial system collapse that ultimately forced him to resign). At no point during the lecture did he express any remorse. For more than an hour he pummeled his audience with the names of those who in his view were to blame: the former government, the European Central Bank, the IMF, the bank boards, and a host of others; not a word about his own incompetence and failures.

- A genuine desire to put things right by moving away from practices that have been proven wrong. Countries in the EM know full well that high public-sector employment keeps economies from reaching their potential; yet few governments have the will to change this harmful practice. Public employment in Egypt made up 30–40 percent of total employment over a 30-year period (1980–2011), yet little was done to reverse a situation that weighed so heavily on the economy. Egypt spent scarce resources on the public sector at a time when it could ill afford the funds. Even now its budget deficit steadily hovers around 10 percent of GDP and the country's competitiveness remains at unacceptable levels (Yehia 2015).
- The development and implementation of a realistic and sound reconstruction plan that can commit the country to a new path, with little chance of reverting to old ways after the situation begins to show signs of improvement. Greece and Cyprus agreed with their lenders to reorganize their economies, involving the privatization of state organizations, downsizing of the public sector, opening up of closed professions, and so on. At the time of writing, uncertainty hangs over the restructuring project because of political wrangling, union opposition, and the public's mistrust of both state and private enterprises. As old habits die hard, one unavoidably worries about the sustainability of the change process.
- A regaining of trust. Under pressure from its lenders, the government of Cyprus broke a major trust link when it asked parliament to enact laws that allowed banks to convert depositor money into useless equity without the consent of the depositors. Bail-ins have serious ramifications on trust irrespective of whether they are justified or not. When depositors put their money in a bank "on trust," they assume that agreements will be honored and that the money will be returned plus the agreed interest. Not even in their worst nightmares do depositors contemplate the possibility of outside third parties, the government and the Troika in this case, forcing the bank to renege on the agreement. Bank depositors feel taken in when bank management and government proudly announce to current and prospective customers that "our banks are now fully capitalized and strong as ever," without telling them the full story of how that capitalization was achieved. The moral equivalent would be for a hotelier to boast to his clients that his hotel is always spic and span because it never runs out of refurbishment money, but to fail to tell them that the project is funded from the proceeds of the sale of customers' jewelry, which

the hotelier removes from their suitcases at night. It is not
surprising that at the time of writing the press reported survey
findings showing that 90 percent of people in Cyprus did not trust
the banks.

**Table 5.2: Relative standing (out of 144 countries) of the performance
of the six Eastern Mediterranean countries on key GCI factors, 2014–
15. Source: Information from Klaus Schwab (Ed.). 2014. The Global
Competitiveness Report 2014–15. Geneva: World Economic Forum.**

Factor	Cyprus	Egypt	Greece	Israel	Lebanon	Turkey
Development stage of the economy (the higher the number the better)	Stage 3	Stage 2	Stage 3	Stage 3	Stage 2–3	Stage 2–3
	Ranking (the lower the number the better)					
Position on Global Competitive Index (1=most competitive)	58	119	81	27	113	45
Imports as % of GDP	78	124	113	108	23	106
General government debt as % of GDP	136	125	142	111	141	53
Pay and productivity	59	131	121	66	60	81
Flexibility of wage determination	108	67	118	78	51	49
Financial market development	83	125	130	20	102	58
Innovation	30	124	79	3	119	56
Capacity for innovation	63	132	109	3	54	77
Production process sophistication	45	120	76	21	84	36
FDI and technology transfer	78	85	105	11	139	28
Quality of overall infrastructure	30	125	57	63	140	33
Quality of management schools	30	114	89	32	17	100
Availability of research and training services	34	124	90	38	67	57
Soundness of banks	143	110	141	18	27	38
Ease of access to loans	109	129	136	51	76	64
Efficacy of corporate boards	90	136	124	89	133	79
Ethical behavior of firms	51	69	99	43	141	68
Prevalence of foreign ownership	84	126	77	52	113	102
Pay and productivity	59	131	121	76	60	81
Business impact of rules on FDI	51	124	133	61	111	71
Property rights	54	104	82	43	108	47
Efficiency of legal framework in settling disputes	51	105	126	46	132	56
Effect of taxation on incentives to invest	18	117	138	70	51	98
Number of days to start a business	39	39	69	69	50	21
Favoritism in decisions of government officials	63	36	109	79	142	59

The performance of the EM on selected factors is summarized in Table 5.2. Careful analysis reveals that the region in general has a long way to go before it gains sustainable economic vibrancy. Israel does much better than the other countries and should be commended for ranking so highly on innovation and capacity to innovate, which are critical to improving economic performance. The Israeli economy also attains a very respectable 27th position on overall competitiveness, even if the economy operates in an unsettled neighborhood. Lebanon should be acknowledged for earning 17th position on business education, another factor important to the development of the region.

Conclusion

Countries in the EM now have a golden opportunity to work toward meeting their economic potential. First and foremost, they need to cooperate in the energy project while meticulously respecting the rule of international law. Such respect will enable the region to work peacefully and in unison to exploit its energy resources wisely. All six countries stand to gain from the enormous revenues that energy can potentially bring. That energy wealth will provide a unique opportunity to transform the six economies and make them more competitive and productive. The restructuring process now in progress in all these countries will need to continue in earnest, irrespective of the comfort that the potential energy revenues might provide. Doing away with restructuring in the belief that the energy reserves will bring in "easy" money would be disastrous.

Cyprus

Cyprus is now under the control of its lenders and its banking system is in disarray, with billions of euros having been taken from depositors' accounts against their will to help support the failing banking system. Although the Troika will leave soon, the situation is unlikely to change because for years the government will continue to owe its creditors immense amounts plus interest. Private, business, and government debts are at dangerously high levels, with the country having gone into deleveraging that is damaging development and consumption. The fact that Cyprus put in place capital controls right after the bail-in of depositors hurt the country's image in financial matters, even if later these controls were lifted. Real estate and land development, which was instrumental in the creation of a calamitous bubble, is now on its knees and will probably stay there while banks try to liquidate borrowers' assets to cover NPLs.

The occupation of 37 percent of the country by Turkish military forces and the never-ending threats from Turkey create instability that hurts the economy.

Cyprus has a very strong tourist product with world-class hotel establishments. It also boasts a strong shipping sector that has much potential. With sound planning and improvement of its agri-relevant infrastructure, it could resuscitate its long-forgotten agricultural sector. The manufacturing sector also has potential provided that innovation takes its rightful place.

Greece and Cyprus are the only countries in the EM that are in the Eurozone; the other four have their own currency and the freedom to apply an independent monetary policy. Greece and Cyprus are required to abide by the rules of the ECB and the policies of the big powers in the Eurozone such as Germany. As a common currency the euro gives Greece and Cyprus many advantages, even if it takes away from their ability to control monetary policy. However, it prohibits them from printing money through their own central banks. It is to the region's advantage, nevertheless, that two of the six countries are in the Eurozone. This might prove particularly helpful to an eventual High Energy Authority (HEA). There were voices calling for the two countries to leave the euro and to go back to the drachma and the Cyprus pound respectively. These voices have to a large extent fallen silent, as most people are now convinced that leaving the Eurozone would be detrimental. Abandoning the euro would mean the adoption of a new and unrecognized currency that would almost certainly create inflation, as the status quo ante would not apply. A run on already weak banks would certainly follow as savers rushed to find more stable economies in which to deposit their money. Once out of the common currency, both countries would open themselves up to currency volatility and speculators' tricks. Potential investors would shun them, worried about the new weak currencies and the exchange controls that would almost certainly apply. Rolling over of government debt would become exceedingly difficult, if not nightmarish, as investors would be unwilling to buy government bonds denominated in two new and unknown cur-rencies; this would most probably lead the two countries to default. Stagflation would most likely also occur, as both inflation and unemployment would almost certainly rise.

What Cyprus needs to do is the following:

- Reduce populism on issues of restructuring so that the restructuring plan can go ahead unimpeded and without the threat of relapse.

- Redesign its economy away from the old paradigm that brought disaster to the country and its people; away from a heavy dependence on real estate and land development and banking services. The country needs to create a healthy, balanced, and diversified economy that is built for the long term rather than on short-term "niches" such as land speculation.
- Improve its tourist and shipping products, which have great potential. The country needs to place the emphasis on quality rather than quantity.
- Continue building relationships and alliances with neighboring countries such as Egypt, Israel, and Greece for joint energy exploration. Cyprus should not be intimidated by threats from Turkey as long as the former continues to operate within international law. Simultaneously, the country must support strongly the creation of an HEA.
- When it comes to a possible solution to the Cyprus problem, the RoC should insist on a plan that creates a fully democratic Cyprus and shies away from an ethnicity-centered "solution"; a democracy like the remaining 27 countries of the EU. The Bizonal Bicommunal Federation (BBF) that is now on the table cannot possibly provide Cyprus with a democratic solution because it is race based and divisive, splitting people into competing ethnic groups and laying the foundation for the formal division of the country into two ethnic entities. A BBF solution is programmed to create a perfect storm and to generate instability and all the preconditions for hostilities that would see the local population (Greek and Turkish Cypriots) forced to leave the island to be supplanted by colonizers from Turkey. The economy of Cyprus stands no chance under a BBF arrangement.

Egypt

Egypt's economy is being held back, partly by a steady rise in its population, which strains its resources and makes it difficult for its GDP growth to keep pace with the need for new jobs. In the last few years, and due to a degree of political instability, Egypt saw a sharp drop in its foreign exchange reserves, which were reduced to only a few months' imports. Political instability, although reduced after the swearing-in of the current government, is expected to continue to cause problems for the economy, as even the slightest instability affects the sensitive tourist sector and discourages investors. Political instability in recent times and sporadic violence frightened many tourists away and will continue to do so, despite Egypt having an enviable tourist product, brilliant ancient history, high-quality hotels, and a helpful and polite people. Unfortunately for Egypt, tourism is very sensitive to security. Every time a violent or deadly act takes place, the negative effects of this on the Egyptian economy are felt immediately.

With roughly 50 percent of its population just above or below the poverty line, Egypt is bound to have continuing social problems that in turn will affect the economy negatively and stretch government finances. Unemployment is consistently high, and would have been much higher had the half-employed and those who perform sporadic, menial jobs for a pittance been included in the unemployment calculation. The country's banking system is weak and loans are not easy to come by. Egypt did however manage to attract a large number of multinationals that invested in areas such as food production, pharmaceuticals, telecommunications, and technology. Agriculture, revenues from Suez Canal transit fees, energy, and transfers from Egyptians employed abroad are expected to continue helping the economy. Financial support from the Gulf States and Saudi Arabia is also helping. The country is working with the IMF for a potential loan of nearly $5 billion provided that Egypt restructures. As more stability is attained, tourism will pick up (provided unrest is controlled), as will FDI. This will help the country achieve sound and sustainable annual GDP growth of between 4 percent and 5 percent. Egypt has much potential and is a welcoming country to businesses and visitors. Egypt is in many ways an attractive and unique country.

What Egypt needs to do is the following:

- Strengthen its political stability further. This will encourage investors to show a preference for Egypt, considering the instability in countries such as Lebanon, Syria, Libya, and Iraq. Egypt is the de facto head of the Arab world and most countries in the EM look up to it for regional leadership.
- Restructure wisely and with social stability in mind. Egypt's many poor could easily erupt if change made them even poorer. The country needs to be very careful when assessing economic plans that are developed in the West but have little relevance to Egypt and its social structures.
- Work very closely with Greece, Cyprus, and, as far as possible, Israel on the energy front. Working together these four countries could defy Turkey, which recently made threatening public state-ments against all the countries in the region. It would be an added

plus if in the end Turkey rescinded those threats and decided to abide by international law and cooperate with the other countries in the EM.

Greece

Greece is experiencing serious economic problems and has been in recession for over five years. The country's high sovereign debt of about 170 percent of GDP has crippled the country and thrown large sections of the population into despair. Many in the community live in squalor. The high rate of NPLs is threatening the banking system, as does low trust in the economy and in the ruling elite. The EU regularly threatens Greece with suspension (or even termination) of the emergency liquidity assistance (ELA) to its banks. High unionization, particularly in the public sector, which in the past led to arbitrary and irresponsible strikes, is still lurking in the background, frightening investors away and reducing confidence. Tax evasion is often put forward by successive governments as a central reason for economic failure. Other commentators accuse successive governments of mismanaging tax revenues and of irresponsible squandering of money, which in the end acts as a disincentive for people to pay their taxes. Political dissent, anti-everyone feelings, and a tense social environment threaten the stability of the economy.

Yet Greece continues to be a leading shipping nation, as it has been since ancient times. Largely on account of reduced prices, 2014 was a record year for tourism, and Greece still boasts one of the world's richest tourist products. It is also home to some of the globe's most cherished antiquities.

What Greece needs to do is the following:

- Restructure urgently, Troika or no Troika. The country needs to break away from the domination of a massive and inefficient civil service that throttles economic progress.
- Become more productive and efficient to improve its export position. This would require innovation and technological upgrading.
- Shed its pessimism and start looking forward to better times, even if the situation is bad.
- Allow the meritocracy to find its rightful place in the country, to encourage some of those who have left to return as things start to improve.

- Take bold steps to harness its energy reserves. This would mean taking reasonable risks and moving away from partnerships that in the past led to a loss of independence.

Israel

Israel's economy is doing well, helped greatly by innovation, high-tech products, and high FDI. Its educated and skilled labor force is an economic blessing. The Jewish community in the US gifts Israel with about $1 billion a year; political support from the US is also always forthcoming and gives Israel a sense of security and invincibility. Its offshore gas reserves are poised to help the economy make new leaps. This will reduce the cost of production of its products and services, adding further to competitiveness.

Defense and security are perennial problems for Israel and burden the real economy, however. Continued conflict in the Gaza Strip is creating undue problems and hurting all facets of life. The unresolved Palestinian problem casts a dark shadow on Israel's economy.

What Israel needs to do is the following:

- Try harder to find a viable and fair solution to the Palestinian conflict. Once that were achieved Israel would have no limits to trading with the Arab world. Considering that its economy is more sophisticated than any other in the region, the country would automatically take its rightful position (perhaps leadership) in the economic activity of the EM.
- Start improving on performance factors that are out of step considering its overall high ranking. The quality of some of its infrastructure needs to be improved, as this is critical to overall economic activity. The efficacy of its corporate boards earns a surprisingly low ranking (89th), and this needs to improve. Israel's bureaucracy affects its ability to meet its true potential and thus needs to improve as well. Its heavy taxation takes money away from private enterprises, but it can be argued that high taxes are unavoidable considering Israel's security concerns.
- Enter into energy alliances with friendly countries in the region, particularly Egypt. This would help Israel maximize its revenue potential from energy. If and when Turkey decides to abide by the rule of law, it could also join in any future alliances.

Lebanon

Lebanon's perennial political problems and its highly divisive constitution are probably the country's most serious drawbacks. A sectarian military build-up and the existence of militias of all types create a feeling of uneasiness, fear, and anxiety, and discourage FDI as well as local investment. Instability is a constant fear for the people of Lebanon. The threat of civil and factional war casts a frightening and menacing shadow. The search for sectarian advantage, continued pivoting for political gain, and constantly shifting alliances make reform (and consolidation of public finances) difficult to achieve. In fact, it is surprising how the country manages to achieve its current performance considering the burden it carries, and that is a credit to Lebanese enterprise. High public debt, often the result of competing publics that must be kept happy, continues to test the country's finances. Lebanon's 143rd place on GCI's macroeconomic environment factor is indicative of the realities on the ground. Its 141st position on government debt as a percentage of GDP also reveals much about the precarious position of the economy.

Regional geopolitical upheavals continue to cause strain in Lebanon and keep the country in continuous tension. The resilient banking system and the continued inflow of funds from the Lebanese diaspora in Africa and elsewhere provide a great boost for the economy and help it bounce back in times of crisis. The recent discovery of natural gas and the agreements that the country is planning to sign with neighboring nations such as Cyprus is very encouraging. When signed, these agreements will delineate the EEZ boundaries and settle any outstanding issues for the good of Lebanon and its neighbors. The ingenuity of business leaders and the presence in Lebanon of academic institutions with regional leadership help the country place itself in a strong position regarding the management education that is so cherished in the area.

What Lebanon needs to do is the following:

- Revisit the country's constitution urgently with a view to making it democratic and unifying. A truly democratic constitution could change its trajectory and catapult its institutions and economy to heights never before seen. Lebanon has great potential and its people are industrious, but it spends much of its effort on discussing the next conflict that might hit rather than on productive activities. Nevertheless, changing the constitution may be an all but impossible task and even an attempt to do so might trigger sectarian violence, as groups inevitably try to consolidate their advantages.

- Build on the strong reputation of its academic institutions and particularly of its graduate business programs. This again is a catch-22 situation, because as long as the country remains unstable international students and professors will stay away. Equally, the best students now have many other options that were not available 50 years ago. Many good schools have sprung up in the last decades in different countries in the Middle East and more particularly in the Gulf area. Equally, more and more top students who can afford the high fees opt for the best US universities at the expense of those in Lebanon. In addition to attracting revenues from strong international students, Lebanon could also benefit from the well-educated cadre that will stay and work in the country.
- Continue improving its superb tourist product. Lebanon is privileged in every sense of the word when it comes to natural beauty, weather, good food, languages, and so on. With improvement its tourist product could compete at a world level, although here again the country's continued instability and threat of violence work strongly against it.

Turkey

Turkey is experiencing troubled relationships with practically all of its neighbors (Syria, Greece, Egypt, Cyprus, Israel), but economically the country is slowly moving into the club of high-income economies and hopes to escape the proverbial middle-income trap. Its public finances are in many respects under control. Continued growth has helped upgrade Turkey's per capita income, though there is much ground to be covered. To complete the transition, the country needs urgently to improve many areas of life, such as the application of the rule of law, democratic institutions, transparency, public accountability, freedom of the press, coming to terms with the Kurdish issue, and other similar concerns. Moreover, it needs to tackle problems with educational disparity as well as geographic inequality. Inflation stands at a high 9 percent and unemployment at a disturbing 10 percent. The current account deficit is a source of concern and is now around 6 percent. Thus there are quite a number of economic danger signals on the horizon. Heavy dependence on foreign capital and high business indebtedness are also worrying signs.

Turkey has demographic vitality and a high density of young people, particularly in the Kurdish areas. Because of its geographic location and large army, it receives the unwavering support of the US irrespective of any malfeasance. Turkey is hoping gradually to become an energy transit hub and in this regard is trying to facilitate the transport of Russian gas via its territory. Political tensions inside and outside Turkey are ubiquitous and continue to create daily problems. The Kurdish problem is as alive as ever and is creating much political instability. The Syrian conflict has involved Turkey, who is accused of fanning the flames of war by supporting anti-government forces and playing a doubtful if not suspicious role in the fight against religious fundamentalists.

What Turkey needs to do is the following:

- Democratize the country and take it out of the Economist Intelligence Unit's "hybrid" classification. Non-democratic regimes tend to under-perform in the long term, while democracies do much better. A cursory review of the GCI ratings demonstrates that of the 10 best-performing economies in the world, 90 percent are fully functioning democracies. Turkey's economy could boom if the country's leadership adopted a democratic posture and lessened the militarism that is taking up its energy and ruining relationships with its neighbors. No one is threatening Turkey militarily. Its aggression is directed against its neighbors, which are also its potential economic partners. It could be said that Turkey's economic progress is inversely related to its militarism. If it manages to come to terms with the fact that international law ought to be respected, its economic future will be guaranteed. Playing the role of American surrogate in the region, however, has no long-term future for Turkey.

- Get into the energy field by mending its relationships with its neighbors, which would allow Turkey to play a major energy transit role in the EM. It could be an ideal energy transit point, with huge benefits to the country and the region. As things stand now, probably no country in the EM would want to trust its energy transportation to an aggressive Turkey that could play havoc with energy security.

- Retune its economic model, focusing on those areas that can lift it out of the middle-income trap in a sustainable way. Light industry, agriculture, and transportation are good starting points in the redesign process. Turkey is not ready to get into the sophisticated arms manufacturing business, which presupposes a high overall scientific foundation and an educated workforce across the country. It is suffering from disparities in education and development, in the sense that its eastern part lags behind the western part in education and economic development. Turkey needs to make full use economically of its entire population and all its territory. Uncontrolled public-sector projects of unknown value may come back to haunt its economy. Such projects include the third bridge across the Bosporus, a new over-sized airport, and the proposed canal linking the Black Sea to the Sea of Marmara. The building of a 1,100-room presidential palace is already attracting all sorts of derisory comments.

- Attend to its GDP growth, which has slowed significantly, from about 12 percent in 2010 to about 3 percent or even less in 2015. This kind of growth cannot solve its high unemployment, which threatens to cause social problems. Relying on short-term borrowing and ignoring current account deficits is not the answer. Its economy is not as strong the Turkish government wants us to believe and the falling value of the Turkish lira (more than 40 percent down in the past two years) is a good indication of the true picture. Turkey is standing on the threshold of a bursting of its property bubble as well (Economist 2015).

Advice to the Eastern Mediterranean from Singapore

Lee Kuan Yew, the "father" of a reborn Singapore, is credited with improving his country's economy and upgrading the living standards of its people. He sets out the following preconditions for countries wishing to improve their economy and upgrade people's living standards:

> A people's standard of living depends on a number of basic factors: first, the resources it has in relation to its population ...; second its level of technological competence and standards of industrial development; third, its educational and training standards; and fourth, the culture, the discipline, and drive in the workforce. (Allison, Blackwill, and Wyne 2013, 83–84)

Some of the countries in the EM appear to fall short on a number of these requirements:

- All of them have natural resources (plenty of sunshine, sea, potential energy finds, etc.), although these are not massive by international standards. Nevertheless, these resources have not yet been exploited satisfactorily.
- Except for Israel, they all have low technological absorption.
- There is low industrial development and low sophistication in production processes.

- Although the region has a good density of educated cadre (particularly in Cyprus and Israel), uncertainty remains about the transfer of learning and the ability to apply at work the skills learned.
- Discipline is low and the organizational culture is poor, as evidenced by the region's low ratings on productivity and competitiveness. The work culture in the public sector of most (if not all) of the countries in the region should be singled out as a major drawback and barrier to development. Shoddy service and low productivity are other manifestations of this ailment.

Thus countries in the EM have promising economic potential provided that they cooperate in energy and their actions remain within the bounds of international law. All these countries need to start restructuring right away and improving their infrastructure. Importantly, they also need to plan for the long term, making sure to keep populism out of the decision-making process as much as possible. The work ethic and organizational culture can, to a large extent, make the difference between success and failure (Landes 1999), so the many and varied challenges here should be addressed with great urgency.

References

Allison, Graham, Robert D. Blackwill, and Ali Wyne. 2013. Lee Kuan Yew: The Grand Master's Insights on China, the United States, and the World. Boston, MA: MIT Press.

Al Monitor. 2014. "Deficit Overpowers Lebanon's Draft Budget." Al Monitor, June 12. http://www.al-monitor.com/pulse/originals/2014/06/lebanon-draft-budget-issued-questions.html. Accessed May 2015.

BBC News. 2014. "UK Interest Rate Could Settle at 3%, Says Bank of England Deputy Governor." BBC News, May 25. http://www.bbc.com/news/business-27563346. Accessed May 2015.

Cross, Rod (Ed.). 1988. Unemployment, Hysteresis, and the Natural Rate Hypothesis. Oxford: Blackwell.

Economics Research Centre. 2014. "Eurostat Data." Issue 14/1, March. Nicosia: University of Cyprus.

Economist. 2014a. "Counting the Long-Term Costs of the Financial Crisis." The Economist, June 14. http://www.economist.com/node/21604188/print. Accessed June 2015.

—. 2014b. "Portugal's Golden Visas: All That Glitters." The Economist, November 17. http://www.economist.com/blogs/charlemagne/2014/11/portugals-golden-visas. Accessed May 2015.

—. 2015. "A Big Moment for Erdogan – and Turkey." The Economist, May 30, 27.

Eurostat. 2015. http://ec.europa.eu/eurostat. Accessed May 2015.

Friedman, Milton. 1968. "The Role of Monetary Policy." American Economic Review, 58, 11.

Furceri, Davide, and Prakash Loungani. 2014. "Can Growth Alone Tackle Unemployment?" World Economic Forum, November 20. https://agenda.weforum.org/2014/11/can-growth-alone-tackle-unemployment/. Accessed May 2015.

Geithner, Timothy. 2015. Stress Test: Reflections on Financial Crises. New York: Broadway Books.

Hall, Robert E. 2014. "Quantifying the Lasting Harm to the U.S. Economy from the Financial Crisis." Working Paper 20183, May. Cambridge, MA: National Bureau of Economic Research. http://papers.nber.org/tmp/34008-w20183.pdf. Accessed May 2015.

Hurriyet Daily News. 2015. "Turkey Eyes Local Jet for Full Independence: Defence Minister." Hurriyet Daily News, May 23. http://www.hurriyetdailynews.com/turkey-eyes-local-jet-for-full-independence-defense-minister.aspx?pageID=238&nID=75619. Accessed May 2015.

Gittleson, Kim. 2014. "Where Is the Cheapest Place to Buy Citizenship?" BBC News, June 4. http://www.bbc.com/news/business-27674135. Accessed May 2015.

Knotek, Edward S. 2007. "How Useful Is Okun's Law." Economic Review, Federal Reserve Bank of Kansas City, Fourth Quarter, 73–100.

Landes, David S. 1999. The Wealth and Poverty of Nations: Why Some Are So Rich and Some So Poor. New York: W. W Norton.

Minsky, H. P. 1992. "The Financial Instability Hypothesis." Working Papers No. 74, May. New York: Jerome Levy Economics Institute of Bard College.

Naughton, Keith, Lynn Doan, and Jeff Green. 2015. "As the Rich Get Richer, Unions Are Poised for Comeback." Bloomberg Business, February 20. http://www.bloomberg.com/news/articles/2015-02-20/unions-poised-for-comeback-as-middle-class-wages-stall. Accessed May 2015.

OECD. 2014. "Foreign Direct Investment Statistics Exlanatory Notes." http://www.oecd.org/investment/statistics.htm. Accessed May 2015.

Rıza, Alper Ali, QC. 2011. "The Law of the Sea: Turkey vs. Cyprus." Talk given at Association for Cypriot, Greek and Turkish Affairs seminar at London School of Economics, November 18. Reported in Today's Zaman, December 13. http://www.todayszaman.com/op-ed_the-law-of-the-sea-turkey-vs-cyprus-by-alper-ali-riza-_265640.html. Accessed May 2015.

Rogers, E. M. 2003. Diffusion of Innovation, 5th ed. New York: Free Press.

Schwab, Klaus (Ed.). 2014. The Global Competitiveness Report 2014–15. Geneva: World Economic Forum. http://www.weforum.org/reports/global-competitiveness-report-2014-2015. Accessed May 2015.

Sdralevich, Carlo, Randa Sab, Younes Zouhar, and Giorgia Albertin. 2014. Subsidy Reform in the Middle East and North Africa: Recent Progress and Challenges Ahead. Washington, DC: International Monetary Fund. www.imf.org/external/pubs/ft/dp/2014/1403mcd.pdf. Accessed May 2015.

Shtrasler, Nehemia. 2013. "Israel's Public Sector Is Getting Fatter, Despite Netanyahu's Ideology." Haaretz, December 27. http://www.haaretz.com/opinion/.premium-1.565696. Accessed May 2015.

Sipri. 2015. http://www.sipri.org/. Accessed May 2015.

Trading Economics. 2015a. "Egypt Foreign Direct Investment 2002–2015." http://www.tradingeconomics.com/egypt/foreign-direct-investment. Accessed May 2015.

—. 2015b. "Greece Foreign Direct Investment 2002–2015." http://www.tradingeconomics.com/Greece/foreign-direct-investment. Accessed May 2015.

—. 2015c. "Lebanon Foreign Direct Investment 2002–2015." http://www.tradingeconomics.com/Lebanon/foreign-direct-investment. Accessed May 2015.

—. 2015d. "Israel Foreign Direct Investment 2002–2015." http://www.tradingeconomics.com/Israel/foreign-direct-investment. Accessed May 2015.

—. 2015e. "Turkey Foreign Direct Investment 2002–2015." http://www.tradingeconomics.com/Turkey/foreign-direct-investment. Accessed May 2015.

—. 2015f. "Countries." http://www.tradingeconomics.com/countries. Accessed May 2015.

Transparency International. n.d. "What We Do." http://www.transparency.org/whatwedo. Accessed May 2015.

—. 2015. "Corruption Perceptions Index 2014: Results." https://www.transparency.org/cpi2014/results. Accessed May 2015.

Wolfson, Martin H. 2002. "Minsky's Theory of Financial Crises in a Global Context." Journal of Economic Issues, XXXVI, 393–400.

World Bank. 2015a. "Bank Nonperforming Loans to Total Gross Loans (%)." http://data.worldbank.org/indicator/FB.AST.NPER.ZS. Accessed May 2015.

—. 2015b. "Unemployment, Total (% of Total Labor Force) (Modeled ILO Estimate)." http://data.worldbank.org/indicator/SL.UEM.TOTL.ZS/countries. Accessed May 2015.

—. 2015c. "GDP per capita (current US$)." http://data.worldbank.org/indicator/NY.GDP.PCAP.CD. Accessed May 2015.

Yehia, Rana. 2015. "EGP 44bn Tax Revenue Increase by End of April." Daily News Egypt, June 6. http://www.dailynewsegypt.com/2015/06/06/egp-44bn-tax-revenue-increase-by-end-of-april/. Accessed September 2015.

Young, Angelo. 2014. "Turkey Is Boosting Weapons Exports with a Focus on Africa, Here's Who Benefits." International Business Times, 8 May. http://www.ibtimes.com/turkey-boosting-weapons-exports-focus-africa-heres-who-benefits-1649300. Accessed May 2015.

CHAPTER SIX

THE ENERGY FACTOR IN EASTERN MEDITERRANEAN RELATIONS: THE CLASH BETWEEN HISTORICAL ANIMOSITY AND REGIONAL COOPERATION

HILAL KHASHAN

From transit pipelines to indigenous hydrocarbon resources: East Mediterranean age of gas dawns

Largely deprived of natural resources, the countries of the Eastern Mediterranean (EM) basin were previously content to have their seaports serve as terminals for Saudi and Iraqi oil pipelines. In 1934 the Iraq Petroleum Company (IPC) laid out oil pipelines to Haifa and Tripoli. It also constructed two oil refineries, one in Haifa in 1939 and another in Tripoli in 1940. Similarly, the Arab-American Oil Company (Aramco) initiated the construction of a Trans-Arabian Oil Pipeline (TAPLINE) to Haifa; however, the creation of the state of Israel in 1948 shifted the company's TAPLINE to Sidon in southern Lebanon, where oil transports started in 1950. Simultaneously, IPC sought to make up for the loss of its Haifa terminal by laying out an oil pipeline to Banias on Syria's Mediterranean coast, which became operational in 1951. Frequent oil transport disruptions thanks to political rivalry between Iraq and Syria, demands for higher transit fees, Arab–Israeli wars, and the inception of the age of supertankers eventually relegated the pipelines and the refineries to dereliction.

Following the beginning of the Iraq–Iran war in 1980, the Syrian regime, which chose to side with Iran against Iraq, closed down the Banias pipeline. In 1982, the Iraqi government collaborated with Turkey to construct an oil pipeline from Kirkuk to Ceyhan as a substitute for Banias. In 2013, the Kurdistan Regional Government (KRG) constructed a pipeline from the Taq Taq oil field to Faysh Khabur, on the Iraqi border with Turkey, where it was connected to the Kirkuk–Ceyhan pipeline that had been disused since the US invasion of Iraq in 2003.

Preliminary offshore exploration in the EM between 1977 and 2002 produced encouraging seismic data about the existence of significant natural gas reserves in the Levant Basin that compromise the exclusive economic zones (EEZs) of Syria, Cyprus, Lebanon, and Israel (Miller and Scaife 2011). Subsequent exploratory studies in the Levant Basin estimate that it contains a "mean probable undiscovered natural gas of 122 trillion cubic feet (tcf)" (EIA 2013). This brings to the fore the great importance of cooperation among the countries of the Levant Basin in jointly exploring and exploiting promising energy resources. This matter assumes priority in view of the fact that the region "continues to discover and develop hydrocarbon resources, [so] the pressure to increase its role as an important energy hub is likely to increase" (EIA 2013). This chapter argues that the ability of the countries of the EM to cooperate on energy matters is constrained by their historical legacy, as well as their inability to resolve lingering political and territorial issues. In view of its stated objective, the chapter seeks to demonstrate that these countries' failure to cooperate is largely determined by the uneven stages of their exploration and exploitation efforts, in addition to their inability to reach compromise solutions to the divisive EEZ issue.

The energy reserves of the EM do not exceed "one percent of the world's total proven reserves of oil and natural gas ... [and their] combined proved reserves – slightly more than 2.5 billion barrels – are far less than those found in other nearby regions, such as Mediterranean North Africa (65 billion barrels)" (EIA 2013). Nevertheless, the Levant Basin could provide for the entire natural gas needs of its constituent countries, as well as part of the growing energy needs of Turkey, Europe, and the Far East. Despite their domestic and inter-state difficulties, the EM countries have no option except to find ways to overcome the burden of history. Even though in 2013, Cyprus and Lebanon did not have significant proven reserves of natural gas, "successful offshore exploration in the Levant Basin over the past several years means that the level of reserves should soon change in Cyprus ... Planned exploration in Lebanon could uncover recoverable quantities of ... natural gas in the coming years" (EIA 2013).

The Levant Basin gas fields

Proven gas reserves in the Levant Basin have been growing steadily over the past few years. In 2000, for example, "Israel held proven reserves of natural gas totalling just 10 billion cubic feet (bcf). As of January 2013, that total was 9.5 tcf, with recent offshore discoveries likely to boost that figure even higher" (EIA 2013). Cyprus's Aphrodite field in Block 12, which was discovered in 2011 by Noble Energy, is set at 7 tcf; Israel's Tamar field of 2009 has a 10 tcf production capacity, whereas its large Leviathan field, discovered in 2010, has 18 tcf gas reserves (EIA 2013). In December 2014, Israel announced the discovery of an estimated 3.2 tcf of gas in Royee field, 150 km offshore near the EEZs of Cyprus and Egypt. This find is Israel's third largest after Tamar and Leviathan gas fields (Reuters, December 14, 2014). The latest discoveries in Israel's EEZ have eclipsed its Mari-B field's 1 tcf gas deposit, which began production in 2004, as well as the Noa and Pinnacles fields, whose total combined reserves do not exceed 1.2 tcf of gas (Knell 2013). Sohbet Karbuz (2014) reports:

> As of January 2014, natural gas resources discovered in Israel and the Republic of Cyprus (RoC) amount to 1,100 bcm. And yet, the region remains one of the world's most underexplored or unexplored areas, despite having good prospects of natural gas – and, perhaps oil – reserves.

Early offshore seismic studies estimate that the southern part alone of Lebanon's EEZ contains about 12 tcf of natural gas. Lebanon's gas reserves have not yet been sufficiently studied, although the government in Beirut believes there are at least 25 tcf in its offshore territory (EIA 2013). Recoverable gas from Gaza Marine, which was discovered in 2000 by BG Group, has meager reserves of 1 tcf. Most of Syria's proven natural gas reserves, which are placed at 10.6 tcf, are onshore in the eastern part of the country (MBendi n.d.). There is no word as yet on Syria's offshore gas reserves. There is little doubt that extensive exploration will reveal more exploitable gas resources. The geological structure of the Levant Basin is similar across its EEZs. Inter-state conflict, political turmoil, and domestic violence have coalesced to prevent the region from realizing its lucrative energy potential.

Traumatic past

The EM region has had a tumultuous history. Its states formed fairly recently, with Greece taking the lead, wresting its independence from the Ottoman Empire in 1832 after an 11-year war of independence. An independent Greece had not buried the hatchet with Turkey, the inheritor of the defunct Ottoman Empire. The Turkish war of independence (1919–23) had widened the chasm between Greeks and Turks, especially in the

Aegean. Memories of hostilities affected the status of Cyprus, which Britain administered from 1878 until it obtained its independence in 1960. It did not take long for the political and security situation in the bicommunal state to implode. In November 1963, Cyprus's Turkish leaders rejected President Makarios's constitutional amendments to reallocate the share of the Greek and Turkish communities in running the machinery of the political system to 70 percent and 30 percent, respectively. Communal fighting ensued immediately and escalated in August 1964, when the Turkish airforce participated in the fighting, especially in Kokkina. In July 1974, Greek Cypriot nationalists committed to Enosis (the union of Greece and Cyprus) staged a failed coup in collusion with the Greek military junta that took charge of Greece after the April 1967 coup d'état. Ankara capitalized on this event to impose Taksim (the separation of the two communities in Cyprus) and invaded the island's northern part. The unilateral declaration of the internationally unrecognized Turkish Republic of Northern Cyprus (TRNC) took place in November 1983. Nevertheless, the Greek-controlled RoC received de jure recognition by the international community, which included jurisdiction over the island's territorial waters and EEZ.

The disintegration of the Ottoman Empire in 1918 brought Syria and Lebanon under French mandatory rule (1920–46), whereas the British mandate of Palestine lasted from 1920 until 1948, when the state of Israel came into existence. The creation of independent states in Syria, Lebanon, and Israel brought stability neither to them, nor to neighboring countries. Israel has been locked in a state of enmity with its Arab neighbors, including those with which it signed peace treaties. In Syria, arbitrary rule and regime despotism eventually put the country into an open-ended civil war that has been raging since March 2011. The introduction of confessional politics into Lebanese politics did not ensure balanced representation. Since independence, Lebanon has endured two civil wars, one in 1958 and another during 1975–99. The Ta'if Agreement of September 1999 aimed at restructuring the Lebanese political system and ensuring fair sectarian representation. Endemic foreign intervention and the prevalence of clientelism prevented the Lebanese from reaching terms on smoothly running national political affairs. Public-sector stagnation and political immobilism have become the order of the day in Lebanon.

Failure to cooperate

Were it not for the notable exception of Israeli–Cypriot relations, the countries of the Levant Basin would have seemed impervious to cooperation. Part of the problem may have to do with the fact that none of these countries has begun to develop its gas export infrastructure. It has been noted that the countries of the Levant Basin are confronted with "a host of trans-boundary problems in terms of getting its output to market, exacerbated by the different stages of development in the region" (Roberts 2014). One would say there is no longer a reason for the Israelis to complain "about how Moses led his people through the desert for 40 years to reach the one place in the region with no oil" (Knell 2013). One of the major gas-related issues that Israel is confronting has to do with the difficulties it is encountering in finding regional partners to cooperate with. In 2001, Ariel Sharon stressed that "Israel would never buy gas from Palestine … and in 2003 he vetoed a deal that would enable British Gas to supply Israel with natural gas from the Gaza wells" (Tagliapietra 2013, 13).

Israel has been unwilling to cooperate with the Palestinian Authority on the utilization of gas off Gaza shore. Hamas's control of Gaza in June 2007 had further complicated the already thorny issue of getting the two sides to work together. There are reasons to assert that Israel

> has been obstructive to the PA's own natural gas exploitation opportunities. Gas was discovered by British BG Group in waters that would comprise Gaza's EEZ. However, political difficulties made it impossible to tap and transport the gas – the PA is not a member of the UN Convention on the Law of the Sea (UNCLOS) and hence has not declared its EEZ. (Knell 2013)

Israel occupied the Gaza Strip between 1967 and 2005 and continues to control its airspace and territorial waters. Palestinians reject Israel's negotiations and describe them as rude thievery in broad daylight. They often compare them to "a modern-day Balfour Declaration" (Knell 2013).

There is no question that both Turkey and Israel understand the need for both of them to cooperate on energy matters, but they have not yet been able to overcome the obstacles, which involve other thorny issues (Cyprus and the 2010 *Mavi Marmara* incident). Both Israeli and Turkish officials have articulated the importance of laying out an Israel–Turkey pipeline for promoting mutual economic and political interests. Israeli policy seeks to improve its economic relations with Ankara, without ignoring the necessity for developing parallel deals with Nicosia. Therefore, the perceived need for a pipeline to Turkey serves as a step that "fits in with Israel's strategy of exploring regional markets first before venturing further afield and is one of the most cost-effective export options for the Leviathan field mooted by the Israeli government and the

Leviathan partners" (Knell 2013). The Israeli view is that such a pipeline gives it access to the largest growing market in the region, as well as the possibility of securing a share of the European market. Israel's interest in the Turkish pipeline does not deflect its attention from the opportunities provided by LNG exports to Europe and East Asia. Because Israel is having difficulty convincing its strong environmentalist lobby about the merits of building an LNG plant on its coast, the "Greek Cypriots' planned LNG terminal is a practical way around this problem given the short distance between Israel's offshore fields and its newfound friendship with the Greek Cypriots" (Knell 2013).

Nicosia has been trying to sway the United States (US) in favor of Cyprus as the place to develop the regional gas infrastructure that in turn would enable Cyprus to become a bridge that can bring the countries of the EM to work together collaboratively. As part of this ambitious endeavor, the Cypriot minister of energy travelled to Washington, where he met with congressmen and Department of State representatives in a bid to enlist their support for making Cyprus a regional energy hub. The RoC sees itself "as an important location to help diversify Europe's energy mix and lessen reliance on producers like Russia and Mideast suppliers" (Kashi 2013a). Cyprus needs to convince Israel that it has more proven gas reserves than Cyprus, to convert its interest in cooperation into concrete measures that would lead to the development of the Vasilikos LNG terminal. As Knell (2013) reports, "Israel certainly has more discovered natural gas resources than Cyprus. The estimated gas in Israel's Leviathan field is around four times larger than the estimates to date for Cyprus' Block 12." Serious hurdles still prevent the concretization of the RoC's gas hub ambitions. This has to do primarily with the fact that "to date, Aphrodite is currently insufficient to justify a major export-oriented project. And Lebanon has yet to even implement its current offshore block award program" (Roberts 2014, 15).

There are seemingly convincing reasons why the RoC believes that the proposed Vasilikos LNG facility is feasible:

> First, LNG can be sold to Asia, where demand is expected to grow much faster than in Europe. Second, LNG, together with the Vitol oil terminal that is currently under construction and due to be completed in July 2014, will bolster the RoC's position as a regional hub, which has related benefits for security. A likely third reason is that Greek Cypriots are probably very wary of depending solely on a route via Turkey for their most promising export ... The grand plan is that this plant would process not only Cyprus gas but also potentially gas from Israel and Lebanon, thus

making it possible to create a world class LNG hub at Vasilikos. (Knell 2013)

Unless it finds more gas in its EEZ, it will be difficult for Cyprus to make the case for building the expensive LNG plant at Vasilikos. If not, the Israelis will most probably go ahead with pumping their gas via "a subsea pipeline across or around Cyprus, or whether it might opt for an LNG facility" (Roberts 2014, 15). Heidi Vella (2015) comments, "Cyprus is an emerging offshore energy frontier worth watching." It faces the tough task of having to deal with domestic issues that have geopolitical ramifications. Even in the remote possibility that no additional gas discoveries are made in its EEZ, thanks to its location in the region Cyprus is a prime candidate for playing a significant role in utilizing the promising EM gas finds.

Cyprus cannot plan its oil strategy on processing Lebanon's natural gas potential in its LNG facility. Lebanese politicians have daunting domestic problems to resolve on sharing the spoils of their gas finds before they can make promises to the RoC. Since an LNG facility is suitable for shipping gas to distant markets, such as those in the Asia/Pacific region, there is a strong need for making long-term export commitments, especially because of the high cost of facility construction, including "shipping, and regasification facilities, and to provide some kind of link to ensure that developers can profit from any subsequent, more-general increase in energy prices" (Roberts 2014, 22). Cypriot officials attach paramount significance to constructing the LNG facility. In fact, this issue has assumed national dimensions and Cypriots equate the fruition of this ambitious goal with the attainment of the country's economic development. Theodoros Tsakiris (2014) explains, "Even if there are a few Greek-Cypriot politicians who would be ready to discuss a 'Turkish' pipeline as a parallel option to the Vasilikos LNG terminal, no one would be ready to drop Vasilikos in favour of a pipeline option, especially if it would end up to Turkey."

In making the case for the Vasilikos facility, RoC officials argue that the proposed Leviathan–Ceyhan Pipeline (LCP) creates for Israel an imbalanced trade relationship with Turkey. Even "if Turkey consumes by 2020 up to 8 billion cubic meters (bcm) annually of Israeli gas [equal to 43 percent of Israel's entire export potential], it would be dependent on Tel Aviv for merely 13.79 percent of its projected demand, estimated by BP at 58 bcm/y" (Tsakiris 2014, 50). Should it be possible to transit Israeli gas through Turkey's National Gas Transmission System (NGTS) all the way to its border with Bulgaria, there is no pipeline available to carry the Israeli gas to Austria's distribution station in Baumgarten (Tsakiris 2014, 55). In view of the Cypriot argument about the impracticality of the

Turkish pipeline option, a Cypriot LNG plant "ensures a higher level [than the LCP] of demand security from the exporter's point of view" (Tsakiris 2014, 48).

Taking the natural gas issue beyond technical aspects, Endy Zemenides, the executive director of the Hellenic American Leadership Council, called for the formation of an energy triangle by Cyprus, Israel, and Greece to usher in "the first Western, democratically controlled source of energy in the Middle East ... an arc of democracies that will serve as a bulwark against [regional] instability" (Kashi 2013a). Cyprus's determination to develop its gas sector has become an overriding issue fueled by the "promotion of the national cause against Turkey [and] the way out of the economic crisis" (Gurel, Kahvechi, and Tzimitras 2014). Greek Cypriot officials are completely opposed to engaging their Turkish counterparts in bilateral talks. For them, the legitimate jurisdiction of the RoC over its EEZ is non-negotiable. They believe that Turkey is trying to put "the unrecognized TRNC [on a par] with the internationally recognized legitimate state, the RoC" (Gurel, Kahvechi, and Tzimitras 2014). Nicosia's decision to exclude the island's Turkish community from gas exploration in its EEZ has upset Ankara, which would like to see an agreement between the two communities on revenue sharing (Knell 2013). Nicosia accepts the principle of revenue sharing, although it adamantly refuses to recognize the de jure existence of the TRNC. This has driven Ankara to opt for retaliatory measures, including signing a continental shelf delimitation agreement with TRNC, "whose president, Dervis Eroglu, described [this] as a precautionary measure to make our Greek counterparts to desist" (Knell 2013).

Despite the official standoff between Lebanon and Israel regarding the delineation of the latter's EEZ, there are reasons to assume that Lebanon's primary problem is domestic and has to do with the country's conflict-ridden sectarian mosaic. According to former Lebanese minister of energy Gebran Bassil, "Israel has no interest in encroaching on Lebanese reservoirs ... But there are local interests that would like to see work in the energy sector delayed further" (Chakrani 2013). The ability of Lebanon to tap its natural gas potential depends on its ability to overcome the "long-stalled offshore bid licensing round" (Tagliapietra 2013, 16). Due to the confessional nature of Lebanese politics, which requires the inclusion of the country's major sects in legislation, it became necessary to establish a petroleum administration. It took two years of difficult bargaining to finally agree on the structure and members of the Lebanese Petroleum Administration (LPA). When leaders of major Lebanese sects finally agreed on it, they decided to rotate its chief executive position on an annual basis in order to maintain a sectarian balance. In view of its overwhelming domestic political constraints, compounded by regional turmoil, it is highly unlikely that the LPA will enable Lebanon to explore fully, let alone exploit, its natural oil resources. Lebanon's sectarian leaders "approach the gas dossier from a narrow tribal perspective that does not take into consideration its technical aspects and economic promise that can benefit the country's citizens with no regard to their sectarian affiliation" (Zaki 2014). Lebanon's stalemate regarding exploring and exploiting its gas wealth encouraged Israel to strike gas deals worth more than $60 billion with Egypt and Jordan (As-Safir (Beirut) March 4, 2015).

Companies interested in bidding hoped that the Lebanese cabinet would approve the necessary decrees that would determine the number of blocks and sort out revenue sharing issues in good time before submitting their bids (Daily Star (Beirut) April 10, 2014). This did not happen and the bidding deadline was delayed for a third time. Oil companies seemed perplexed by the unnecessary and inexplicable delays, and bemused by the strict "financial stipulations set out by the Lebanese government … [that] may dissuade oil companies to drill for gas" (Associated News Agency April 7, 2014). It has been aptly noted that:

> The tax regime proposed by Lebanon, which includes the imposition of taxes on profits – is exorbitant in view of the existing dangers. Sounds like trying to sell the fish before catching it. Instead of assuring the oil market about the political dangers, the Lebanese scared everybody. (Al-Hayat (London) April 6, 2014)

The Israeli government was taken aback by the unexpected Egyptian decision in 2012 to abrogate its natural gas export agreements, which provided Israel with 40 percent of its total supply needs (Al-Hayat April 6, 2014). Israel is concerned about the increasing political and security instability in the EM and the deterioration of its close ties with Turkey since the Justice and Development Party (AKP) rose to power after its first landslide victory in the 2002 general elections. Untoward developments related to insecurity and the attendant unpredictability "have precipitated a build-up of naval forces in the Levant basin from a number of state actors wanting to get in on the action" (Saidel and Kasdin 2014). Cut-throat diplomacy appears to have convinced the countries of the region to invest more funds in developing their navies. For example, Israel is currently in "the process of creating the most technologically advanced fleet in the eastern Mediterranean" (Saidel and Kasdin 2014). Not missing an opportunity to contribute to the already tense regional environment, in

2011 the then Turkish Prime Minister Recep Tayyip Erdoğan warned Israel that it "cannot do whatever it wants in the Eastern Mediterranean. They will see what our decisions will be on this subject. Our navy attack ships can be there at any moment" (Kashi 2013a).

Exploration and exploitation efforts

Israel has been in front of the other countries in the Levant Basin in exploring and exploiting gas. In April 2013, it embarked on exploiting the reserves of the Tamar field, which has the capacity to fulfill its domestic consumption for at least two decades (Knell 2013). Israel has plans to exploit the huge Leviathan field by 2017. Officials in Nicosia aim to capitalize on the exploration success in Block 12 to pursue additional resources in Cypriot waters, and hope to discover between 30 and 40 tcf of additional natural gas (EIA 2013). In response, Turkish Petroleum (TP) launched an effort to drill for gas off the TRNC coast (Knell 2013). Lebanon's exploration is in its early stages of licensing and there are no indicators that exploration will get under way any time soon, whereas exploration in Syria is postponed pending the end of its civil war, which appears to be protracted.

The government of Lebanon completed a pre-qualification bid for exploration in the country's territorial waters in April 2013. Chevron, Total, ExxonMobil, and Shell were among the 52 companies that applied for pre-qualification, and 46 of those had their applications accepted, although not much has happened since (Knell 2013). Endemic internal divisions and the scramble to win the biggest chunk of the hoped-for gas dividends have invited acerbic criticism from Lebanese commentators:

> In order for Lebanon to defend its right to its natural resources, especially against Israel ... it must at the very least respect its own plans and timetables ... when approving the decrees on EPAs [exploration and production agreements] and offshore blocks, and then granting concessions, exploration and drilling must begin in the southernmost part of the EEZ, because there are no sovereign issues in the north or the centre. (Chakrani 2013)

Aside from the promise of additional natural gas finds, and despite the hitherto unresolved exploration and exploitation issues, the EM region has shale oil, which is still considered an unconventional energy source. However, the shale oil resources there "have not developed to the same extent that they have elsewhere in the world" (Saidel and Kasdin 2014). Syria's oil shale resources approximate 50 billion tonnes, and Jordan's about 65 billion tonnes (EIA 2013). Israel's shale reserves are about the equivalent of 250 billion barrels (Gold 2011). Israel is already considering the large-scale development of its shale deposits, which may position it as a leading shale developer and utilizer after the US and China (Gold 2011). New technologies are making the processing of shale oil cleaner and more efficient.

Israel has not shown a real interest in cooperating with the Palestinian Authority to explore the gas potential off Gaza's coast. The EIA (2013) notes, "In September 2012, the Palestinian Authority and Israel discussed developing the offshore Gaza territory, although no firm agreements are in place." The non-state status of the Palestinian Authority serves as a disincentive for Israel to negotiate gas matters seriously, especially since Hamas continues to control the Gaza Strip.

The exclusive economic zone dilemma

Political analysts warn that the enormous problems with which the countries of the EM find themselves struggling to cope will be exceptionally difficult to resolve. It seems that their acrimonious historical memories stand in the way of compromising and reaching reasonable policy outcomes (Oilprice.com 2013).

In 2010, Lebanon supplied the United Nations (UN) Secretary-General with its "geographical coordinates for the delimitization of [its] ... EEZ. Obviously, these coordinates [based on the 1949 armistice line between Israel and Lebanon] do not coincide with those used in the agreement between Cyprus and Israel," based on the working Blue Line of 2000, following Israeli withdrawal from southern Lebanon (Abi-Aad 2014). In supplying these coordinates, Lebanon filed a claim concerning a 250-square nautical mile area with Israel, and sought both UN and US assistance in resolving the dispute. The two countries, which are officially in a state of war and do not exchange diplomatic missions, went to the extent of resorting to issuing belligerent statements. Thus, in July 2011 Israel Minister of National Infrastructure Uzi Landau threatened to resort to military action "to protect not only the rule of law but the international maritime law" (Abi-Aad 2014). A year later, Hizbullah chief Hasan Nasrallah warned that it would "target Israel's gas facilities should it encroach on Lebanon's EEZ] and steal ... [its] resources" (Abi-Aad 2014).

A US diplomat who sought to bridge the gap between Lebanon and Israel could not hide his frustration and disappointment at the seemingly insignificant EEZ dispute between the two countries:

> There is nothing complex about the Lebanon–Israel case in terms of their coastline or the methodologies they used in assessing conflicting claims. Indeed, if they had had diplomatic relations this relatively minor disagreement would have either been long-since resolved or may not have arisen at all. (Hof 2014, 73)

It recently transpired that Amos Hochstein, US deputy assistant secretary for energy diplomacy, worked out in April 2013 an undisclosed agreement between Lebanon and Israel regarding the establishment of a maritime security zone (MSL) as a buffer where no energy-related activity could take place without the consent of both governments (Daily Star August 11, 2014). Cyprus sought to use its good offices to resolve the standoff between the two countries, although its efforts to break the impasse made no headway. It has been claimed that Cypriot interest in resolving this dispute emanates from Nicosia's wish to involve Israel and Lebanon in its energy plans, especially the LNG facility (Abi-Aad 2014). The Lebanese should not self-flagellate because of the 860 sq km area in dispute with Israel, since about half of the world's EEZs remain undelineated (Saida Online 2015). There is no question that the incentive for regional cooperation far exceeds an inauspicious collective memory that applies to intra-Cypriot relations as well.

It might be difficult to rationalize former Lebanese energy minister Bassil's warning about the likelihood that Israel "might steal Lebanon's share of [gas]" (Aziz 2013), considering that he previously played down the matter. Bassil, a Maronite Christian, was actually trying to create an atmosphere of urgency in Lebanon to convince Lebanese Shiites to yield to his preference for granting oil companies exploration licenses in blocks not contested with Israel; that is, off the Maronite-populated Lebanese coast. In connection with his efforts to invite bidders for two blocks other than those off the southern Lebanese coast that the Shiite leaders oppose, Bassil sought to enlist the backing of the Lebanese president, the acting Prime Minister, and the speaker of the parliament in order to convene cabinet and parliamentary sessions to approve his bidding plan. He reasoned that this would be "the only way for Lebanon to safeguard its offshore resources and prevent them from being appropriated by others" (Aziz 2013). When his efforts failed to impress leaders of the Shiite and Sunni communities who respectively control parliament and cabinet, Bassil claimed that Israel might be involved in horizontal drilling to encroach on Lebanon's EEZ, but "a geologist with PetroServe International noted that it would not make sense for a company to employ horizontal drilling to blindly move from one reserve in search for another" (Nash 2013). Carole Nakhle, an energy economist at British Surrey

Energy Economic Centre, shrugs off Lebanese politicians' squabbling and procrastination. She says that "investors in the oil and gas sector are used to taking risk and companies take a long-term perspective ... But if I look at the maritime borders this can be a disincentive for investors in Lebanon" (Knell 2013).

It is unlikely that gas finds in Israel's Aphrodite-2 well will create problems with the RoC. The two countries have already shown great capacity for cooperation in the realization that they need each other. Even if "the Aphrodite-2 prove[s] to be part of the same structure as Cyprus' field [which may have over 3 tcf of technically recoverable resources] ... the two countries should be able to negotiate a utilization agreement before production begins" (EIA 2013). Whereas the EEZ delimitation between Israel and Lebanon is more of a domestic problem in the latter's political system, the RoC maritime travails lie with Turkey, which never ceases to describe "Nicosia's exploratory drilling as nothing but sabotage of the negotiation process between Turkish Cypriots and Greek Cypriots" (Knell 2013).

Parting with the past and transcending the present: The logic of collective action

Russia's annexation of the Crimea and the turmoil in Ukraine are prodding the European Union (EU) to expedite the search for substitutes for Russian gas. The countries of the EM have a unique opportunity to take advantage of their natural gas potential to bury the hatchet and usher in an era of collaborative work that could be in their best interests. Cyprus's energy minister expressed his hope that the "discoveries of hydrocarbons in the eastern Mediterranean are definitely now an incentive, and it could be a catalyst for peace for the region" (Kashi 2013b). Likewise, Yossi Abu, chief executive of Israeli Delek Drilling, posits that even though "Leviathan is actually the reservoir that can potentially bring Israel to be totally independent from an energy perspective and also position ... [it] as an exporter of natural gas rather than importer ... [it] can use the new gas discoveries as a bridge to have a better relationship with our neighbours" (Knell 2013).

In its bid to reduce its heavy reliance on gas supplies from Russia, Turkey has become central to shifting the EU's energy policy. In connection with the new energy thinking, the EU is developing a Southern Corridor alternative that "aims at supplying Europe with gas directly from the Caspian basin and the Middle East," thus bypassing Russia (Gurel and Mullen 2014). It is widely believed that the EM is likely to become a source of gas feeding the Southern Corridor, provided that it can be linked to the planned Trans-Anatolian Natural Gas Pipeline (TANAP; Knell 2013). The former executive president of the Cyprus National Hydrocarbons Company (KRETYK) has said that with much more gas expected to be found offshore to Cyprus, the EM region could supply up to a third of the EU's additional gas needs, which are expected to reach 100 bcm by 2025 (Gurel and Mullen 2014).

Gas alone is not a strong incentive to resolve the Cyprus problem, despite the fact that such a development would improve Turkey's relations with the EU. The parties to the conflict have to understand that they need each other. Any negotiation process that is not predicated on reciprocal respect and placing oneself in the position of the other is bound to fail. It is only logical to propose that the discovery of natural gas in Cyprus's EEZ – even if more gas finds need to be made – is bound to expedite the peace process and convince the two parties to the conflict that the fruits of cooperation exceed ungainly polemical bickering. To be sure:

> [the] reasoning behind this question is that the commercial benefits of mutual cooperation on gas, as well as the geopolitical benefits of supporting the diversification of EU gas supplies, could constitute strong enough incentives for all parties to reach a settlement. (Gurel and Mullen 2014)

There are indicators to suggest that this has not been the case yet: "Not only has unilateral exploration of natural gas … led to mutual tensions, it was arguably an underlying cause of the delay in the re-launch of the UN-sponsored inter-communal negotiations for a settlement of the Cyprus problem" (Gurel and Mullen 2014). The RoC has been incapable of thinking about the gas issue with the TRNC except in terms of being the only internationally recognized government on the island. Therefore, it has "the sovereign right to explore for natural resources in the Republic's EEZ" (Gurel and Mullen 2014). The economic situation in both RoC and TRNC is such that they can no longer afford to block each other. By 2010 TRNC debt to Turkey was estimated to exceed 80 percent of its GDP, whereas the debt/GDP ratio of the RoC is expected to peak at 126.2 percent in 2015 (Gurel and Mullen 2014). Cyprus has still to recover from the 2013 banking crash, which caused unprecedented socioeconomic woes and loss of trust in the country's financial institutions. One aspect that hinders reaching a gas-for-cash deal has to do with the realization that "each side perceives the other side's need to be greater than its own and hence presumes that the other side has a greater need to solve the Cyprus problem" (Gurel and Mullen 2014). This type of wishful reasoning must be curtailed in the interest of the island at large.

The Lebanese are pinning their hopes "on hydrocarbon revenues to turn around the country's weak economy, which has one of the highest rates of public debt to gross domestic product (GDP) in the world" (Gurel and Mullen 2014), although they have not shown a modicum of willingness to cooperate outside narrow sectarian and personal interests. The upheavals in the broader region do not create an atmosphere that encourages divided Lebanese politicians to come to terms with one another. The stabilization of the region is a sine qua non for bringing the Lebanese together, since they often report to regional patrons before committing themselves to any policy proposal. The same can be said about the relationship between the Palestinians and the Israelis. Even if there were no territorial issues with the Israelis, the Palestinians simply cannot develop their own gas infrastructure on their own. As Anais Antreasyan (2013, 31) reports, "Palestinian gas consumption remains negligible, at 45 million cubic meters per year (0.0001 tcf) ... exploring the gas could lead to Israeli-Palestinian cooperation ... They need each other for the efficient development of ... offshore reserves."

Ideology still stands in the face of regional cooperation in the energy sector. Sooner or later, the countries of the EM will realize that they need to put their differences aside. If they really want to secure international gas investors, they mush convince these investors that these countries are trustworthy and predictable. Unlike oil whose prices are international, gas prices tend to vary substantially across the world. At present, gas investors have reasons for reluctance to enter into such joint ventures. The downward trend of gas prices raise questions about the commercial viability of investment in new gas projects. It is the responsibility of the countries of the EM to convince investors otherwise.

Such a realization may not be enough to get these countries to cooperate, however. What they seem to lack is the will to act. The propensity of the Lebanese to resolve their own domestic problems and cooperate among themselves remains debatable. Similarly, the enigma of Cyprus's Greek and Turkish communities' ability to overcome the burden of history has yet to be resolved. What is clear, however, is that, with or without a regional vision on energy cooperation, Israel will proceed with its ambitious energy plans either collectively or individually.

References

Abi-Aad, Naji. 2014. "The Conflict between Israel and Lebanon over Their Exclusive Economic Zones." In Sami Andoura and David Koranyi (Eds.), Energy in the Eastern Mediterranean: Promise or Peril? Egmont Paper 65, May, 69–71. Brussels: Egmont Institute.

Antreasyan, Anais. 2013. "Gas Finds in the Eastern Mediterranean: Gaza, Israel, and Other Conflicts." Journal of Palestine Studies, 42, 29–47.

Aziz, Jean. 2013. "Will Offshore Gas Spark New Lebanon-Israel Conflict?" Al Monitor, July 10. http://www.al-monitor.com/pulse/originals/2013/07/lebanon-israel-gas-exploration-dispute.html. Accessed November 2015.

Chakrani, Hassan. 2013. "Lebanon's Gas under Threat: Israel Drilling near Southern Fields." Al-Akhbar (Beirut), July 7. http://english.al-akhbar.com/node/16348. Accessed November 2015.

EIA. 2013. "Overview of Oil and Natural Gas in the Eastern Mediterranean Region." August 15. Washington, DC: US Energy Information Administration. http://www.eia.gov/beta/international/analysis_includes/regions_of_int erest/Eastern_Mediterranean/eastern-mediterranean.pdf. Accessed November 2015.

Gold, Dore. 2011. "How Israel Could Revolutionize the Global Energy Sector." Jerusalem Post, November 3. http://www.jpost.com/Features/Front-Lines/How-Israel-could-revolutionize-the-global-energy-sector. Accessed November 2015.

Gurel, Ayla, and Fiona Mullen. 2014. "Can Eastern Mediterranean Gas Discoveries Have a Positive Impact on Turkey-EU Relations?" Global Turkey in Europe, Policy Brief 12, March. Istanbul: Istanbul Policy Center. http://ipc.sabanciuniv.edu/wp-content/uploads/2014/03/GTE_PB_12.pdf. Accessed November 2015.

Gurel, Aula, Hayriye Kahvechi, and Harry Tzimitras. 2014. "How to Build Confidence over Energy Issues in the Context of a Cyprus Settlement?" In Sami Andoura and David Koranyi (Eds.), Energy in the Eastern Mediterranean: Promise or Peril? Egmont Paper 65, May, 59–68. Brussels: Egmont Institute.

Hof, Fred C. 2014. "Lebanon and Israel: A Line on the Water." In Sami Andoura and David Koranyi (Eds.), Energy in the Eastern Mediterranean: Promise or Peril? Egmont Paper 65, May, 73. Brussels: Egmont Institute.

Karbuz, Sohbet. 2014. "How to Frame and Develop the Necessary Cross-Border Energy Infrastructures between Cyprus, Turkey, and Israel?" In

Sami Andoura and David Koranyi (Eds.), Energy in the Eastern
Mediterranean: Promise or Peril? Egmont Paper 65, May, 29–37.
Brussels: Egmont Institute.
Kashi, David. 2013a. "Huge Natural Gas Fields in the Eastern
Mediterranean Are Set to Transform Cyprus into European Energy
Hub." International Business Times, September 12.
http://www.ibtimes.com/huge-natural-gas-fields-eastern-
mediterranean-are-set-transform-cyprus-european-energy-hub-
1404582. Accessed November 2015.
—. 2013b. "Israel, Lebanon and the Eastern Mediterranean's Oil and Gas,
a Source of Conflict or Peace?" International Business Times, October
7. http://www.ibtimes.com/israel-lebanon-eastern-mediterraneans-oil-
gas-source-conflict-or-peace-1415718. Accessed November 2015.
Knell, Yolande. 2013. "Gas Finds in East Mediterranean May Change
Strategic Balance." BBC News, May 13.
http://www.bbc.com/news/world-middle-east-22509295.
Accessed November 2015.
MBendi Information Services. n.d. "Natural Gas Liquid Extraction in
Syria – Overview."
http://www.mbendi.com/indy/oilg/gas_/as/sy/p0005.htm.
Accessed November 2015.
Miller, Richie, and Gary Scaife. 2011. "Offshore 'Frontier' Basins in
Spotlight." American Oil & Gas Reporter, June.
http://www.aogr.com/magazine/editors-choice/offshore-frontier-
basins-in-spotlight. Accessed June 2011.
Nash, Matt. 2013. "Is Israel Stealing Lebanon's Gas?" NOW News,
August 19. https://now.mmedia.me/lb/en/reportsfeatures/is-israel-stealing-
lebanons-gas. Accessed November 2015.
Oilprice.com. 2013. "Natural Gas Discoveries in the Eastern Med Reignite
Old Rivalries." Oilprice.com, June 26.
http://oilprice.com/Energy/Natural-Gas/Natural-Gas-Discoveries-in-the-
Eastern-Med-Reignite-Old-Rivalries.html. Accessed November 2015.
Roberts, John. 2014. "The Eastern Mediterranean Energy Conundrum:
Options and Challenges." In Sami Andoura and David Koranyi (Eds.),
Energy in the Eastern Mediterranean: Promise or Peril? Egmont Paper
65, May, 15–27. Brussels: Egmont Institute.
Saida Online. 2015. "Information Indicating That the Gas Wealth in
Lebanon More Than $41 Billion So Far." Saida Online.
www.saidaonline.com/newsapp.php?go=fullnews&newsid=50201.
Accessed April 6, 2015.

Saidel, Nicholas, and Julian Kasdin. 2014. "With Natural Gas Fields in the Eastern Mediterranean, Israel Now Has a New Front: The Sea." Tablet Magazine, January 17. http://www.tabletmag.com/jewish-news-and-politics/159738/israels-new-front. Accessed November 2015.

Tagliapietra, Simone. 2013. "Towards a New Eastern Mediterranean Energy Corridor: Natural Gas Developments between Market Opportunities and Geopolitical Risks." Note di Lavoro, December. Milan: Fondazione Eni Enrico Mattei.

Tsakiris, Theodoros. 2014. "The Leviathan–Ceyhan Pipeline: Political and Commercial Arguments against the Construction of a Turkish–Israeli Pipeline." In Sami Andoura and David Koranyi (Eds.), Energy in the Eastern Mediterranean: Promise or Peril? Egmont Paper 65, May, 47–57. Brussels: Egmont Institute.

Vella, Heidi. 2015. "Offshore Cyprus: Navigating Geopolitical Issues in the Levant Basin." Offshore Technology, January 20. http://www.offshore-technology.com/features/featureoffshore-cyprus-navigating-geopolitical-issues-in-the-levant-basin-4487876/. Accessed November 2015.

Zaki, Rasha Abu. 2014. "Lebanese Oil Expert for 'Al-Araby al-Jadeed': Israel Is Stealing Lebanon Gas." Al-Ankabout, April 29. www.alankabout.com/lebanon_news/55492.html. Accessed November 2015.

CHAPTER SEVEN

THE CHALLENGES
OF THE EASTERN MEDITERRANEAN

MIGUEL ÁNGEL MORATINOS CUYAUBÉ

The region's past

Writing on the Mediterranean at the beginning of the twenty-first century inevitably evokes memories of the many conflicts that still bedevil this region of the world and that unfortunately have not been solved yet. It also means highlighting the new challenges that loom large on the horizon of this area, which historically conveyed hope and tragedy. This composite region, so perfectly defined and studied by Fernand Braudel, fully reflects the many contradictions of this world that stand at the crossroads of our destiny.

The Mediterranean has inspired thousands of works and studies, focusing mainly on the geographic, cultural, historical, or sociopolitical aspects of the region. However, except for the great work of the French scholar Fernand Braudel, there has been no recent comparable comprehensive and complete study of the Mediterranean basin's current realities and challenges. This task deserves the time and effort needed because of the importance of the project. A multidisciplinary and multicountry Mediterranean team, under suitable political direction, would give meaning to such a valuable piece of work. This could in the end potentially give us a guide for the future.

If this lack of interest in the Mediterranean issue is indeed true, then the indifference shown to the eastern part of the Mediterranean must surely stand out as a great oversight. Indeed, the Eastern Mediterranean (EM) is most often referred to as the "Near East" or "Middle East," thus leaving out the Mediterranean nature and identity of this part of the world. The Arab–Israeli conflict attracts most of the interest of Western governments, at the expense of the EM component, which has been relegated of a secondary role.

However, the secondary role that the West has assigned to the EM does not do justice to the position and importance of the region, particularly if one were to think of the major role it has played throughout history. Downgrading the EM basically means leaving out the very origin of our culture and our history. The Ancient Mediterranean, as described in *Mediterranean: A Story to Share* by Mostafa Hassani Idrissi (2013, 74), is rooted in "Mesopotamia, the region of the great rivers which stretches to the East of the Mediterranean. ... The invention of writing and of the city, that is, the development of complex societies, occurred in the Eastern Mediterranean."

This historical reminder helps highlight the strategic importance of the region. This geographic space, the "Lighthouse of the Mediterranean" in the words of historian David Abulafia (2012), is where Alexander the Great established his center of gravity with respect to Persia and Egypt. Geopolitical interest in the EM returned in force in the late nineteenth and early twentieth centuries. David Abulafia refers to the "fifth Mediterranean" that began its journey from its eastern boundary and culminated as the "Eastern question."

Turkey is at the center of the strategic challenges across the region. The "sick man of Europe" shook the whole sub-region with its decadence and finally its demise at the end of World War I. The disintegration of the Ottoman Empire caused a succession of crises that stretched from the Balkans to the Middle East. Both the Treaty of Versailles[1] and the Treaty of Lausanne[2] clearly illustrated the strategic importance of this area and the evolution of the new states that emerged. Cyprus deserves special mention due to its geographic location and its use as a platform for military bases. This island was in the grip of British ambition. The Treaty of Lausanne in 1923 managed to confirm Britain's position on the island with the formal agreement of Turkey and Greece. Since then, the main concerns of the region have centered on Middle East issues and the Greek–Turkish rivalry over Cyprus, in this way overlooking the broader Mediterranean. Consequently, for many years the Mediterranean was not a priority on the agenda of that time.

Nevertheless, Greece returned to the forefront. The Hellenistic spirit regained momentum with the arrival of Eleftherios Venizelos. His leadership and political skills brought Greek influence to the decision-making process at the Paris Conference; many of his positions were largely incorporated into the Treaty of Versailles. However, apart from the personality and political and diplomatic capabilities of this Cretan nationalist, as Margaret Macmillan puts it in her book *Peacemakers*, "the First World War changed the landscape completely. The Ottomans had chosen the losing side in the war and Venizelos and Greece the winning side" (Macmillan 2001, 360). These circumstances facilitated the change of strategy of most of the major players, particularly the British:

> The English, who for so long had supported Ottoman Turkey, were now in need of an alternative partner to keep the Eastern side of the Mediterranean safe for their ships. It was clear that the British did not wish the French Empire to expand there and equally, if possible, they did not want to spend their own money. This made a strong Greece attractive. Principles and interests conveniently overlapped. Greece was Western and civilized, while Asian Ottoman Turkey was barbaric. And Venizelos was admirable, 'the greatest leader of Greece since the time of Pericles' in the opinion of Lloyd George. A stronger Greece would then be a perfect ally. (Macmillan 2001, 364)

This British–Greek alliance was so strong that even on complicated subjects such as Cyprus, the Greek authorities and Venizelos himself agreed to give satisfaction to British interests. As Macmillan (2001, 364) notes, "If the English wanted to return Cyprus to the Greeks, it would be wonderful and of course Greece would let the British forces use bases there, if the British wanted to keep them, it was also very understandable."

All these historical references help us to better understand how the EM gradually reclaimed a central role in the early twentieth century, but especially since the end of World War II and as the strategic stakes were raised. The fall of the Ottoman Empire, the new shape of the Middle East, and the various crises in the Balkans drew the attention of major powers to the sub-region again.

The end of World War II and the new balance of power in the region changed once more the main geopolitical axes of the EM, establishing new counterbalances. Bipolar dialectics were imposed. The Cold War and the division of the world into two blocs were reflected in the position and interests of every country in the region. The East–West confrontation became apparent in the Balkans, the Middle East, and especially Cyprus. The creation of the North Atlantic Treaty Organization (NATO) and Turkey's membership in this political and military alliance, as bulwark and policeman of the interests of the United States (US) throughout this region, weakened the Mediterranean resonance in national policies, replacing it with the distant concept of "Atlanticism" that is foreign to the region. The Mediterranean was thus left without its own policies and became entangled in the hegemonic struggle to control navigation in its waters. The presence of the Russian fleet and the Sixth US Fleet were the sole noticeable elements in the EM until the fall of the Berlin Wall.

We need to analyze the political developments in the EM with reference to the above context, while acknowledging its limitations and constraints.

The case of Cyprus

Cyprus is very relevant to our understanding of the realities of the EM. Throughout its history this island country, close to the East, has received many (often unwelcome) visitors and has been influenced by many different cultures and civilizations. Starting in the Neolithic period, about 3700 BCE, it was colonized by the Phoenicians and later by the Achaeans, who brought the Greek language and religion. Then came the Assyrians, Macedonians, Egyptians, Persians, Romans, Byzantines, and Saracens. Cyprus has always been coveted by major powers and inevitably suffered directly from the confrontations between different actors who wished to enforce their hegemony throughout the island.

This "paradise island," which fully justifies its mythical character, did not escape the fate of the Greek tragedy. As Jean-François Drevet (2000, 13) notes in his book *Chypre en Europe*, "The recent history of Cyprus is tragic … Being at the crossroads of varying interests that are larger than themselves, its inhabitants pay a heavy toll, without even being able to decide their fate." This collective consciousness of national impotence has always been present in the history of this nation – a sense of injustice, conspiracy, and sordid interests always looming large over the collective imagination of Cyprus. Although this chapter does not wish to reawaken the "conspiracy" theory (on which read O'Malley and Craig 2001), it underscores the general feeling of the Cypriot population, who consider that they have always been mistreated by the superpowers.

The failure of negotiations to achieve the unification of the island after Cyprus's accession to the European Union (EU) has not helped change this mindset. Forty-one years after the occupation of the northern part of the island by the Turkish army and eleven years after Cyprus's entry into the EU, the situation seems frozen. As time passes, the status quo consolidates. The recent financial and economic crisis that Cyprus has endured has not improved the overall attitude of Cypriot society. The serious mistakes in the EU's management of the Cypriot financial crisis (see Moratinos 2013) have caused the great majority of Cyprus's population to move away from their European vocation. And this comes at a time when the only hope for a solution to the Cyprus problem rests on a greater and more intense involvement of Europe.

The unveiling of a new policy in the coming years should take into consideration the new realities of the EM. Cyprus will always be at the center of developments in the region, so this should be taken into account in the formulation of a different policy.

Which are the new challenges in the Eastern Mediterranean?

Undoubtedly the world, and inevitably the EM, is now facing major challenges. Aside from the influences of globalization, the Mediterranean region is facing its own strategic changes that mark the end of this chapter of its history and the beginning of another. One hundred years after the outbreak of World War I and the fall of the Ottoman Empire, the EM is tormented by multiple crises that are likely to change the political balance of the entire region.

A new geopolitical setting

For a moment we thought, wrongly as it appears, that the Cold War was completely buried. It is now reappearing, as evidenced by the positions taken over several territorial disputes (including Ukraine) and geopolitical disagreements. The Syrian crisis marks the beginning of the revival of Russian diplomacy in the region and the return of a more active foreign policy from Moscow. The financial crisis in Cyprus and the measures taken concerning Russian deposits in Cypriot banks are evidence of the continued lack of agreement between Russia and the West. NATO is increasingly active, but more toward Central Europe and the Caucasus than toward the Mediterranean and the Balkans. In any case, we are heading for a new East–West confrontation that is entirely unnecessary and costly for everyone, especially for Europe and the Russian Federation. This mutual suspicion and lack of trust will not contribute in the least to the development of the EM region.

Although the traditional context of geopolitics has changed and the influence of the East–West axis is again casting a shadow on the geopolitical landscape, the most significant changes for the region are likely to take place in the east and south of the Mediterranean.

The EM region is closer to all the changes now taking place in the Arab–Muslim world. After all, it is in this part of the Mediterranean that the major crises have taken place and the so-called Arab Spring started; although technically the origins of this political tsunami were in Tunisia, which is in the central Mediterranean region. Nearer to the eastern part of the Mediterranean, Libya suffered the consequences of domestic revolts, and Egypt and Syria, at the heart of the EM, set the pace for all the events that followed.

Nothing will ever be the same, including the relationships between the different countries. The process of reform and political participation is irreversible. Even if there are ups and downs on this road to modernity, there is no turning back. This does not mean that political Islam will be the winner of this paradigm shift; not at all. We need to believe in the maturity of Arab societies that will allow them gradually to move toward their own modernity, different from the one that Westerners wish to impose, but also away from Islamic theocracy, which has failed to find and will have difficulty finding legitimacy as a political alternative in all these countries.

This eruption of desire for change among Arab–Muslim societies should not frighten European and Western governments. Rather, all of Europe should mobilize urgently to support these societies and respond to the many challenges faced by each one of these countries. The case of Egypt is crystal clear. After the failure of an Islamic transition, the second authoritarian transition should be able to prepare the country for a genuine process toward democratization that will apply the principles and rules of modernity.

Syria and Libya are at the bottom of the abyss and it is difficult to say how these societies will evolve. These social and political upheavals present us with a Mediterranean region that is fragmented and difficult to unify, but which is also crying out for help; more democratic countries should hasten to provide this.

Instability also prevails in the East. The Middle East is still unable to find a much deserved stability. Almost a century after World War I, the region continues to be immersed in violence and suffering. It seems that the Promised Land remains an unfulfilled promise. Those directly involved in the Arab–Israeli conflict are failing to find a solution, while the international community is not genuinely making a commitment that can help find a settlement that is so essential for everyone. Admittedly there is a certain "diplomatic fatigue" and exhaustion of new ideas on how to bring about the end of the Arab–Israeli conflict. Israel, as a major EM power, is still unable to build a vision and a strategy for its future. It ignores the Mediterranean dimension and concentrates only on the issue of the survival of the State of Israel. It prioritizes a policy that is restricted to the defense of its state, when it ought to be living in peace and security with its neighbors. The delay in adopting a two-state solution does not contribute to building a prosperous and stable region. Regrettably, peace seems to be drawing away, while radicalism fills the gap and stifles the efforts of those who want peace and have worked for it for years. Fear, hatred, disparagement, and exclusion are gaining ground, while tolerance, coexistence, and peace, increasingly considered part of a utopian project, are ruled out.

New ideological issues

New ideological goals find their way into the current geopolitical context of the EM. Behind the political and military confrontations in the region hide different visions and perceptions of the future. Simplification would lead us toward the theory of the "Clash of Civilizations" put forward by American sociologist Samuel Huntington. Without approving of his reasoning, and even decrying it, we must inevitably admit that we are now facing a new reality that was not there 40, 30, or even 10 years back. The US military intervention in Iraq opened Pandora's box and brought out all the myths and frustrations of the Muslim world, which has been subjected to double standards. All these found expression in Islamic radicalism, now increasingly present throughout the region. We are witnessing ideological struggles more exacerbated than ever before: Shiites against Sunnis, Muslims against Christians, and so on. We are now seeing the use of religion as a means of seizing political power. We are, regrettably, witnessing manipulation. The absence of a vision that would help avoid these cultural and religious conflicts is totally absent. The "Alliance of Civilizations" attempted to reverse the downward spiral but, regrettably, lacks the required political momentum and determination to reverse the situation and bring normality back.

The false dialectic of "Islam vs. the West" has made inroads, extending to Afghanistan, Iraq, Iran, the Middle East, the Sahel, and Central Africa as jihadist fighters multiply. The EM is at the core of these developments and at the vanguard of Western interests. This new geopolitical reality is expected to take center stage over old East–West theories, bringing to the EM new geostrategic responsibilities.

New economic challenges

The EM has never had any particular economic appeal. The region has always served mostly as a transit point and passage to other more economically attractive destinations, such as the Silk Road, the East Indies, the Suez Canal, and so on. Adventurers and traders had to take the EM sea route to gain access to their "Eldorado." The big economic bounty was not in the EM but farther away, in regions such as the Gulf, Asia, and the Pacific. Moreover, the economies of the Mediterranean sub-region had always been directed toward meeting their own national needs, without reaching large production capacities. Agriculture and modest mineral resources were the standard economic outputs of the region. The recent discovery of energy reserves, considered by some experts as among the largest in the world, may well change radically the situation and the geostrategic interests of the EM.

The "Oil for Security" agreement signed at the time between the Al-Saud family and the US is still in place. This reality might change, however, on account of the new production capacities that shale gas through fracking provides the US, and of the potential for oil and gas exploitation that the EM offers. Israel, Lebanon, Egypt, Turkey, and Cyprus are all claiming their legitimate interest over these resources and demand control over their exploitation. International law must prevail under any conditions and the sovereignty over resources that is guaranteed by the law of the sea must be scrupulously observed. These new-found resources provide the region with a golden opportunity to reach a historic agreement that could change for the better the geopolitics of the whole area. For once, oil and gas could serve as a catalyst for uniting people and solving disputes rather than for creating confrontation and conflict, as has been very often the case in the past.

It would be sensible for the countries in the EM to create a High Energy Authority (HEA), putting mutual suspicions to one side. This could be modeled after the High Authority that was created in 1951 for coal and steel, which allowed the production and exploitation of these two resources by Germany and France. This helped avoid a new war between these two countries and in the process created the beginnings of the European Union. In my opinion, Cyprus could play the leading role in this initiative by putting forward to its neighbors and partners a solemn statement supporting the creation of this historic enterprise.

New geostrategic interests

Each country of the EM would need to examine and clearly identify the new geostrategic issues that are at stake. They need to come face to face with the new realities and challenges they are now facing. The East–West axis is no longer the main challenge. The outcome of Russian–American relations will not affect these countries as much as it did in the past. Countries in the region need to start acting in full independence, assessing their geostrategic potential on merit, and stop acting as superpower subcontractors. Only through the formulation of sovereign and independent policies will they be able to determine their future actions.

It is clear that events in the Middle East and the evolution of the Arab world will be paramount to the agenda of the countries in the EM. Neighboring countries could be called on to allow quick access and provide support during emergencies and political or humanitarian crises, or to act as logistics platforms for the management of these crises. Countries in the region would need to change their foreign affairs policies, adopting a more independent posture when managing their oil and gas resources. The EM ideally integrates the multiple and heterogeneous qualities of the whole Mediterranean. The region includes in its ranks countries that are members of the EU and others that are candidates for EU membership, such as the Balkan states and Turkey. Turkey represents, in many ways, the diversity of the region in that it has a Muslim population but also wishes to agree to and implement the Copenhagen criteria. This could open the door to EU membership. The region also includes Arab countries and Israel, which sooner or later will have to take a stand on their mutual coexistence.

The time has come for all the countries in the region to take responsibility for developments and act accordingly. To date, the major Mediterranean initiatives that have seen the light concerned the Western Mediterranean countries. France, Spain, and Italy have launched their own initiatives. No major Mediterranean initiative has come out of the Turkish or Greek foreign affairs ministries. Only Egypt has made an attempt to counteract the proposals from Western Mediterranean countries (the 5+5 Dialogue) through the creation of the Mediterranean Forum in Alexandria. Maybe now is the time for one of the countries of the EM, such as Cyprus, Greece, or Turkey, to attempt a new initiative.

Europe is the solution

History teaches us that the golden age of the EM came when the region showed a willingness and capacity to decide for itself. Today some of the states in this sub-region are members of the EU. The EU has been quite active concerning economic and social development, but, it must be said, has done little in the direction of solving disputes. All the major problems that have conditioned the development of the area, such as the Turkey–Cyprus and Israel–Palestine conflicts, have been left to the responsibility of the great powers and especially the US. Recent events and developments have highlighted the limitations of the superpowers in solving the region's problems; a new strategy is therefore necessary. A fresh approach needs to be developed and implemented and the new political personalities in Europe must also understand the latest dimensions of the EM. However, priority must first be given to solving the two major ongoing conflicts.

The unification of Cyprus must clearly be a European affair and should not be managed and manipulated by former colonial powers or their successors. One fails to understand why Britain should maintain military bases in Cyprus and thus occupy a substantial proportion of the country's territory. Equally, one fails to understand why it should be impossible to establish a collective security system that surpasses the constraints of NATO and implements a new and more efficient European defense and security policy that can ensure peace and stability throughout the region.

Achieving lasting peace in the Middle East is absolutely critical. This is an urgent issue that needs to be addressed immediately. The recognition of the two states of Palestine and Israel and the establishment of a regional economic integration process on the model of the EU should be feasible. On the initiative of the Mediterranean countries, Europe can help in the creation of a major space of peace, stability, and regional cooperation in the form of the Helsinki accords signed in 1975. An initiative would need to be started that would establish a security and cooperation organization in the region, which would include Israel, Iran, and all Arab and European countries, as well as the US, Russia, China, and Japan.

These ideas could help the Mediterranean region take back its leading role in defining its future. In this regard, the EU must take the role of coach and guide of this new endeavor. What is now needed is the will of one or several of the countries in the region to embark on this voyage. I do not think that the Phoenicians, the Cretans, and the Byzantines had it any easier. I encourage the people of the EM to row hard toward a new horizon of peace and prosperity. It can be done.

Notes

1. Signed on June 28, 1919 between Germany and the Allies in the aftermath of World War I. It announced the creation of a League of Nations.
2. Signed on July 24, 1923, it was the last treaty resulting from World War I.

References

Abulafia, David. 2012. The Great Sea: A Human History of the Mediterranean. London: Penguin.
Drevet, Jean-François. 2000. Chypre en Europe. Paris: L'Harmattan.

Hassani-Idrissi, Mostafa (Ed.). 2013. Méditerranée: Une histoire à partager. Marseille-Provence: Bayard éditions.

Macmillan, Margaret. 2001. Peacemakers: The Paris Peace Conference of 1919 and Its Attempt to End War. London: John Murray.

Moratinos, Miguel Ángel. 2013. "Défendre Chypre." miguelangelmoratinos.com, 31 March. http://www.miguelangelmoratinos.com/index.php/fr/politique/europe/item/227-defendre-chypre. Accessed March 2013.

O'Malley, Brendan, and Ian Craig. 2001. The Cyprus Conspiracy: America, Espionage and the Turkish Invasion. London: I. B.Tauris.

CHAPTER EIGHT

FUNDAMENTALS OF A HOLISTIC
APPROACH TO CRITICAL SITUATIONS

ARIS PETASIS AND THEODOROS KYPRIANOU

The Eastern Mediterranean (EM) is facing problems because the countries in the area have generally decided to go for "national interest alone" rather than for "national interest through regional interest." In the last 100 years the region has seen more than its fair share of wars between neighbors, with two major conflicts still outstanding (the Palestinian and Cyprus problems), making the region less than peaceful. One of the region's powers (Israel) is in open conflict with two of its neighbors. The other powerful country in the region (Turkey) is occupying the territory of one of its neighbors (Cyprus), threatens with impunity another neighbor (Greece), and at the time of writing was engaged in bombing two further neighbors. The two most powerful countries in the EM (Turkey and Israel) are also at odds. This does not auger well for the region and its future. "Might is right" is clearly not the way forward.

In the absence of close cooperation, these countries are failing to reach their economic potential because they fail to understand their inter-relatedness and the power of unity. Inter-relatedness and working in unison have been strong drivers behind the creation of the global economy and other large economic blocs such as the European Union (EU). Economics can bring countries together and can also cause them to quarrel – particularly when some countries try to grab their neighbour's share. Strong regional powers typically fall into the trap of trying to frustrate the ambitions of their weaker neighbors, in this way pushing them into forming alliances with others for their own protection. This finally creates a vicious circle, which more often than not ends up in one or more superpowers exploiting everyone in the region.

The authors of this chapter believe that the interests of the countries of the EM are closely inter-related and that the region has more to gain from all countries working in unison rather than striving to protect their individual "national interests" no matter what. The true national interest is sometimes best served by yielding it to the overall regional interest, which in the end can multiply every country's national interest. Internalizing the fact that the countries in the EM are inter-related is a good starting point. This internalization then needs to translate into the belief that regional cooperation can ultimately lead countries to enter into a closer relationship that can get the region to work together as a meaningful whole. Once this is achieved, the likelihood of conflict between neighbors reduces and the economic outlook of the region improves markedly. The discovery of energy and more specifically gas has the potential to create a unified whole of countries in the region that would work together harmoniously in areas such as energy exploration, exploitation, transportation, research and development, and so on. Peaceful and wise exploitation of these energy resources could have a healing effect on some of the bad experiences of the past. Equally, it could bring great wealth and a bright future to the region.

In this chapter we bring to bear our background and work in medicine, business, the economy, strategy, and governance to try to explain what lies behind wholes and holistic approaches to issues. Employing an inter-disciplinary approach, we try to define the characteristics of wholes, their susceptibilities, the attacks that they are liable to suffer, and the interventions that need to be brought to bear to heal systems in trouble. As stated, the EM is an ailing region and as such cannot reach its potential or even attain acceptable levels of output. Its condition needs to be improved through appropriate interventions that have to be holistic in nature and take into account all the varied parameters and interests that have impacts on the functionality of this particular whole. A major, therapeutic intervention to restore the EM to health would be the creation of a High Energy Authority (HEA) for the joint and peaceful exploitation of the energy resources of the region. For this to happen, however, a host of other smaller, though important, interventions need to take place, the prime among which is acceptance of the rule of law, which would ultimately lead to a fair solution of the region's two overwhelming issues (the Palestinian and Cyprus problems). This would help restore the trust among nations that is so necessary to unity. Although the creation of trust is an intervention in its own right, it could also be a by-product of the therapeutic intervention of solving these situations fairly. To benefit most from reading this chapter, we recommend that readers continuously make mental reference to the EM region during the analysis of wholes, holistic approaches, system characteristics, therapeutic interventions, management of economies and organizations, ethics and ethical behavior, greed, and the self-interest that afflicts almost every country in the world. For the purposes of this chapter, we view the EM region as the set (the whole) and the countries of the region as sub-sets (the parts).

We address the term "system" from two different vantage points:

- From the economic/business theory point of view, which defines a system as: "An organized, purposeful structure that consists of interrelated and interdependent elements (components, entities, factors, members, parts etc.). These elements continually influence one another (directly or indirectly) to maintain their activity and the existence of the system, in order to achieve the goal of the system" (Business Dictionary 2015).
- From the physiological point of view, which defines the system as a social structure that exhibits properties and characteristics of living organisms existing in a certain milieu, trying to survive by resisting entropic forces and external threats.

In this respect, we focus on the fundamental principles that ought to be followed and the methodologies that ought to be applied to enable the system to manage malfunctions and threats effectively. In this context, the goal of the system encompasses the welfare of country, citizens, and the person. We should not forget that after all, economic and business activity is expected to serve all of the above publics if it is to have long-term legitimacy. We aim to extend the goal of the system to include the welfare of all EM countries and their citizens. The region is facing turmoil and a host of other problems that cause each country to perform well below potential. The region is critically ill when one considers the great animosity that exists between countries and the resultant negative impact on economic cooperation. Conflicts and malfunctions can best be rectified if countries are convinced to work together as a meaningful whole rather than as competing, and often conflicting, parts. We work on the premise that the benefits that the whole (the region) will generate for its parts (the countries) will be far greater than the benefits that each part can generate for itself working alone.

We try to explain the importance of holistic management under the following headings:

- Lessons from the health sciences
- Lessons from history
- Open vs. closed and simple vs. complex systems
- System entropy and dynamic homeostasis

- People and systems
- Holistic view of the Eastern Mediterranean as a complex system
- System characteristics and the need for balance
- Pitfalls and system dysfunctions
- Time for a new "therapeutic" paradigm?
- Conclusion with reference to the High Energy Authority

Lessons from the health sciences

Hippocrates was among the first to recognize the complexity of the human body and to stress the inter-connectivity between each and every part (organ/body system, "the four humors" in Hippocrates' theory) of this complex super-system. Much water has flowed under the bridge since then and an immense amount of helpful work has been generated. The impact of failure of one or more parts of the body (from cellular to organ level) on the proper functioning of a person and their health has been studied and documented in depth in medicine and sociology as well. Importantly, the often neglected inter-relationship between physical, emotional, and psychic/spiritual health is now a favorite subject of investigation in psychology (experimental psychology in particular) and religion.

Factors in the environment such as the social and financial standing of the individual, social instability, and the social turmoil one experiences have also been identified as having an impact on human health. These factors were neglected in the past because of the belief that they were unconnected to medicine. Conventional wisdom now supports the notion that we cannot understand health simply by looking at blood markers and images of the body; we also need to look at human behavior benchmarks and perceived life satisfaction. It is now common knowledge that human behavior (particularly that connected to the "evil twins" of greed and fear) influences human micro- and macro- environments, which in turn have an impact on human health.

Critical illness (system disorganization) is perceived as a health status where one (or more) organic system(s)/organ(s)/physiological mechanism(s) is so disordered that it ceases to perform adequately to maintain vital body functions (consciousness, airway patency, breathing, and circulation), to the extent of imminent death. Critical illness can result from either external insults or internal pathological processes with or without an underlying chronic illness (acute or chronic illness exacerbation). In a pathophysiological context, external insults can be classified broadly as:

- Acutely or chronically acting poisons and traumas

- Infections (endemic or transferred through the process of globalization; more or less contagious)
- Acute or chronic unsustainable deviations from "normality" in one or more environmental system(s), e.g., serious temperature dis-regulation
- Lack of essential food and water supplies (hunger and thirst)

Similarly, internal chronic diseases can be classified as:

- Immunity and cancer (parts of the system attack and in this way tend to destroy the system itself)
- Degeneration and senescence (prevalence of entropic forces)

Before such insults/processes can cause maximum damage, they need to be powerful enough to overcome the existing "defense" mechanisms (usually multifaceted and multilevel) and/or saturate the existing balancing (bio-feedback)/buffer systems (usually overlapping and cross-reacting).

In this chapter we examine critical illness as a pathophysiological model of system disorganization that has remarkable similarities to failing and poisoned relationships, either between ethnic/religious groups within countries or between neighboring countries. Every system failure requires wise and skillful management of threatening situations that endanger personal welfare, lives, societies, countries, and so on. Evidence-based (Sackett 1996), abstract descriptions (concepts/dictums/axioms of critical illness pathophysiology) are included where necessary.

The gist of the matter is that the medical and scientific community now realizes that unless the (critically) ill patient is viewed as a whole (considering the inter-relationships between body organs/systems), the patient cannot be adequately studied, protected, and restored to health. It is a matter of going beyond blood and tissue indices. It is our deep belief that this approach applies, possibly with a few adaptations, to practically all dysfunctions that afflict human organizations (social, economic, political, military/defense, and so on).

Holistic approaches demand serious questioning regarding the nature of the problem or derangement/disease, the particularities of the environment (social, cultural), the treatment plan, and the timeframe of therapeutic effects. Equally, holistic approaches measure the effectiveness of the therapy against the acuity and virulence of the illness and the severity of the complications manifested in the recovery process. A methodologically sound analysis and practice enhance our ability to plan and carry out successful interventions that aim to restore a threatened or grossly imbalanced system. Most of the chapters in this book aim to analyze one or more aspects of the EM situation in an effort first to identify the severity of the illness and then to offer suggestions regarding possible interventions. The suggestion of creating an HEA is one way of rectifying the many ailments of the region and constitutes the apex of interventions to attempt to bring the region back to normality, stability, and efficiency.

Lessons from history

Alexander the Great was one of the first to recognize the complexity and inter-relatedness of military, economic, and political systems. He was quick to identify the interplay between internal and external forces that threatened to disturb the balance and vitality of his kingdom. Although he himself did not build the core/basic military and political system of the Greeks, it was Alexander who fashioned what he found from his father Philip and the great military strategist Parmenion into a formidable structure that would outlive him for centuries, leaving a strong legacy to this day. In their drive for great achievements, the Macedonians realized quickly that unless alliances were put in place, little could be achieved. Philip, and later Alexander, worked tirelessly to get all Greek city-states on board. Both knew that without a broader alliance of fellow Greeks, there was little that could be achieved. Alexander used all sorts of means (including coercion) to get everyone to agree to his broader plan. The Spartans refused to join in, but he ignored them in his attempt to create a "Greek High Authority" (as explained later) that would fight together and share the benefits of the spread of Hellenism to the East. It was simple: the Greeks had to work together as a well-oiled machine. Hellenization was all about synergy and common cause. Alexander and most of his companions were educated by the great Greek philosopher from Stagira, Aristotle, in the great school at Mieza (near the modern Greek city of Naousa). There they learned all about inter-relationships and inter-dependencies, parts and wholes, systems and sub-systems, philosophy and mathematics, and how all these were woven into a meaningful whole. There they learned that things do not stand alone and that inter-dependence is a rule of life.

By understanding the broader properties of systems, Alexander managed to build the world's most integrated and formidable force of his time. This organization was destined to liberate fellow Greeks of the East from tyranny and to pass on Hellenistic thought to countless countries, stretching as far as Bactria (in modern Punjab, India). The Greco-Bactrian Empire (set up mostly by Athenians) lasted for about 200 years after

Alexander's death. Alexander's system of nations and peoples was sturdy and generally peaceful. His understanding of systems, organizational working patterns, the inter-relatedness of parts, and alliances went beyond common comprehension. The fact that he recruited Callisthenes (Aristotle's nephew) to record history and to study and categorize the flora of the nations that were to fall under the Greeks speaks volumes about Alexander's understanding of what is now known as the "holistic" approach to a task.

The great king of Macedon understood full well the human side of the military. He built a political machine by bonding everyone together through camaraderie in the armed forces. He extended the hand of friendship to the peoples who came under his empire and refused to view the vanquished as conquered people; rather, they were new co-patriots. Through his masterful management of the Hellenistic organization, he succeeded in ruling without a single revolution from the non-Greeks whom Alexander integrated into the Greek military, economic, and political structures in the areas under his command. He understood clearly and at an early stage the enormous importance of a unifying language, without diminishing other languages, and quickly introduced the *koine* (Hellenistic Greek) for easier understanding and communication, as many people found the rigors of ancient Greek too much to handle. Little did Alexander know at the time that the New Testament would be written in Greek and that the great books of Orthodoxy and the eastern Roman Empire would be written in the language that he helped fashion. In an effort to unify the then known world, he did unimaginable things that ultimately led to great synergies.

Alexander's concern went beyond the army, the companions, the cavalry, the archers, and the navy. He wished to set up a system that would go beyond just the military and that would blend together successfully a multitude of properties and functions: military strategy, psychology, religion, spirituality, the sciences, culture, language, geopolitics, and so on. His understanding of system complexities was incredible. Alexander was a genius par excellence. His gifted personality, courage, and nimble brain enabled him to build a system that was to last and that would act as a model to this day for business, politics, linguistics, strategy, and leadership (Arrian 2003).

Partha Bose (2003, 1) presents Alexander as "[a]rguably the greatest military strategist, tactician, and ruler in history, Alexander's achievements have influenced many military, political and business leaders." Bose goes on to say that Alexander's system of governance influenced Roman leaders and emperors (Pompeii, Julius Caesar), Carthaginians, Indians, the

Medici of Italy, the Habsburgs of Austria, and a pleiad of leaders in world history. Alexander had a mission to build a truly magnificent system that would help him achieve unity among people of differing backgrounds and to fulfill his dream of Hellenization, passing on to others the Greek culture, ideas, and traditions. With a sense of history he carried with him a copy of Homer's *Iliad* (to Alexander Achilles was a direct ancestor).

Alexander has been an influence in one form or another for nearly 2,500 years and will probably continue to be so for thousands of years to come. Just like his father, his vista transcended Macedonia, Thrace, Epirus (his mother's birthplace), and the rest of the lands of the Greeks. He had a truly global understanding at a time when most people of his generation had a parochial mindset. He could see the then known world as a unified whole and himself and the Greeks as the champions of unity for nations that were to come under Hellenistic influence. He had the capacity to harness the strengths of diversified peoples for the broader good. He saw countries and people as parts of a wider and more advanced global system. He viewed the resources of countries under his influence as tangible and the varying religions, customs, beliefs, and philosophies as soft intangibles that had to be managed creatively. One must not forget that before Alexander's time the Persians had attacked the Greeks repeatedly, including the three calamitous (for the Persians) showdowns at Marathon, Salamis, and Plataea; while Leonidas designed Thermopile to be a demonstration of the indomitable Greek spirit. In his drive to forge alliances with the mighty Persians, whose empire at the time went back 200 years, Alexander was willing to forgive and forget. He concentrated on managing all countries, regions, and resources. In pursuit of his objective, he did not shy away from foreigners (non-Greeks) or people who were alien to the Greek culture. As such, he encouraged his officers to inter-marry and in fact promoted non-Greeks to officer rank (much to the consternation of some of the Greek officers). He himself was married to the non-Greek Roxana (of Tajik/Uzbek/Persian origin), who gave birth to their son Alexander IV. As Macedonian and Persian custom allowed multiple wives, Alexander also married Stateira, the eldest daughter of the Persian king Darius, and Parysatis, younger daughter of Artaxerxes III. His great general and friend Hephaestion married another of Darius's daughters, Drypetis. Alexander hoped to see the unifying effect that any future children of this mixed marriage would bring to Greeks and Persians and others in the region. As it turned out, Alexander had two confirmed children: Herakles with his mistress Barsine, widow of general Memnon, a Greek general in the service of Persia, and Alexander IV with his wife Roxane.

Open vs. closed and simple vs. complex systems

Open vs. closed systems

In thermodynamics, isolated systems cannot exchange energy or matter with their environment. Closed systems are able to exchange with their environment energy (heat and work) but not matter. An open system allows the transfer of energy as well as matter between it and its surroundings (ChemWiki 2015). Analogously a human being (or organization/society) exhibits a set of functions that allow it to receive input internally as well as from the external environment. This input is in turn processed to produce an output (i.e., an action/status change), which conversely influences the internal/external environment (Daft 2001). Closed-system models tend to focus on internal events when explaining a system's actions and behavior, while open-system models focus on events that occur externally (as well as internally) and influence change within the system. In fact, the human body and psyche are by definition an open system exchanging energy and matter with the environment. Students are dismayed when they first hear that we humans are in fact completely "recycled" in every aspect of our being!

In the course of a critical illness, an organism/organization fails to respond adequately to an unusually abrupt change in the settings of the internal and/or external environment; the organism's buffering systems become overwhelmed by the force and magnitude of the change, frequently undermined by pre-existing, internal (usually) chronic dysfunctions. Typically, the restoration of the *internal* equilibrium of an ill system to a different but viable and stable state (but not necessarily back to "normal") is absolutely necessary if the system is ultimately to be able to interact successfully and beneficially with the external environment.

Modern-world economic systems that are no more "isolated" or "closed" than those in the example from medicine could benefit substantially from the insights that human physiology and pathophysiology provide us, because through these insights we can better understand the dynamics and ailments of economic systems (or other societal structures, for that matter). Countries that are "isolated" or "closed" ultimately degenerate and become ineffective and/or are dangerous to their neighbors; they invariably face problems with their neighbors because interaction and cooperation are not fundamental traits of closed systems/countries. Conversely, countries that meet the requirements of openness interact with other countries and particularly with their neighbors. They communicate and share information; they deal with problems proactively or as they arise, providing continuous feedback to one another.

Defining the boundaries of an open economic system

Open economic systems communicate with practically the whole world and as such their boundaries are difficult to define. Within an open system, all countries have the opportunity to create and share innovative ideas with others in their surroundings. Ideas go both ways and to the advantage of everyone who wishes to glean what is good from a concept. Within a truly open system, technology eliminates boundaries and provides every country with the opportunity to set up economic and other relationships with countries far and near. As such, economies can benefit from the boundless good of inter-relationships and exchanges with other economies. Countries define their operating boundaries analogously with how open they wish to be. At the two extremes, their boundaries could be limited to their own geographic boundaries (closed system) or the world (fully open system). No one could have imagined 20 years back that imported fruit and vegetables from countries with just a few weeks of sunshine a year such as the Netherlands would be inundating with their produce traditional agricultural countries that enjoy almost year-round sunshine. The EU and the openness among member countries that this union has brought about made this possible, in this example, for the Netherlands to expand its boundaries.

Simple vs. complex systems

Not all systems have the same complexity and not all systems that are complex necessarily have a large number of component parts. Most complex systems have the capacity to adapt, learn, and rejuvenate. Adaptive systems are capable of receiving feedback, evaluation, and acting on information that can help the system adapt and survive. Organizations are typically adaptive in nature, although not all manage to adapt correctly or in a timely fashion.

On the one end of the spectrum are very complex, adaptive, and intricate systems and on the other are simple and uncomplicated systems that have the capacity to adapt as well. The human body is naturally an open, very complex, and adaptive system, but can this be said of an economy or a business enterprise or a country or a set of countries in the EM, for example? The economies of the United States (US), China, and Germany are large and complex, while those of small and tiny countries and islands are typically small and simple. On the one side of the complexity spectrum are economies that encompass military industrial complexes, complex services, technology, health industries, and practically every imaginable business activity, and on the other side are unsophisticated economies that rely on a few business activities.

System failure can hit small and large, complex and simple structures, old and young enterprises, big and small countries, sophisticated and simple economies, and so on. Behind most of these failures typically lie inherent system weaknesses, speculation, and bad management. Debilitating recessions are typically preceded by real estate and stock exchange bubbles and weak financial institutions. The collapse of Lehman Brothers in 2008 lit the fuse that brought the global financial crisis to a crescendo and led to a loss of confidence and trust in many financial institutions. This started a chain reaction on housing loans (confirming Marx's dictum that housing and land are likely to bring the capitalist system down), non-performing loans, and so on. Bad management is almost always the product of incompetence, greed, fear, individualism, and human frailty.

System entropy and dynamic homeostasis

As already seen through examples from physiology, history, strategy, and the economy, human systems tend to die as internal equilibria tend toward imbalance and eventually to non-reversible, non-sustainable deviations from normality. In the case of the human body, death constitutes an inevitable yet hardly acceptable reality, despite the great achievements of medicine. In the case of economic systems, death may be postponed for a while if the system rejuvenates and reinvents itself by adapting to the new demands of the publics it serves and the new challenges of the environment. However, rejuvenation and reinvention require wise and visionary leadership, which is not always available. The reality is that in the end all systems are doomed to die, with new ones ready to take their place.

Entropy

Entropy brings disorder and randomness (typical characteristics of closed systems, even if open systems run a similar danger). Entropy renders a system inefficient and continued entropy incapacitates or even kills the system. In this section we discuss how human nature along with micro/macro-environmental changes can create the circumstances for critical illness to afflict a system. Equally, we consider how dynamic homeostasis mechanisms could be reinforced to alleviate "poisonous" effects and unnecessary human suffering.

Systems employ feedback as a control and improvement mechanism. Feedback improves the stability of the system and creates the preconditions for self-improvement. Feedback mechanisms influence the system and protect it from failure and disaster. They help to sustain equilibrium through self-regulation. Homeostatic mechanisms recognize the value of the self-regulation process and employ this to good effect. Homeostatic control mechanisms typically provide negative feedback to help bring the system back to its preferred state by controlling variables that go out of line. The thermostat, for instance, tells the air-conditioning unit that the required/ideal temperature has been exceeded and asks it to turn itself down. In this case the output (temperature) of a sensor affects the regulatory center (air-conditioning unit) and instructs it to reduce activity so as to return to equilibrium. Positive feedback mechanisms work in reverse to negative systems because system output enhances the activity of the stimulus rather than toning it down; for example, increased sweating triggers the body's cooling mechanisms to provide equilibrium.

Dynamic homeostasis

Dynamic homeostasis is perhaps the most potent characteristic of effective systems, as it allows the necessary change to happen while the system continues to maintain its stability. Dynamic homeostasis is analogous to an airplane moving at great speed without the passengers noticing its continuous shift of position. In fact, passengers get to feel that the airplane in flight is in a static position. Keeping a system in equilibrium while changing and rejuvenating it is not an easy task, particularly as regards complex systems. Change typically entails turbulence. Russia provides a good example of how equilibrium can be lost in the midst of change. Perestroika brought with it tumultuous changes to a system that had been relatively stable for about 70 years. With the break-up of the Soviet Union the Russian economy went into a spin and chaos erupted, accompanied by all the horrors of economic malaise. It took decades before the Russian economy and its military defense structures could reach a state of equilibrium. China avoided Russia's fate because economic change was gradual and controlled. According to Mao Zedong, the cycle of change is endless and takes the country from equilibrium to disequilibrium and back to equilibrium, with each cycle moving the country to a higher level of socioeconomic development.

People and systems

People are an integral part of economic and business systems. Get the people side wrong and you end up with a malfunctioning social system. Here again, the way the people factor operates varies from country to country, company to company, and culture to culture, rendering solutions and "treatments" highly individualized. In 1981, Ouchi put forward the idea that the secret to Japanese success lay in the way the people factor was handled. He considered that with limited natural resources, Japan owed its success to its people management more than to its technology. He noted, "This is a managing style that focuses on a strong company philosophy, a distinct corporate culture, long-range staff development, and consensus decision-making." He stressed that commitment to the human factor ultimately leads to increased job commitment, lower turnover, and, most importantly, higher productivity. Broad participation in most stages of the decision-making process is central to the Japanese system. Communication and exchange of information (at a level probably unknown to most companies outside Japan) are essential to the management function. The Japanese system takes it for granted that people should be respected and their contribution acknowledged. Ideas should not be sourced from management alone; the ideal system needs to encourage wider employee involvement and contribution. It depends on well-trained and competent employees who are capable of participating meaningfully in the management of company affairs.

Ouchi coined the term "Theory Z" to express the system under which the Japanese work. Theory Z places the emphasis on knowledge, training, and organizational practices that render the employee valuable to many departments and functions rather than a few. Job stability and tenure are also central to this approach. Organizations are expected to provide employees with job security and in turn employees are expected to give their loyalty and commitment to the company. It is assumed that stability of tenure, experience of the full range of business activities, and knowledge of the organization prepare employees well for higher managerial roles. In contrast to some of the systems that one finds in Western countries, where emphasis on specialization typically takes precedence over more general skills and where a reasonable percentage of labor turnover is desired, the Japanese system favors a more people-centered approach and respect for age.

Holistic view of the economy as a complex system

The economy as an integrated system/whole attracted the attention of thinkers from antiquity, although the systematic and "scientific" study of the economy as a unified whole is thought to have started only some 500 years ago. As a subject of study, holism (from the Greek word *holos/ὅλος*), or the idea that the whole is made up of component parts that need to work in unison if they are to be efficient and avoid ruin, gained prominence relatively recently (although holism was well known in Ancient Greek times). The *Oxford English Dictionary* defines holism as:

> The theory that parts of a whole are in intimate interconnection, such that they cannot exist independently of the whole, or cannot be understood without reference to the whole, which is thus regarded as greater than the sum of its parts ... the opposite of atomism.

Within a medical context, it defines holism as: "The treating of the whole person, taking into account mental and social factors, rather than just the symptoms of a disease." Parts influence each other within the context of an integrated whole. As such, the value of each component part when working inside the system is much greater than the cumulative value of each part when outside the system. In fact, specialized/dedicated parts in particular have little or no value outside the system.

The Cartesian way of understanding systems has been to break the whole down to its component parts and to study each part rationally and independently. Within this context, the system/whole needs to be studied through its individual component parts and not through its unified properties. Although in certain cases this approach might work well, it is difficult to see how it can work in the social sciences, considering that humans are unpredictable and in some respects irrational. Decomposing the system into its component parts to help gain an understanding of the properties of each part and then putting them back into a whole clearly does not guarantee total understanding of the system and its workings.

For better results, the whole needs to be viewed as the master that unifies its component parts rationally and efficiently. Clearly, the whole cannot be understood adequately through the properties of its component parts. The function of the heart cannot be understood in isolation from the body. The heart's function gains meaning when seen as a working part of the human body and as a contributor to the workings of the other parts of the body, which in the end keep the body functioning and healthy. Reductionism, the processes of decomposing the whole into parts, cannot explain the whole.

By accepting that prices rise as demand increases and supply remains constant, we cannot fully understand how the economic system functions. Supply and demand do not operate in a vacuum and outside the broader economic framework. To understand the economy we need to go beyond supply and demand. We need to understand concepts such as inflation, fiscal and monetary policies, price elasticity, factors of production, government policies, consumer behavior, unemployment, economic growth, social welfare, savings, and a host of other factors. We need to understand the parts as well as the unified whole. Touch one part of the economic system and you trigger a process, sometimes with unwanted consequences because of the factor of inter-relatedness.

Similarly, we cannot understand how a business enterprise works by simply understanding piecemeal how marketing and pricing work. To understand the business organization we need to understand, among other things, how the following work within the context of the organization: employees, finance and accounting systems, storage and purchasing, logistics, raw materials, human behavior, consumer habits, marketing and sales, management systems, technology, equipment, and productivity, which together with a host of other parts make up the corporate milieu. One also has to understand how corporate and economic systems are created in the first place and how disease can set in over time. Equally, we need to understand how systems can be restored to health through the application of thoughtful, evidence-based, and individualized (personalized) treatment plans.

The economy as a system

The ancient Greek philosopher, historian, and military strategist Xenophon is credited with making the first attempt at helping us understand how the economy works as a system. He concentrated on the workings of home economics in his seminal work *Oeconomicus*, which was probably written in the early 360s BCE. The *Online Etymology Dictionary* records that the Latin "oeconomia" comes from the Greek word "οικονομία" (οίκος = house/dwelling + νόμος = management). Much later, others attempted to explain more systematically and scientifically how the economic system works. Among the first to write about "scientific economy" was the French politician and minister of finance Jean-Baptiste Colbert (1619–83), who attempted to introduce order in the workings of the economy and government. He approached his subject through systematic study and analysis of the complexities of the economic system and the role of bureaucracy. Probably one of the most universally acknowledged economists and philosophers who tried to explain the workings of the economy and the inter-relationships that lie behind it was Adam Smith (1776). Smith wrote on nearly all issues surrounding the economic system, including, but not limited to, division of labor, wages and labor, pricing and commodities, interest rates and stock prices (including stock of money), accumulation of capital, and political economy.

Political economy as a system

Of the classical economists, the British David Ricardo (1772–1823) proved to be one of the most influential in explaining the "science" of economics and how complex functions come to form a viable economic system. He wrote in the early nineteenth century (see Ricardo 2004) and was evidently influenced by Adam Smith. Ricardo's contemporary, Jean-Baptiste Say (1767–1832), published his famous work in 1803, later published as *A Treatise on Political Economy* (Say 1971). Alexander Hamilton, the first secretary of the economy of the US, also attempted to explain the workings of the economic system and in so doing relied on the work of many of his predecessors (see Hamilton 2011). A little later, Max Weber (1826–1920) addressed the workings of bureaucratic systems (see Weber 2013). Weber, Karl Marx, and Emil Durkheim are considered by many commentators to be the architects of modern social science (and sociology) and among the first to have seen clearly the role of the economy within the overall social system.

Corporate management system

In the area of corporate management, Frederick Taylor (1855–1915) led the development of "scientific management." In his seminal work, *The Principles of Scientific Management* (see Taylor 1997), he attempted to use measurement and observation (both scientific processes) to define the best way of doing things so that the overall system can work efficiently and beneficially. Taylor saw clearly the inter-relationship between events and organizational functions. His work was so influential at the time that even Vladimir Lenin considered his ideas useful to building socialism. Taylor's near-contemporary, engineer Henri Fayol (1841–1925), was one of the first to put forward fundamental principles in the art of managing the corporate system (see Fayol 2013). He expounded on how best to organize a business entity if utilization of its resources is to be maximized (Cunningham and Wood 2002). Fayol concentrated mostly on the administrative (management) side of running an organization, while

Taylor centered his work on what came to be known as the science of management. Both attempts were focused on running the business enterprise system effectively. Fayol gave us his 14 functions of management – division of labor, discipline, unity of command, and so on – and helped us understand better the workings and functions of the corporate body.

Mary Parker Follet (1868–1933) and Lillian Gilbreth (1878–1972) are considered among the first to have contributed greatly to the study of management and particularly the social system of organizations. They stand alongside Taylor and Fayol as great contributors to our understanding of the corporate body (see Parker Follett 2013; Gilbreth 2010).

"Social ecologist" Peter F. Drucker (1909–2005) left a lasting legacy for business and is probably the most quoted management leader in the history of management (see Drucker 1999). He helped us understand the complex workings of the organization and the ramifications of good management on the corporate body and society. He is rightly hailed by many as the architect of modern management. While Taylor and Fayol helped enhance our understanding of organizational systems, through his 39 books, countless articles, and lectures Drucker helped push our comprehension of business systems to levels not seen or experienced before. He had a formidable ability to predict developments long before they materialized. One could go so far as to say that Drucker was the Aristotle of management thinkers. Terms such as information society, decentralization, privatization, the knowledge economy, innovation, and a host of other concepts are credited to him. Drucker (2006) predicted the coming of the services explosion and the need to train people in knowledge and skills that can be meaningfully applied. As a thinker, he explained masterfully the real world of management and gave substance to words and ideas that formerly were poorly understood. As such, he suffered the envy of many an academic who berated him (much to the amusement of people in the real world of business, who greatly respected him) as not adding enough academic rigor to his work. His critics went so far as to label him a communist because of his thoughtful positions that management ought to take account of the people factor in the decision-making process, and that organizations ought to balance profit with good citizenship if they are to have a future in the long term. Balance and equity formed the mainstay of Drucker's work: balance between short- and long-term needs, balance between profit and social responsibility, balance between business needs and people's expectations, balance between the individual and the group, and balance between freedom and responsibility.

All of the above pioneers viewed the world of business and economics as a system that needed to be managed properly. Sound decision making (the ability to evaluate today's events against future outcomes) lay at the heart of their work. They believed that every action we take, no matter how isolated and how confined to one's area or function, influences the system in its totality. These thinkers were among the first to appreciate the complexity and inter-relatedness of economic, business, and social systems and to make recommendations on how best to manage them. Nevertheless, most suffered the typical fate of pioneers: they were attacked for their "outlandish" views (for example, Adam Smith's work was criticized by none other than Ricardo). In the end, the work of these people left an indelible mark on the economic and enterprise management and gave us an indispensable frame (a systems approach) through which to view the workings of the economy.

System characteristics and the need for balance

Coordination and discordance

The brain coordinates organ systems through an extremely complex matrix of sensors and afferent/efferent mechanisms that guarantee effective coordination and maintain physiological functions in order. Likewise, coordination mechanisms are central to the viability and operation of economic systems that require a vast array of functions and sub-functions to work in unison. Differing ministries, often with competing objectives, need to be coordinated toward the overall objective. Multiple countries have to coordinate activities when engaging in joint projects or other activities that have an impact on the regional economic system. Unavoidably, coordination sometimes fails because of internal conflicts. Conflict arises because of power plays and the pull and push between centralization and autonomy, but equally because of the need for power that some people exhibit in abundance.

Synergy

Synergy is a central property of every effective physiological and economic complex system. The term comes from the Greek συνεργία, which derives from συνεργός, working together. With synergy 1+1 becomes >2 because the system outperforms the cumulative mathematical output of its parts. The benefit of synergy is often put forward as a reason for merging the activities of companies or even countries, for that matter. The European

Union (EU) was primarily created to stop conflict between countries and to create economic and other synergies (unified market, abolition of trade barriers and import/export taxes, free movement of capital, goods, and people, and so on). Synergies are ubiquitous features of well-functioning and efficient systems.

Synergy invariably creates new properties and new value structures and, most importantly, synergy tends to unify around common interests and benefits. People in the corporate world know full well the difficulties of creating an economic surplus unless there is joint and cohesive action. Products do not sell on their own, no matter how good they are. Customer needs have to be taken into account first; then the cost of the goods to be sold has to be competitive; and production, marketing, and selling capabilities need to be in place; but most importantly, all of the above have to work in unison before an economic surplus can be created. The health of an economy or enterprise cannot be predicted simply by looking at each economic function independently and without regard to the whole.

Optimality and sub-optimality

Despite the beauty and perfection of the human body, optimal physiological functioning is generally unattainable in real life because of the inherent frailties of the human body and the attacks it experiences. Nevertheless, just like all other systems the human body is designed to survive several concurrent deviations from normality and the sub-optimal performance of one or more of its sub-systems. It does this by recruiting its physiological reserves and (as already noted) by deploying buffer and compensatory systems. Likewise, economic and business systems (and most other complex systems) hardly ever work optimally (at 100 percent performance or at 100 percent of potential). Systems have inherent weaknesses that prevent them from reaching optimality. One major such weakness lies with the limitations of human cognition and emotions, perhaps even more so in situations that require decisions from elected representatives, some of whom are more concerned about being reelected than the merits of a particular case. In such situations, warped ambitions and dodgy moral values make optimization unachievable.

The limitations of the human brain and weaknesses in human behavior cause systems to fail repeatedly and almost predictably. At the extreme, serious external and internal threats, limitations, imbalances, and sub-optimal performance render the system non-viable. When, for example, one part of the community lives at the expense of another, inescapably the economic system fails under the weight of injustice. When governments tax excessively and illogically in order to maintain the high lifestyles of the ruling class and the bureaucrats who serve them, again the system suffers. It weakens when those who are supposed to pay their taxes fail to do so and in the process cause great hardship to others. Greed, bounded/limited rationality, and human emotions and passions render optimality a phantom-like and meaningless concept.

In 1956, Herbert Simon put forward the concept of satisficing, which is close to that of sub-optimality (March and Simon 1958). In effect, what this means is that economic and business systems can only generate acceptable, not optimal, outputs. Put simply, when the human brain evaluates alternative options, it ends up choosing the one that meets acceptable requirements rather than the one that maximizes. The preferred option cannot thus be optimal because of the nature and limitations of the decision-making process. Human thought processes are bounded/limited and cannot therefore meet full potential. Human beings operate and decide within the confines of "bounded rationality" (to use Simon's terminology), which makes optimal decisions impossible. Decision-making weaknesses are not only due to biological or cognitive limitations; emotional and spiritual dimensions also play a significant role. Human beings are emotional and are often guided by self-interest, self-aggrandizement, and limited spirituality, all of which prevent a decision from being optimal. Dishonesty in the workings of governments, bureaucracies, and private enterprise makes sound (let alone optimal) decision making difficult, if not impossible.

For instance, Cyprus ranks 31st on the World Transparency Index (Transparency International 2015), having slipped from 29th in the 2011 index. Other countries in the EM generally have a less enviable record; indeed, Cyprus ranked 16th among the EU countries that took part in the survey. Transparency International sites corrupt practices between political parties and businesses. It also mentions a lack of regulation designed to prevent corruption from happening, as well as weaknesses in the areas of follow-up, tracking, and penalization of corruption. Thus corruption interferes in the decision-making process as individual interests override other, more important matters.

Forecasting

The need to look into the future perhaps presents the biggest challenge and limitation to optimal decision making. Human beings simply do not have the capacity to see the future absolutely clearly and in all its dimensions; perfect forecasting of multiple factors and imponderables is humanly impossible. Decisions that are taken now are meant to work in the future and to yield results on the basis of what actually happens in the future, which is of course unknown. Yet business and political environments change fast and in certain sectors, such as technology, changes never take a break. What held yesterday does not necessarily hold today and probably will not hold tomorrow. Extrapolating from past data is no longer helpful in some industries at least, because the future is unlikely to look the same as before. While Wall Street forecast a shrinkage of 0.5 percent of the US economy for the first three months of 2014, the final shrinkage was double that (an annual rate of 1 percent). Strikingly, the projections were made only a few months before the actual figures were released.

Sometimes decisions fail because of the human inability to differentiate small from big, important from unimportant, and good from bad. Governments and businesses often take decisions that in the fullness of time prove to be hopeless and irrational. Take the decision of Cyprus to continue financing the government-owned Cyprus Airways, the former national airline, in the full knowledge that it was a white elephant in need of continuous subsidization (often outside EU rules). The need to close the company down was obvious even to the uninitiated. What transpired is perfect proof of decision making guided by vested interests and petty interferences in the proper and rational evaluation of options. As the first signs of trouble began to appear, some of those involved suggested that the company be sold. With political party interests in mind, one of the actors in the saga took the position that the company should not be sold because "it would end up in the hands of capitalists." With their comfort zone in mind, some pilots also opposed the sale with vehemence. They were worried that they would have to look for work abroad, just as many of their colleagues had done once they realized that the airline was not viable. Forgetting that the airline was in fact bankrupt, pilots facing redundancy put forward the curious position that "the government is trying to barter away state property for the benefit of private interests and party hacks." Most political parties in this chronicle prevaricated and hoped that the political cost of shutting a state company down would be borne by someone other than themselves. The taxpayer fell victim to propaganda and kept pouring money down a bottomless pit.

The limitations of human memory and, most critically, the difficulties in human conceptualization make optimality impossible to achieve. Suffice to say that some of the most horrendous decisions ever taken were by people who ostensibly had a high intelligence quotient and were thought to be rational. Referring to the Vietnam War in his memoirs, the former US defense secretary Robert McNamara noted, "we were wrong, terribly wrong. We owe it to future generations to explain why" (McNamara and VanDeMark 1995, 373). He goes on to lament the fact that in the decision-making process some of the best brains in the country failed to understand what ought to have been done and plunged the US into a terrible, humiliating, and debilitating war that cost hundreds of thousands of lives on both sides and devastated Vietnam.

Herbert Simon's bounded rationality and acceptable-goal attainment are proven almost daily by decisions on the economy and business, and particularly by those on public policy. Political correctness, the need of politicians to be reelected, and the desire for political gain often force politicians to take decisions that are grossly damaging. Economic decisions more often than not are contaminated by electoral politics, the desire for political gain, and the need to balance the varied competing requirements (often greed based) of the manifold publics that politicians serve. In 1963, Cyert and March talked about *aspiration levels* in the decision-making process (see Cyert and March 1992). They basically said that governments, institutions, and people have differing aspiration levels that effectively determine the level at which goals are achieved. High aspirations call for higher levels of goal achievement and low aspirations for lower. In both cases the system is programmed to stop once the aspired-to achievement levels are met; optimization takes second place and in fact ceases to exist. Apparently, we achieve at the level that meets our aspirations and not any higher.

Interaction

Interaction between parts is critical to systems and closely relates to (in fact it is a prerequisite for) coordination and synergy. Systems need to interact internally and with the outside environment if they are to remain healthy. Closed systems limit interactions internally and as such ultimately suffer from ever-increasing entropic forces. Their inability to communicate limits their propensity for change when this becomes necessary. Systems need to receive feedback to enable them take action in the right direction and at the opportune time. Starve the organization of information and you kill its power to change and adapt. Economies and businesses need innovation to survive. However, innovation requires information and ideation, which in turn presuppose interaction with the environment. Closed economic systems, which often strive to protect vested interests, sooner or later realize that remaining closed leads to the system's ultimate death. Exchange of information and adaptation need to be continuous to allow the system to rejuvenate and survive.

Stilted, inflexible, and unbending bureaucratic systems are programmed to fail in their mission. Interactions affect and are affected by the system and its component parts. For many years before its accession to the EU, sections of Cyprus's economy were closed to outside competition through protective tariffs and duties. This was done in the mistaken belief that tariffs would protect Cypriot industry. Unavoidably, it led to the withering away of the industrial base of Cyprus and to its ultimate near-demise. With the opening up of markets after accession to the EU, many of these protected organizations melted away as they were unable to compete. To (supposedly) protect the locally produced aluminum products, the government of the day slapped a crippling import duty on imported aluminum products. For example, one needed to pay two to three times the price of Italian-made aluminum products for much inferior Cyprus-made items. As expected, once import duties were abolished, the industry went into panic.

The same happened to, among others, the garment and shoe industries, where customers were forced through import duties to buy expensive and often shoddy products ostensibly to protect local industry. A characteristic example of this monopolization or oligopolization follows: with union support, a handful of hotel musicians managed to force on hotels the employment of local musicians only. This in turn forced hotels to hire Cypriot musicians from a very limited pool of often doubtful talent. The reader can imagine what happened as the many hotels in the country vied for the services of a handful of local musicians. With demand for musicians high, the market saw an influx of unqualified and amateur "musicians" offering a cacophony of services. As the hotels began to experience client complaints, the practice was abandoned; but not before it had caused much damage to the industry.

Disproportionality

Disproportionality (the expression of non-linear properties) is another cha-racteristic of complex systems. Change a part and you influence the system in a given way. Change another part and you get a different influence on the system. Repeat these two changes a year later and you end up with still different results. This phenomenon is paramount from the human pathophysiology point of view, considering that a therapeutic intervention or bundles of interventions can cause multiple effects (quantitatively and qualitatively) that may shift in time, rendering the intervention more or less ineffective or even detrimental to the patient, depending on the circumstances and the timeframe of its deployment

(Hussar 2013). An upgrade of 1 percent on the totality of factors in the system does not necessarily yield a 1 percent change in output. Upgrade the marketing budget by 1 percent and you may end up with a 4 percent increase in sales. Repeat the exercise some time later and you get some other result; maybe falling sales. Make the same change to the sales incentive budget and you get something else. Make a marginal change in job content (to make the role more interesting and emotionally rewarding to the employee) and you get a significant improvement in the morale, productivity, and profitability of the firm. Repeat the intervention a year later and you obtain something else.

Repeated attempts were made to introduce improved performance management systems in the Cypriot civil service. All attempts failed because:

- political patronage protected employees from the consequences of poor performance;
- line managers failed to engage themselves in an exercise that they considered dangerously near the boundaries of their comfort zone;
- high unionization provided ample protection to low-performing staff and discouraged the equitable treatment of high performers, who were browbeaten by the union into "not rocking the boat."

Similar changes in the performance management scheme were made in companies operating abroad, but owned by Cypriots and employing mostly Cypriots, with phenomenal results in terms of enhanced employee performance and company profitability. The same intervention in two different settings/organizations yielded two diverse results because of differences in culture and work ethic. In the first the work culture encouraged indifference, whereas in the other case the culture encouraged vibrancy, creativity, and healthy competition. In the first instance reward went to everyone equally (deservedly or not), whereas in the second reward was based on merit.

Changes in one or more parts of the system can conceivably lead to unintended consequences, with the real outcome being different to that expected. The Hawthorne experiments (Mayo 1949) are good proof of unintended consequences. Here the fact that attention was paid to staff, in the process of carrying out observations for research purposes, caused higher employee interest, which in turn led to an unintended improvement in short-term performance.

Deming (2000) saw training and innovation as necessary tools for meeting the ever-changing environment in which economies and businesses find themselves all the time:

> Long-term commitment to new learning and new philosophy is required of any management that seeks transformation. The timid and the fainthearted, and the people that expect quick results, are doomed to disappointment.

Deming gave the literature of business and economics helpful guidelines for instituting management transformation. These guidelines include consistent improvement of product and service quality; emphasis on sound leadership capable of dealing with change; emphasis on cost minimization; building long-term relationships with suppliers; improving quality and productivity; engaging in on-the-job training, education, and self-improvement; and getting everyone involved in the transformation process.

Economic benchmarks

In the world of economy and business, equilibrium is typically represented by what are commonly known as benchmarks or economic indicators. The markers of a stable economic system are many and varied. Unless these markers stay within prescribed ranges, the system becomes unstable. By analogy with physiology, benchmarking refers to the mechanisms that allow critical economic indicators to remain within delineated ranges. There are no universally accepted markers of "economic health," but from experience one could say that an economy is considered healthy if it registers, for example, growth rates of above 4 percent, keeps unemployment in the region of 3 percent and inflation in the region of 1–3 percent, a positive or near-positive balance of trade, national debt in the region of 70 percent of GDP (or lower), and a budget surplus or even budget deficit (of less than 1 percent of GDP). Other benchmarks could include innovation and creativity levels, good education and health systems, adequate research and development, high productivity (4+ percent annually), a balanced tax system, and so on. This list is not exhaustive, as many other factors such as military expenditure, income distribution, quality of living, and life expectancy have also to be taken into account.

Pitfalls and system dysfunctions

System breakdown

System breakdowns are not easy to reverse, particularly if the affected system is complex in nature. Indicatively, the Japanese economy has been in recession for the past 15 years and all well-meaning attempts to revive it have basically failed. The country's debt to GDP ratio now stands at roughly 200 percent. Typical of what can happen when an intervention is initiated, when the Japanese consumption tax increased slightly the country's growth rate immediately receded. The American economy went into recession in 2008 and six years later was still fighting to regain lost ground. Five or more years into the "economic recovery process" and many of the countries of southern Europe continue to reel under the pressure of high unemployment, cash shortages, crippling private and corporate debt, inadequate investment, and low business/bank system confidence. Greece is bearing the brunt of the austerity measures that the economic crisis brought to the country. The inability of the political elite to introduce long-awaited changes made matters worse.

Growth rates in the EU are now below 1 percent and countries such as Italy, Greece, and France are stagnating and seem to be in a quagmire, with new investments nowhere to be seen (Economist May 24, 2014). Culture is often at the center of economic and business or social systems and their workings. Countries that put much emphasis on social cohesion and social support (socialist governments?) operate in a culture that differs from that of countries with a strong private enterprise/capitalist/laissez-faire sentiment (conservative governments?). Recession and the accompanying human suffering brought back the ubiquitous debate over the role of government and its capacity to intervene in the market. The Western world has to a large extent adopted the capitalist system and as such unwittingly introduced business cycles, recessions, unemployment, and other system failures that are typical of capitalism (not that socialism/communism does not suffer from business cycles). On the positive side, many economies benefited materially from capitalism, which helped them increase their overall wealth.

Attitudes, mindsets, political orientations, and ethics play a vastly important role in the functioning, survival, and efficiency of economic systems. Weber approached this problem with great enthusiasm in his seminal work on sociology and economics, *Die protestantische Ethik und der Geist des Kapitalismus* (see Weber 2002). He put forward the view that the capitalist system and its breakdowns started as Protestants, and more particularly Calvinists, succeeded in penetrating the minds of sufficient numbers of people influencing them to take on secular work, entrepreneurship, commerce, and trade, and more specifically to adopt the business of accumulating wealth and investing surpluses as part of their divine worldly "calling" and proof of commitment to God's will. As the Protestant ethic began to be translated into action, capitalism started to develop, bringing with it wealth creation, recessions, and unemployment as well as business cycles.

Economic failures are often rooted in the failure of leaders (in politics, government, business, education, and so on) to behave in a just and equitable manner and according to the spirit of God. The Judeo-Christian ethic is characteristic of these philosophical arguments. The principles that govern decent behavior can lay the foundations for the creation of the preconditions that can lead to healthy economic and business systems. The adoption of fair-mindedness can act as a barrier to economic system failure, recessions, and unemployment (or at least can help delay such untoward outcomes). Speaking about America, James P. Eckman (2012) summarized well what happens when an economic system departs from basic ethical principles:

> Some business leaders have been motivated by greed and selfishness ... The ethical foundation of American culture that prevents business leaders from engaging in unethical activity is gone. I would strongly argue that as the ethical foundation of the American financial system has crumbled, the state has stepped in and rewritten the rules for financial and business dealings. The result is an economic and financial system overseen by impersonal bureaucrats, who first write and then seek to enforce literally volumes of rules and regulations. Those rules and regulations replace the simplicity of God's moral law ... The more we depart from God's moral law, the historic foundation of our civilization, the more onerous and complicated government regulation will become. The more this occurs, the more the American economy will no longer be able to compete, and its capacity to generate innovation and wealth will be gone.

Eckman is talking about ethical behavior, and the lack thereof, which to a large extent explains many of the ills of our economic system. Chicanery, deviousness, love of money, greed for material things, and lack of scruples have catapulted economic failure to new heights and have lain the foundations for a repeat even if the recession has been reversed for now. Disregard for ethical standards has been a major cause of the economic desolation we are experiencing in many countries. Fair-mindedness has been to a significant degree absent from the lives of many who hold positions of leadership in politics, business, education, entertainment, the military, and in almost all fields of endeavor. The concept of self-imposed constraints on recalcitrant behavior is all but missing in many areas of business and politics. Deviant and unethical behavior is sometimes rewarded with bonuses for short-term, often fictitious, business gains (see the banking sector). Instant gratification as expressed by borrowing and rising debt has also guided many people's actions in the Western world and elsewhere. In many cases the state is the villain that insists on collecting taxes without much accountability as to their proper use. Some politicians even become irritated when asked about accountability, considering that in their minds they have a God-given right to misuse other people's money. Hearing about corruption in government and by people holding high positions no longer shocks, as many of us have become numb to such messages.

Pitfalls of management from the pathophysiological point of view

One size fits all appears to be the current default "treatment" recommended by the money lenders (the Troika) to their patients (failing economies): aliquots of cash in the form of loans, crippling austerity measures, higher taxes, and lower social benefits. In the case of Cyprus, the smallest of the troubled economies, the Troika also forced depositor bail-ins through deposit haircuts. It dispensed its (default position) bitter elixir (its "panacea" medical potion) for all ailments and without regard to the patient's social and economic make-up: population size, culture, religious orientation, history, societal circumstances. Importantly, the Troika was not interested in knowing the roots of the problem in the first place. To many in Southern Europe its approach looks like an almost primal and insensitive approach to solving problems, even if the crisis was caused by the very actions and failings of countries now in trouble. To mention just a few of the counter-physiological outcomes of treating economic sufferers, not much attention was paid to reinforcing "buffer systems" that would have maintained critical social parameters within acceptable (viable) limits; interventions were frequently ill timed and were not sufficiently targeted; and patient complications were not monitored in a safe and meaningful way.

Worryingly, the team of practitioners can cut off the potion (loan tranches and emergency liquidity assistance) if they judge that the patient is not toeing the line. They do this by first attacking banking liquidity, making it difficult for banks to operate and survive. At times the Troika behaves like the proverbial medical practitioner who threatens the patient with abandonment the moment the patient has no recourse to other medical assistance, or because of worries that the patient may be unable to pay the mounting bills. This has been the case in Cyprus and Greece. The Troika wields a great deal of power and, just as a powerful medical insurance provider can cut off all access to hospitals, medical treatment, and the like, the Troika can cut off a country from international financing. It asks for its money to be paid back as agreed, with little regard to the societal needs of the debtor country. It has the power to cut off from the money markets a wayward debtor and even bankrupt the country in a sudden-death fashion. Of course, patients in this paradigm have a lot to answer for: their irresponsible actions and misbehavior over time and their enjoyment in the past of a lifestyle that was beyond their means.

Time for a new "therapeutic" paradigm?

Economic systems evolve all the time, making the skill of forecasting an essential tool of the trade for economists, governments, strategists, and managers. In some cases precedent helps the prediction process, while in others it can prove disastrous. Even though economic systems typically have in-built mechanisms to deal with change, these mechanisms do not always work well, largely because of the limitations of decision making discussed earlier in this chapter. Moreover, change sometimes comes quickly and with little notice, finding people unprepared. For example, within a very short span of 40–50 years the Cypriot economic system moved away from an agrarian model that served the country for thousands of years, to a quasi-sophisticated model. In the end the new model destroyed the economy, largely because those managing the system and the public in general were unable to understand its requirements and unready to deal with them. The agrarian Cypriot economy was turned into a service economy at a dizzying pace (tourism, shipping, and financial services including all financial peripherals replaced agriculture). The evolution of the banking industry was swift, haphazard, amateurishly managed, risky, and consequently destined to fail.

Cyprus was living under the illusion that it was operating as a sophisticated financial services center, even though it was not recognized as such by even one of the world's major financial players: London, Frankfurt, New York, Zurich. The Cypriot banking system depended heavily on high-interest-paying deposits that primarily came from three sources: local depositors, businesspeople from the former USSR, and to a minor extent developing-country depositors. The Cypriot government and bankers failed to understand that sophisticated banking systems draw deposits and investments from a wide spectrum. To the trained eye the collapse of Cyprus's financial industry was waiting to happen because it was working without a strong rudder. For example, while other countries in the EU offered depositors interest rates in the region of 1.5–2.5 percent, Cyprus paid double this rate, making it an attractive proposition for short-term investors as well as speculators. These deposits had to be loaned out even to unworthy borrowers. This, coupled with corruption from various sectors, created the situation in which Cyprus now finds itself. Cyprus's financial system was in many ways working by its own rules and not necessarily within conventions. It was marked by *excess*:

- The financial industry became obese quickly, with "financial diabetes" setting in and dangerously raising the risk of amputation (the financial sector's balance sheet of 7–8 times GDP will in the end fizzle down to a fraction of that).
- Over-sized deposits clogged the banking sector's arteries while the banking witch doctors looked on in amazement.
- Over-sized and risky loans ended up as toxic, non-performing loans that crippled the sector, just as high blood pressure does to a patient.

The Cyprus paradigm raises the question: "How can a social system be restored to health?" The quick answer is that it all depends on whether society is ready for the unavoidable and painful surgical operation that will hopefully revive the patient and restore health. Most critically, is society ready for the serious introspection that can lead to the abandonment of behaviors that were at best doubtful and proved to be harmful? The crux of the matter lies in behavior change and the abandonment of approaches that promise easy gains. Rebuilding a failed system and putting it on a path of sustainable growth is not an easy task. Such situations typically entail the adoption of a new therapeutic paradigm that encompasses at least these basic stages: a new mindset; the refusal of quick fixes; and putting in place appropriate checks and balances to protect the system from regressing to its old ways, putting special emphasis on the ethical dimension.

Conclusion with reference to the High Energy Authority

This chapter has brought together a broad amalgam of disciplines to help the reader better understand the essence of holism, inter-dependability, system ailments/dysfunctionality, and system functionality. Equally, it has tried to demonstrate that every ailing situation is unique and that any planned intervention ought to be well thought out to help the system survive all the attacks that it will inevitably suffer and all the dissonances that are likely to appear and threaten the system. In so doing, it borrowed from the fields of pathophysiology, history, the economy, management, and ethics. All systems are prone to illness and decay, no matter how well designed they may be. As such, system failures need to be assessed correctly and treated holistically. Entropic forces (which tend to disrupt and cause chaos) and buffers (dynamic homeostasis mechanisms that maintain balance) should be identified and their particular characteristics analyzed. Interventions ought to be planned accordingly, with a view to reducing and if possible eliminating entropic forces and reinforcing dynamic homeostasis. Each sick person is sick in their own way, just as each failing economy or business or country fails in its own particular way. Each geographic region for that matter fails in its own unique way and the treatment thus needs to vary accordingly. The EM is no exception to this rule. All eight contributors to this volume consider the region to be dysfunctional and ailing and in need of treatment. Undoubtedly, the recommended treatment ought to be targeted to the uniqueness of the illness, which is none other than the failure of countries in the EM to address fairly its particular problems and to work together to help the region meet its full potential.

Human nature (and its great iniquities, fear and greed) can make the difference to the workings of a social system. The human factor, people's strengths and weaknesses and the way they are managed at all levels, is critical to how economic and other systems develop, succeed, or fail. The EM failed on two counts: it failed to address and resolve inter-country conflicts and to get the regional economy to achieve its potential. Hence the wobbly EM system of nations is not working well. The regional system does not have one strong, unifying objective that appeals to all countries, and strong checks and balances are not embedded so that they can come to the defense of the system when it is attacked. Controls can help detect disease in a timely manner, allowing the necessary preventive measures to take effect and stop the contagion from spreading. It is axiomatic that patients and ailing systems recover faster if the illness is detected at an early stage.

As an economic system of nations, the EM has much to answer for in relation to its failures and particularly its inability to get its countries to work together for the common economic good. Most importantly, this loose regional economic system fails to defend itself from attacks, most of which come from its own constituent parts, which fail to cooperate in any meaningful sense. National greed (often masquerading as national interest) had the better of the countries in the region. In the same way as biological systems fail when they are attacked and unable to defend themselves, regional economic systems need methods of control (hence sensors and overlapping afferent/efferent mechanisms and pathways) for defense purposes. The much-needed defenses were not there in the case of the EM and this allowed attacks to play havoc with the system. Coordination, synergy, optimality, forecasting, recognition of disproportionality, and proper interaction are crucial parts of these monitoring and change mechanisms; they are the "sensors" that control and protect systems from performing the wrong functions that are inimical to the system. The EM regional system in many ways also failed miserably to develop a common vision that would unite countries and allow them to support each other.

The economic events of the last seven to ten years have not helped the situation at all, since at least two countries (Greece and Cyprus) fell under the economic management of unelected third parties and more particularly the Troika, which set the boundaries within which they would be able to act. The Troika prescribed the standard treatment for both economies, which is injections of cash (loans) and crippling austerity measures. These approaches were presented as a panacea for all ailments irrespective of size, culture, religious background, history, societal circumstances, or anything else. The treatment did not work as planned because the mindset of the people affected was not examined, nor was it addressed. People's mindsets are absolutely central to how an economic system is designed in the first place, how it is operated, and how it is managed. Greece, which is now going through its worst crisis since World War II, is another classic example of how the Troika failed totally to understand the current mindset and the difficulties that people in a conservative country experience when asked to make radical changes. Greece is no Britain, no Russia, and no Albania. Greece is Greece and should have been viewed as such by those treating the patient, however guilty of neglect. One would have thought that the economic crisis would have been reason enough for both these economically ailing countries to cooperate with and come closer to their EM neighbor, Turkey. However, this failed to happen because Turkey has claims on both these countries and their resources and keeps pestering them militarily. Once more, the politics of the region worked against cooperation; instead of the economic crisis helping cement the current loose economic system, it worked in the opposite direction. Nor did the economic crisis in Egypt bring Israel and Egypt any closer either, although the two countries now cooperate more than they did when the latter was ruled by the Muslim Brotherhood, which was supported by Turkey.

Regional economic systems evolve all the time, just as the Western world's Calvinistic capitalism is also evolving. It is not unreasonable to say that therapeutic strategies and interventions for failing systems such as that of the EM should also evolve, adapting accordingly but always remaining helpful rather than harmful (Ὠφελεῖν ἢ μὴ βλάπτειν), as Hippocrates says in Epidemics 1.11. In this respect, the therapeutic strategy for the ailing EM would need to take into account individual country interests, country-related strategic considerations, perceptions as fashioned by history, real and imaginary threats, and a host of other factors. In the first instance, humanitarianism and public-spiritedness (both Ancient Greek traits) are unlikely to be part of the intervention strategies, but in due course one would hope to see them playing a helpful role. In the end, the EM system of countries will stand or fall on the strength of the ethical standards they apply, particularly as regards the decision-making process. With the help of the twin tools of probity/responsibility and ethical behavior, the EM region will be able to overcome its economic and related failures without the individual countries losing their identities. A holistic approach will be necessary if the ailments of the region are to be addressed. This approach needs to blend well the tangible with the intangible, the economic with the social, the financial with the spiritual, the strategic with the tactical, the national with the multinational and the regional, and so on.

If the countries of the region can come together and form a larger unit, at the center of which will be an HEA, then many of the conflicts that afflict the EM will be eclipsed. This in turn will allow the full exploitation of the region's resources to go full steam ahead. In this way the EM countries can hope for a better future, in terms of both the vastly important issue of security as well as their economies, all of which have failed to achieve their potential. Of course, this presupposes the setting up of a new system that encompasses all countries in the region. Within this new arrangement, individual countries will need to transform themselves into productive, cooperative, and caring units of the EM network. Each needs to appreciate that it stands to gain more through cooperation and peaceful coexistence than through working alone or using violence against its neighbors. Through this cooperative approach, all countries in the region will be better placed to enjoy the multitude of synergies that will inevitably arise. An HEA will provide each country with the opportunity to add its individual strengths to the regional system, thus helping improve an area that has seen more than its fair share of conflict. Politically and militarily troubled relationships will hopefully become part of the past. Energy finds provide a unique opportunity for these countries to start sharing rather than coveting their neighbors' riches.

The issue of limited independence looms large in the debate over closer cooperation. As seen already in Chapter 2, although Greece and Cyprus are free on paper, in reality their independence is qualified. They are restricted from acting freely, particularly on matters of great significance to them. Lebanon's independence is limited by its very constitution, which makes decision making subject to all sorts of factional constraints, causing paralysis, suspicion, and anger. Its internal problems are far too numerous to allow the country to operate freely and to decide issues on merit. Egypt's independence is less constrained, but the country is poor (in GDP terms) and to some degree dependent on aid, some of which comes from the US. Aid also comes from the Gulf and Saudi Arabia, depending on political circumstances. Israel is small and powerful, but is heavily dependent on the US for its military apparatus, which again qualifies its independence to some extent. Without the help of the US, Israel would find it difficult to meet the continuous pressures it faces from its neighbors. The country's resources are constrained by virtue of its small size and the absence of a large internal market that can help sustain its industrial base. Land for agriculture is also limited on account of the country's size. To a degree Turkey is also dependent on the US, although it tries not to show it. Of course, America is in its turn dependent on Turkey for support in the enforcement by force of its policies in the regions neighboring Turkey. It is clear that on the dependence/independence index, America is the common denominator and therefore one can expect the US to play its role in the event of countries in the region deciding to work under a HEA. This means that these countries should be extra careful to ensure that the region's interests take precedence over those of America, and other third-party countries for that matter.

Building a regional energy-sharing system as a way to improve the conditions of the EM is not going to be easy. The recommended therapeutic intervention will not necessarily go down well with everyone, largely because of historical developments and the way in which each country perceives its national interest. A new mindset therefore needs to be adopted that favors cooperation and forgiveness. Countries first have to shed attitudes that encourage national greed, national aggression, and unwillingness to abide by international law. The new watchwords need to be cooperation, sharing, system synergies, dynamic homeostasis, support, peace, and harmony. Use of power and aggression should have no place in the new system. The EM countries know full well that in the past aggression begot misery, desolation, and loathing rather than economic growth. Fair-mindedness has to dominate the thought processes of people in positions of leadership in the region (elected officials, military, business, education, and other leaders). In summary, these countries stand to gain much more from rebuilding their economies and improving their citizens' welfare if they are part of a broader peaceful regional arrangement rather than acting alone in pursuit of "national interest."

Although the creation of an HEA appears to be the best way forward, one ought to remember that a new system would have to be created and put in place from scratch. At the beginning, this system would need to deal with all the ailments and ambitions of member countries. As a regional system it would be exposed to new illnesses that would call for interventions and cures. Much would depend on how the venture was managed because, as has been demonstrated earlier in this chapter, good management is not an off-the-shelf tool that the region can acquire from the West or the East. Classic management approaches would need to be adapted to the needs of the HEA and those of member countries to ensure workability and, most importantly, to ensure consonant relations between member countries. At its core, the new system would essentially be an economic enterprise created to help countries exploit their economic potential. It would also be a geostrategic enterprise that encouraged countries and people to work together in peace. A key question in the minds of the visionaries behind the HEA project would surely be the association's future performance and how far this would go in solving the region's political and economic problems. It would take much goodwill from founding members to keep the system on an even keel. Pull and push forces would be at work continuously, some of which would inevitably threaten the system's stability and others that would push it forward. The HEA would have all the traits of systems, explained earlier in this chapter.

The envisaged HEA would provide a platform for countries in the region to work together on energy matters and, as such, it would unavoidably have an impact on their economies. Each country would strive to enhance its economic position through membership in the HEA rather than going it alone. However, getting six or more countries to dovetail their economic activities so that they remain in harmony with the management strategy of the HEA would certainly be difficult. The six economies are similar neither in strength nor in development. The Israeli economy leads in most performance factors, including per capita GDP. Turkey's economy is large in relation to those of other countries, Egypt's economy is at the bottom of the scale in terms of performance, and Greece's economy is under the control of the Troika, as is Cyprus's. Lebanon is in continuous political turmoil, which has a heavy negative impact on the economy. The way in which the HEA is put together and subsequently managed will determine to a large extent the growth levels (and frustrations) of the economies of all these countries.

There is no guarantee that the creation of the HEA would be an automatic success, as the existence of six or more countries under one umbrella is likely to generate tension. All we have to do is look at what the refugee crisis is doing to the EU right now. This means that the leadership of the HEA would need to be extra careful in the way it managed the whole system, paying particular attention to the maintenance of a sustainable equilibrium. The legal system that would apply to the HEA would also be critical. Well-functioning economic systems typically operate within sound and stable legal systems. Among other factors, a well-functioning legal system guarantees property rights, secures patents and copyrights, and deals with litigation speedily and justly. Investors shun enterprises that have malfunctioning legal systems. In addition, the HEA and member countries would need to have in place tax systems that are efficient and fair and that incentivize people to invest and work hard.

The success of the envisaged HEA would depend heavily on how people of different backgrounds, religions, and languages managed their affairs within the new system and how capable the system proved to be in synthesizing these variables and constants into one working whole. The different work ethics that the HEA brought together would test and strain the fabric of this new social system. The success or failure of the HEA would depend largely on how the people factor performed and whether people opted to work together for the common good or for the narrow interests of their own country while feigning love for the system. The "Mediterranean culture" that all people in the area share and would bring to the HEA system would hopefully help the bonding process. At least four different individual cultures would have to blend together meaningfully: Arab, Israeli, Greek, and Turkish. If this blend were successful, then one could expect great things to come. If the blending failed, then the whole exercise would be likely to experience difficulties that would need masterful handling.

The EM region is well endowed with skilled people and has relatively good universities that could help the system operate as planned. Lebanon in particular can be singled out for its management education and its high rank on the Global Competitive Index on the factor of management education. The youth of the region need opportunities to apply their skills. These are not easily forthcoming at the moment. The newly found oil and gas reserves may provide a lifeline for some of the scientists, technicians, and administrators who are now performing meaningless tasks or are looking for some pointless bureaucratic role in the public sector. Just as unnecessary wastage of physiological reserves can be detrimental in the context of human pathophysiology, wastage of human talent can be harmful to the organization, the economy, and the social system. Some of the EM countries pride themselves on having one of the highest densities of university graduates in the world (some with education from highly respected institutions). Yet some of these countries fail pitifully to exploit the potential of their talented workforce, mostly because they fail to innovate and to offer more options and avenues to their educated cadre. The work culture also creates destructive influences because of the laid-back attitude of staff in some settings, such as the broader public sector where there is little relationship between reward and performance. As within the context of a system all parts are inter-related, we see the fruits of the anomaly in the public sector: shoddy work, irresponsible attitudes, delays, loss of competitiveness, citizen frustration, and so on. The oil and gas industry will require new skills and new attitudes that the available cadre will need to adopt quickly. Thankfully, the region has plenty of energetic people who are willing to quickly adapt to the new requirements.

The EM region is ready for change and improvement; in fact, change is well overdue. The creation of an HEA will inevitably bring great transformation to the region for the good of all. If the HEA is set up with care and with fairness to all countries, then any negative fallout of this unprecedented development will be controlled and the reaction of those opposed to the idea will be restrained. The new system will take time to be implemented and will require stewardship and leadership. Former belligerents will become economic allies and the former occupied but now free will sit on equal terms with their previous masters. This will not be an easy task to achieve without jerks and relapses that will threaten the new system. This explains why the necessary controls need to be put in place to ensure the stability of the system. It will be in the interests of the EM countries to ensure that it works well and efficiently, because the better the system works, the more benefits will accrue to each member country. Interaction and exchange of ideas are likely to improve the innovation that is so essential to the performance of the HEA. The equilibrium at HEA and country level is likely to be protected by the member countries themselves acting in unison and in support of each other. Greece would have been bankrupt a long time ago had it not been for the support it received from fellow members of the EU.

The idea of creating an HEA, as suggested in this book, stems partly from the premise that nations need to work together, because as long as they work in isolation and in closed systems, with national interest as the only guiding light, unwilling to interact and work with others, there will be no real peace and no chance of realizing the region's economic potential. The sooner the EM countries rise to the challenge the better. Each country needs to take bold action by first expelling fear (one of two major sins) from their mindset and psyche. They should not be frightened by the possibility of the venture failing, because success will depend on their willingness to work together. Also, they should not fear any loss to their independence, because most of these countries already have qualified independence in one sense or another. This will unavoidably require the shedding of the other major sin: greed. Greed could cripple and destroy the new system in record speed. In fact, it could make the project a non-starter from day one. The issue of greed rightly looms large in this chapter because greed (of members as well as outsiders) lies behind many attacks on social systems. Greed will unavoidably play its role in the workings of the envisaged HEA. The degree, shape, and intensity of that greed will be instrumental to the performance of the EM and the viability of the HEA. Equally, the project's viability will to a great extent depend on the goodwill each country shows at all stages. Nevertheless, this promising project has no chance of taking off unless Turkey removes its occupation troops and settlers from Cyprus, and unless the Palestinian–Israeli conflict is resolved fairly and democratically, paying due respect to the human rights and freedoms of all people in the conflict. The manner in which Alexander's empire collapsed should serve as a somber reminder of the immense difficulty of builing unity and the great ease with which unity can be crashed by greed. No sooner had Alexander died and his successors (diadochi/διάτοχοι) began the violent dismantling of the newly unified system, each carving up a piece for himself only to see their piece go to the Romans less than 200 years later.

References

Arrian. 2003. The Campaigns of Alexander, edited by J. R. Hamilton, translated by Aubrey De Selincourt. Harmondsworth: Penguin Classics.

Bose, Partha. 2003. Alexander the Great's Art of Strategy. Harmondsworth: Penguin.

Business Dictionary. 2015. "System." http://www.businessdictionary.com/definition/system.html#ixzz354V YlSUa. Accessed June 2015.

ChemWiki. 2015. "A System and Its Surroundings." ChemWiki University of California, Davis.

http://chemwiki.ucdavis.edu/Physical_Chemistry/Thermodynamics/A_
    System_And_Its_Surroundings. Accessed July 2015.
Cunningham, John, and Michael C. Wood (Eds.). 2002. Henri Fayol
    Critical Evaluations in Business and Management. London: Routledge.
Cyert, Richard M., and James G. March. 1992. A Behavioral Theory of
    the Firm. Hoboken, NJ: John Wiley.
Daft, R. L. 2001. Organization Theory and Design (7th ed.). Mason, OH:
    South-Western College Publishing.
Deming, W. Edwards. 2000. Out of the Crisis. Boston, MA: MIT Press.
Drucker, Peter F. 1999. Management Challenges for the 21st Century. New
    York: HarperBusiness.
—. 2006. The Practice of Management. New York: HarperBusiness.
Eckman, James P. 2012. "Issues in Perspective: The Judeo-Christian
    Tradition and Capitalism." Omaha, NE: Grace University, March 3.
    http://graceuniversity.edu/iip/wp-content/uploads/2012/03/2012_0303-
    0304.pdf. Accessed August, 2014.
Fayol, Henri. 2013. General and Industrial Management, translated by
    Constance Storrs. Eastford, CT: Martino Fine Books.
Gilbreth, Lillian. 2010. The Psychology of Management. New York:
    Qontro Classic Books.
Hamilton, Alexander. 2011. Alexander Hamilton: Writings, edited by
    Joanne B. Freeman. Library of America. New York: Penguin Putnam.
Hippocrates. 5th century BCE. Hippocratic Corpus: Ancient Medicine.
    http://classics.mit.edu/Browse/browse-Hippocrates.html.
    Accessed Noember 2015.
Hussar, Daniel A. 2013. "Efficacy and Safety." Merck Manual, Professional
    Version.
    http://www.merckmanuals.com/professional/clinical_pharmacology/co
    ncepts_in_pharmacotherapy/efficacy_and_safety.html.
    Accessed May 2015.
March, James G., and Herbert A. Simon. 1958. Organisations. Hoboken,
    NJ: John Wiley.
Mayo, Elton. 1949. Hawthorne and the Western Electric Company: The
    Social Problems of an Industrial Civilisation. London: Routledge.
McNamara, Robert, and Brian VanDeMark. 1995. In Retrospect: The
    Tragedy and Lessons of Vietnam. New York: Vintage Books/Random
    House.
Ouchi, William G. 1981. Theory Z. New York: Avon Books.
Parker Follett, Mary. 2013. Dynamic Administration: The Collected
    Papers of Mary Parker. Eastford, CT: Martino Fine Books.

Ricardo, David. 2004. Principles of Political Economy and Taxation. New York: Dover Publications.

Sackett, D. L. 1996. Evidence Based Medicine: What It Is and What It Isn't. British Medical Journal, 312, 71.

Say, Jean-Baptiste. 1971. A Treatise on Political Economy. New York: Augustus M. Kelley. (First US edition 1821, Philadelphia: Claxton, Remsen & Haffelfinger.)

Smith, Adam. 1776. An Inquiry into the Nature and Causes of the Wealth of Nations. London: W. Strahan.

Taylor, Frederick Winslow. 1997. The Principles of Scientific Management. Charleston, SC: Biblio Bazaar Reproduction Series.

Transparency International. 2015. "Corruption by Country/Territory." http://www.transparency.org/country. Accessed May 2015.

Weber, Max. 2002. The Protestant Ethic and the "Spirit" of Capitalism and Other Writings, edited by Peter R. Baehr and Gordon C. Wells. Harmondsworth: Penguin Twentieth Century Classics.

Weber, Max. 2013. Economy and Society, vol I, edited by Guenther Ross and Claus Wittich. Oakland, CA: University of California Press.

Xenophon. 2012. The Science of Good Husbandry, translated by R. Bradley. Farmington Hills, MI: Gale.

CHAPTER NINE

TEMPEST AND TRANQUILITY IN THE EASTERN MEDITERRANEAN

ARIS PETASIS

The East Mediterranean (EM) is now facing one of its biggest challenges. Perhaps for the first time in the region's history, the countries in the area are invited by nature and destiny to find ways to share a vast common wealth that has the potential to change for the better the lives of their people. The region now has proven energy reserves, the magnitude of which, although not fully known, appears to be substantial; enough potentially to create a sea-change in the fortunes of the energy-rich countries. The challenge now is for these nations to decide whether they wish to work alone to exploit their own energy reserves or to work together, guided by a unified objective. The first option focuses on narrow, "national interests," while the second focuses on broader, inter-country interests that ultimately serve national interests as well, and possibly better. If the first option wins the debate, all countries in the region stand to lose, so it appears, from not reaching their economic potential. If they decide to work together, then their economic fortunes will most likely change substantially. Those in the region do of course appreciate the difficulties of building cooperation and harmony in a neighborhood with a strife-filled history, ongoing conflicts, and two major unresolved issues.

Several factors seem to stand in the way of reaching broad agreement on bilateral or multilateral cooperation, with history taking first place in the ranking of barriers. Already there are feuds between countries over the delineation of exclusive economic zones (EEZ). The question of who owns what remains unanswered in some cases. It is not unreasonable to think that the region's countries may not quite be ready to work in collaboration despite the obvious advantages of collective action. More optimistically, it would also be reasonable to think that because of the immense economic and political rewards that are at stake, they will ultimately be convinced to work together and amicably for mutual benefit.

Mutual interests may ultimately prevail over individual interests simply because this is the sensible thing to do. Cooperation is likely to deliver better results than disunity.

The region's economies

None of the economies of the countries in the EM are meeting their potential (see Chapter 5), mostly because the conflict in the region stands in the way of full development and because economic restructuring is not taking place. Even Israel, which has the best-performing economy and boasts the highest per capita income in the region, is not reaching its potential because it is focused on vital defense and security matters. Egypt suffers from its own economic ailments, one of which is the high birth rate that eats up any growth in GDP. At one point its foreign currency reserves reached rock bottom because the economy was the first victim of the unsettled political situation. This demonstrates how strongly inter-related are politics and economics. Egypt suffers seriously from problems of hidden unemployment and high subsidies that need to be curtailed, but no one knows how best to go about it considering the many social repercussions of doing so. Reducing subsidies risks creating social upheaval that the country can ill afford, particularly as the government is now engaged in a political tug of war with religious fundamentalist opponents. The economic situation of Greece and Cyprus, as measured by real unemployment, is also desperate and Syria's economic problems are beyond description. Although Turkey is experiencing growth, a careful analysis of its economic fundamentals reveals dangerous signs of major impending problems. High consumption fueled by borrowing and a crippling current account deficit are just some of these. Lebanon is in the grip of permanent political turmoil (and paralysis) on account of its highly undemocratic, faction-centered constitution. At the time of writing the country had been without a president for about a year because of the veto power of various religious factions. Its garbage disposal problem has already reached its eighteenth year of being debated with no agreement between the factions, which in the process is endangering people's health. Armed militias are everywhere in hiding and ready for action at short notice.

Defense

Defense expenditures in the region are high and take money away from the countries' other priorities. The Stockholm Peace Research Institute (2015) puts Turkey in 14th place in the league of countries with the highest military expenditure. The country currently spends \$19 billion a year or 2.3 percent of its GDP on defense. Israel's economy is badly hit by military expenditure, considering that this small country spends \$14.6 billion on defense, or a staggering 6.2 percent of GDP. Lebanon is not in any better a position seeing that it spends 4.1 percent of GDP on defense, not counting the cost of private funding of a multitude of private militias. Greece's outlay is 2.5 percent of GDP, although the Troika is pressing for reductions, disregarding the open threat from Turkey, a fellow member of the North Atlantic Treaty Organization (NATO). Greece has traditionally been one of the highest defense spenders among NATO members (European NATO allies spend on average 1.6 percent of GDP on defense). It is generally accepted that in the event of countries in the region cooperating on energy, the vast expenditures on defense would be reduced massively, making money available for the rest of the economy and in particular social benefits.

Unemployment

Greece, Cyprus, and Egypt are experiencing unprecedented unemployment levels, even if one were to rely solely on official data, which often under-estimates the problem. Actual unemployment is typically much higher than that officially reported for a variety of reasons. Large numbers of unemployed fail to register once they stop receiving unemployment bene-fits, many migrate, and others take on meaningless jobs. The World Bank (2015) reports that the unemployment rates in the EM over the period 2010–14 were:

- Cyprus 11.8% (now estimated at 17%)
- Egypt 11.9%
- Greece 24.2%
- Israel 6.9%
- Lebanon 8.9%
- Jordan 12.2%
- Turkey 9.2%

Unless the economies of these countries grow at a faster rate than normal (for the region, 2+ percent) the current unemployment figures are not likely to drop to acceptable levels (e.g., 3 percent). Nevertheless, all countries in the EM are desperate to see unemployment fall because of the immense social and economic problems it causes.

Unemployment is a debilitating and humiliating experience that often forces people to emigrate, even though they do not want to do so. The people of Greece and Cyprus can testify to this. Those in Egypt and Lebanon can also bear witness, even if both countries face residency restrictions in the European Union (EU) and most other countries.

Will to cooperate

Countries in the region understand that by cooperating they all stand to gain vast economic advantage. Yet a great question mark hangs over whether they have the *will* to cooperate. Sadly, history appears to cast a dark shadow over the prospects of collaboration and hence of joint exploration and exploitation of resources. Hilal Khashan (see Chapter 6) seems less than sanguine about the readiness of EM countries to cooperate at this juncture because of the poisoned history of the region and its open wounds. Old quarrels, bad blood between current and former antagonists, and wrongly defined and wrongly perceived national interests that are often seen through a narrow nationally defined prism are just some of the reasons that weigh against cooperation. Equally, heavy meddling in the region by outsiders, particularly by the United States (US), complicates matters. In addition, there is the tug of war between the American-led West and Russia, with the former trying to lessen its dependence on Russian energy and the latter viewing this position as inimical to its interests. The Ukrainian crisis is not helping matters either and is forcing countries to take sides whether they like it or not.

Stephanos Constantinides (see Chapter 1) sheds light on the big power games in the region, as does William Mallinson (Chapter 2). One therefore wonders whether the big powers wish to see the EM countries cooperating or whether they view that as detrimental to their interests and their meddling presence.

Mallinson brings out the fear of Russia syndrome that afflicts the Americans and the British. The recent testimony in the US Congress of America's top military that Russia poses the biggest threat to the US tends to confirm in a panegyric manner what he is saying. The way the Ukrainian debacle has been handled by the US and its rush to arm countries in the region serve as additional proof. In this maelstrom of antagonism between Russians and Americans, Cyprus becomes the victim as the US pushes hard for a political "solution" to the Cyprus problem that will be to the benefit of US and Turkish interests, and NATO of course. America is worried that as long as unoccupied Cyprus has its own foreign policy, there will always be a danger that Cyprus will move closer to

Moscow. The solution therefore, in American minds, is to dismember the Republic of Cyprus by creating two states, in a country of about 12,000 sq km, with suffocating veto powers that would render the country impotent to carry out any foreign policy decisions, and with America's close ally, Turkey, ultimately filling the vacuum.

The Russian factor makes Turkish–Israeli strategic cooperation in the Middle East, particularly over Syria, another vital US objective. Both Greece and Cyprus continue to be political pawns in a dangerous game between outside players. This has been the fate of the region for centuries, with EM countries often reduced to mere pieces in the geopolitical chess game. All these realities make it harder to achieve cooperation in the region without first satisfying American interests in particular. This does not augur well for Greece and Cyprus, in that they are both weak and impotent (and half-bankrupt) and cannot even exploit their resources on their own because of Turkish belligerence, of which America is tolerant.

Choosing sides

Sanctions imposed against Russia by the US (and grudgingly by the EU after heavy American pressure) have complicated the situation and angered those who see this move as reflecting double standards, considering that the US keeps silent on Turkey's continued occupation of 37 percent of Cyprus for over 40 years. Not surprisingly, Cypriots are weary of any American attempts to solve the Cyprus problem, knowing full well on whose side the scales will tilt. The protection of the energy reserves in the EM is forcing countries in the region to choose sides and to engage in security arrangements to protect themselves. This ultimately hurts the chances of regional cooperation.

George Georgiou (Chapter 4) sees Greece, Cyprus, and Israel as working together in a beneficial manner, but doubts whether this relationship has much of a future considering that relations between Turkey and Israel inevitably will improve at the expense of the Greeks. It is more or less accepted in the region that US policy breathes through two lungs: one Turkish and the other Israeli. The corollary is also true, of course, as both countries depend heavily on continued American support, in particular military aid. Some observers suspect that the US will continue to put more and more pressure on both Israel and Turkey to toe the American line and make up, a chokehold that they will probably find difficult to resist. America needs friends as its influence over many countries in the region (Greece, Cyprus, Egypt, Lebanon, and Syria) is steadily waning, certainly at grassroots level. As Cyprus works through its worst economic crisis since the Turkish invasion of 1974, it continues to seek an economic lifeline via its gas reserves. Without Israel's active participation and support, Cyprus's energy options remain limited given its current weak economic and by extension political situation. Unfortunately for Cyprus, already there is talk of Turkey cooperating with Israel on energy transport. Some commentators fear that the brutal reality may one day soon make Cyprus a mere footnote in Israeli foreign policy manuals.

In the conflict between the Greeks (Greece plus the free areas of Cyprus) and Turkey, the US unreservedly and as a default position sides with Turkey, irrespective of the merits of the argument. Simply put, America sees its national interests aligned to those of the Turkish and not the Greeks. In a private conversation with one of the world's most prominent human rights lawyers (in the presence of a former high-ranking politician), I asked, "If the US had to choose one hundred times between Turkey and the Greeks, what would the score be?" The terse response was, "One hundred for Turkey and zero for the Greeks." To the follow-on question "Why so?" the reply was:

> Because American interests lie with NATO-member Turkey that maintains a standing army three to four times larger than that of Britain and because Turkey controls one of Russia's main sea pathways and borders with Iran, Iraq, Syria, and a host of other potential conflagration points. So, forget all about ethics.

The Greeks are expendable and they know that. They have had plenty of bad experiences already, thus they are always looking around for real and meaningful alliances. Relationships between the Greeks and the Russians have always been good and to the majority of the Greek people Russia is a natural and historical ally. With American support secured, Turkey has little reason to obey international law whenever it can get away with arbitrary (and often violent) action. American influence in Syria is in reality non-existent. The balance of power in Lebanon and particularly the strength of the forces in southern Lebanon reduces US influence there to a minimum. Egypt is not particularly happy with its relationship with the US and the old Sadat–US relationship is like a long-forgotten dream. So the US concentrates on strengthening its relations with Israel and Turkey, the two strongest military powers in the region. Unavoidably, the Greeks are likely to be big-time losers in this regional tug of war unless Russia starts making serious inroads into the area, bringing with it its massive military presence.

Transit route

Solon Kassinis (Chapter 3) reports that the EM region has the potential to
develop into a "second North Sea" and to become the fourth largest region
in hydrocarbons production globally (after Russia, Qatar, and the North
Sea). This in itself should have been enough to rally the countries in the
region around a common cause, that of exploiting their common resources
together. Yet worries about past bad behavior by some countries make it
difficult for people to warm up to the idea. For example, Kassinis is wary
of an export pipeline from the EM to Europe going through Turkey
because of Turkey's past and current aggressive behavior toward its
weaker neighbors. This view is probably shared by the vast majority of
Greeks, who feel that transport security and reliability and respect for
international law must take precedence over energy economics. They
reason that transit through Turkey automatically makes EM oil and gas
hostage to a country that already holds hostage the Euphrates water supply
to Syria.

Opinion seems to converge around the view that occupiers of other
people's land in no way qualify as energy transit partners. Only if Turkey
changes its behavior dramatically for the better and unequivocally starts
respecting international law will this change. Aggression and cooperation
do not mix well.

Cyprus and Greece to take the lead

Miguel Moratinos (Chapter 7) goes to the heart of what needs to be done
in the EM if countries in the region are to exploit their resources for the
benefit of their economies and regional peace. He traces the conflict-
ridden past of the area and highlights its geostrategic importance today.
The chapter refers to the impact on the region of the fall of the Ottoman
Empire, the end of World War II, the creation of NATO, and the US and
NATO's assignment to Turkey of the role of regional policeman. The
effects on the area of the Cold War and its aftermath following the fall of
the Berlin Wall are appropriately stressed, as are the new challenges the
region is now facing. As regards Cyprus, Moratinos notes that the major
powers have always coveted the island, causing it to fall victim to
confrontations between actors who want to exercise their hegemony.

The new geopolitics of the area have brought about a new and entirely
unnecessary East–West confrontation that is costing everyone in Europe,
Russia, and the EM. Economic issues such as energy reserves are creating
new tensions. Looking to the future, Moratinos suggests the creation of a

High Energy Authority (HEA), just as France and Germany did with coal and steel in 1951, an entity that ultimately gave rise to the EU. He offers ideas on how the countries in the region can successfully meet their current challenges, at the center of which lie the unresolved conflicts between Turkey and Cyprus and between Israelis and Palestinians. As the future of Russian–US relationships will inevitably affect the region, it behooves all EM countries to act together and in full independence, if possible, from the big powers. Therefore they need to review their geostrategic potential on merit rather than in relation to how much pressure the major powers exert on them. Acting together and in accord, the countries of the region will cease to be subcontractors for and proxies of other powers. With the help of Europe, accords can be reached for the overall good of the EM and Europe as a whole.

Moratinos goes on to suggest that Cyprus and Greece take the lead in bringing together the energy-rich countries in the region for common benefit. They are friendly with all the other EM countries apart from Turkey, and are also members of the EU. Both are peaceful countries and have no claims on other people's land. Their military is modest and of a defensive nature and therefore not a threat to anyone. As such, they are in a good position to get the project off to a head start.

Bringing in Turkey

Turkey has no proven energy reserves in the Mediterranean part of the country and as such could easily have been largely ignored in the debate over joint action on the region's energy. However, Turkey has a long shoreline, is near to the energy reserves of other countries, and could be a useful transit hub to European energy markets. It already plays host to a network of gas pipelines that transport energy. Turkey also has a large army, a comparatively huge military budget in absolute terms ($19+ billion), and a long history of causing trouble to its neighbors if it does not get its own way. Furthermore, it has the unwavering support of America, acting as Turkey's power multiplier. Additionally, Turkey is a good international chess player, playing one country off against another. The recent disloyal Turkish role in the Syrian affair and its unwillingness to cooperate fully with US actions in the region give us a good picture of reality.

At the time of writing, Turkey has turned its guns against the Kurds of Turkey, Syria, and Iraq under the guise of fighting the Islamic State of Iraq and the Levant (ISIL). With a nod from America, it is now trying to set up a buffer zone to separate the Turkish Kurds from those in Syria, for fear that contiguous Kurdish lands that are now in different but neighboring countries could make the creation of a Kurdish nation easier to achieve. America's erstwhile allies, the Kurds of Syria and Iraq, are now being pummeled by Turkish bombs, while the US remains silent. Here is what *The Times* (London, August 10, 2015) had to say on Turkey's current myopic position after Ankara began attacking the Kurds: "the Erdogan line [put] him on a policy collision with almost all Turkey's neighbours, as well as his NATO allies."

Turkey is large in both geographic size and population and has the possibility of playing a number of roles, for instance energy customer of the energy-rich countries in the region; energy transit hub for energy producers; and troublemaker and threat to weaker neighbors, in effect forcing them abide by Turkish wishes on energy matters. The US Energy Information Administration (2014) notes:

> Turkey's importance in world energy markets is growing, both as a regional energy transit hub and as a growing consumer. Turkey's energy demand has increased rapidly over the past few years and likely will continue to grow in the future.

Turkey's proven oil reserves are limited and no one can say with confidence how large they are or whether their exploitation makes financial sense. Coincidentally, the energy potential lies in the southern part of the country, but onshore. Currently the national oil company is cooperating with international companies through joint ventures to explore energy reserves in the Black Sea. Turkey hopes that commercial production will start in a few years' time. While not a big energy consumer per capita, Turkey has a huge appetite for energy because its economy is growing and because it has managed to avoid the major economic downsides that European countries have experienced. Its energy consumption is expected to double in the next decade, according to the International Energy Agency (2013). This partly explains why Turkey is so keen in getting involved in the EM energy game and why it cannot be easily ignored by the other countries.

It would therefore be advantageous to the EM project if Turkey were to join the club of countries in the region as a peaceful partner. Is this possible? Maybe yes, but it is unlikely if Turkey's past record is to be trusted. For instance, a few years ago Turkey declared a policy of "zero problems with neighbors," but ended up with the exact opposite and is now at loggerheads even with fellow Sunni Egypt. If Turkey can antagonize a great country like Egypt, one can imagine what might happen to smaller countries. Egypt's history stretches back to Pharaonic times, it has a large landmass, and its population exceeds that of Turkey. Most importantly, it is acknowledged by nearly all countries in the region as the de facto historical leader of the Arab world (Thompson 2009). If Egypt decides that it does not wish to join an energy league with Turkey, the HEA project will either stumble or will have to downsize significantly. At the time of writing, Italian firm ENI had announced a new and massive energy find in Egypt, which, if true, would make the country's membership of an HEA essential.

Turkey's attacks on Iraq and Syria are attacks on Egypt's fellow Arab countries and its bombing of Turkish Kurds is an attack on Egypt's Sunni brethren. The Turkish airforce is also violating Greece's sovereign airspace almost daily. At the time of writing, the Turkish president had made an illegal visit to the occupied part of Cyprus, landing in an illegal airport, to salute the tens of thousands of occupation troops that Turkey maintains illegally on the island. While America remains mute, Egypt is observing Turkish aggression and taking action, including increased cooperation with the Greeks.

Turkey is also verbally aggressive with Israel, another major military power in the region, and calls its leadership all kinds of derogatory names. Given Turkey's aggressive history, Israel looks like an indispensable partner for any alliance because of its willingness to use its power. Turkey is also violently opposed to Syria and is involved in a deadly and bloody exercise of regime change there. Syria is thus unlikely to accept Turkey in any fraternity unless it can see a massive shift for the better in Turkish policy. Comfortingly, Turkey's nemesis, Russia, is now in the region.

Bringing in Israel, Lebanon, and Jordan

Israel has a good relationship with the Greeks and a tolerable relationship with Egypt. Its relationship with Lebanon has its ups and downs, however, and is unlikely to change in the near future, mostly because of Lebanon's sectarian mix and the existence of Lebanese factions who are strongly anti-Israel. The sporadic violence on the border separating Lebanon with Israel is indicative of the uneasy relationship between the two. Yet Lebanon could join an alliance with the Greeks, Egypt, and even Israel if it were done covertly enough.

Although in a strict sense Jordan is not a Mediterranean sea country, it too could play a useful role as a valuable partner in a future alliance, considering its position on the Gulf of Aqaba. The peaceful cooperation at the Eilat–Aqaba and Eilat–Taba crossings is an encouraging sign for the future. Jordan is poor in energy reserves, with ENI (2014) reporting natural gas reserves of slightly more than 200 billion cubic feet. Shale may have more potential there, but many experts are worried about the environmental damage from shale exploration. At the moment Jordan is a heavy importer of crude oil, natural gas, and petroleum products, the cost of which accounts for roughly 40 percent of its national budget.

Two major hurdles

Those of us who support the creation of a High Energy Authority (HEA) acknowledge several major sticking points that could derail the drive toward cooperation:

- Turkey's poor relationships with its neighbors, its military occupation of part of Cyprus, and the ease with which it uses violence.
- The unresolved Palestinian–Israeli conflict, which inevitably creates serious problems in Arab–Israeli relationships.

In fact, the solution of these two problems is a prerequisite to any broad all-country alliance in the EM basin. They need to be resolved amicably and fairly and without a doubt within the provisions of the United Nations (UN) Charter and international law.

Arabs and Israelis

Although at the moment Israel is militarily invincible, the Israelis are well aware that military might alone can not provide the long-term security and stability they desire. The Palestinians in their turn want to have their own country and the security that this would bring to present and future generations. The 1973 war of Israel with Egypt was a signal to Israel of what can happen when things go wrong, even if momentarily. Israel is also aware of the Russian resurgence and the developing US–Russia military equation in Europe. Russia is gradually moving into the EM and no one knows what this may ultimately mean for the balance of power.

In the same way that some form of peace between Israel and Egypt was found through the Camp David Accords of 1978, one would hope that a final peace agreement could be signed by the Israelis and the Palestinians, despite the bloodshed that stands between them. Israel and Egypt fought four wars: the first on the establishment of Israel in 1948; the Suez Canal war of 1956, with Britain and France involved directly on the side of Israel (Kyle 2011); the Six-Day War in 1967; and the Yom Kippur war of 1973, which saw the US setting up an air bridge to supply Israel with much-needed military hardware after a calamitous start to the war and the threat of intervention by the Soviet Union. At the end of this conflict the Agranat Commission recommended the dismissal of the Israeli Defense Forces chief of staff for mishandling the war (for more see Rabinovich 2004).

Through the accord between Israel and the PLO (Palestine Liberation Organization), the world saw some progress in the sense that the weaker side got something back from the stronger. A "Declaration of Principles" was signed in 1993 after a year and a half of secret negotiations, leading to self-rule in the Gaza Strip (for a brief account of the peace process, read Office of the Historian n.d.; and for a longer treatment Bauck and Omer 2013). However, this agreement left many major questions to be answered at a later stage, including the rights of Palestinian refugees and the status of Jerusalem.

Jordan, which fought Israel during the 1967 war, also signed a treaty with the Israelis. The Washington Declaration of 1994 put an end to belligerence between the two countries and granted Jordan a special role in Jerusalem's Muslim holy places. The peace offensive continued with the Oslo II agreement, which made possible the withdrawal of Israel from major West Bank cities such as Nablus, Jenin, and Ramallah, and allowed the Palestinian National Authority to take over their administration. The Wye River Memorandum of 1998 allowed for the transfer of an additional 14.2 percent of the West Bank to full Palestinian control. Left unanswered, nevertheless, were major questions such as the final borders, the rights of Palestinian refugees, and water sharing. Even on the Syrian–Israeli and Lebanese–Israeli fronts there was discernible progress, which saw movement toward the resolution of the Golan Heights issue and the impasse in the southern part of Lebanon.

Cyprus and Turkey

While some progress was made in Arab–Israeli relations, no progress at all was made on the Cyprus problem. Not an inch of Cypriot territory has been freed, not one refugee has returned home, and there remains the same number of Turkish soldiers in Cyprus, while illegal settler numbers are rising dangerously. In fact, the situation continuous to worsen as Turkey is pouring new colonizers into Cyprus, aiming to change the demographic balance of the country once and for all, even if this constitutes a war crime. As the dominant power in the conflict, Turkey continues to push for complete control of the island using soft and hard power as necessary. In effect, it is waiting for Cyprus to accept capitulation and sign the surrender instrument.

The Cyprus conflict is as obdurate a problem as that between Palestine and Israel, except that the balance of power in Cyprus's case is overwhelmingly in favor of Turkey, which is in no mood to abide by international law. Cyprus is at the mercy of Turkey, while America and Britain (Cyprus's guarantor power under the existing constitution) pretend to see nothing wrong. Turkey's expressed objective for the last 60 or more years has been "to regain Cyprus," which the Ottomans lost to the British in 1978 (for more see Mallinson 2005). As long as Turkey has the support of its two major NATO allies, little is likely to move in the direction of a fair solution. Under the undemocratic London and Zurich agreements of 1959 that the British forced on the hapless people of Cyprus, the United Kingdom (UK) is allowed to maintain bases on the island that occupy 254 sq km or nearly 3 percent of Cyprus's territory. Through these agreements the Cypriots lost the right to self-determination, which all people in the world should enjoy.

The 1959 agreements saddled the unfortunate Cypriots with three "guarantor" powers: Britain, Turkey, and Greece. All three played their own distinct and mostly unhelpful roles in the conflict: Britain and Turkey have played a destructive role, while Greece has remained passive at best. With the unspoken support of its NATO friends Turkey has managed to stay out of the discussions, although it is the occupying power and the source of the island's woes. Consequently, these discussions are now carried out between Greek Cypriot and Turkish Cypriot representatives, under the shadow and powerful grip of the Turkish occupation army; more surrender talks than free negotiations. This charade gives the impression that Cyprus is faced with an inter-communal dispute in which Turkey is a benign and caring observer.

Greece remains weak and often unreliable, giving Turkey a free hand to do as it pleases. The approach of Greek governments to Cyprus's misfortunes is predicated on the absurd doctrine of "Cyprus decides and Greece stands by Cyprus," which in effect tells the Cypriots, "please do not bother asking us for help." Turkey is laughing, because:

- Greece is nowhere to be seen, apart from making the odd noise here and there.
- It has unwavering American and British support.
- Some in the UN hierarchy are taking a Pontius Pilate stance by using their neutrality as a third party to avoid supporting the truth.

- The EU is happy to do the minimum necessary to appear caring about the partial occupation of a fellow EU member, while taking great pains not to jeopardize lucrative commercial deals with Turkey.

It has to be said, nevertheless, that as long as Turkey occupies part of Cyprus, the door to its EU membership remains slammed shut, much to the delight of those EU members that secretly oppose Turkish membership.

The current discussions over the Cyprus problem are nothing but a farce that helps promote Turkey's objective of bringing the entire island under its suzerainty. Turkey would be happy to see Cyprus turned into a non-state, with the former controlling the island's foreign affairs and defense through the veto power of its vassal the "Turkish Cypriot Founding State." The new Cyprus is designed to have two largely autonomous entities (one no larger than a big farm) that would be brought together to form a new state with a flimsy central government that would be run on vetoes every step of the way, essentially by a foreign judge who would be airlifted in to solve any deadlocks. The new arrangement is designed to fail, largely on account of these vetoes, which would allow Turkey to paralyze the government of Cyprus and itself to fill the vacuum. Turkey has stated repeatedly that it is adamant about maintaining a permanent military presence in Cyprus and the right to intervene militarily whenever it deems necessary. If Cyprus finally falls under the de facto control of Turkey, the decisions on its energy will indirectly be Turkey's, including that concerning a potential HEA.

The Annan Plan of 2002–04 (which euphemistically takes its name from the former UN Secretary General Kofi Annan) was ostensibly drafted to solve the Cyprus problem fairly. In essence, though, it was drawn up by the US and the UK to serve NATO objectives through Turkey. The plan was served up to the people of Cyprus with the signature of the UN Secretary General to give it a semblance of objectivity. Had it been accepted, Cyprus would have basically been turned into a Turkish dependency (Palley 2005). However, the plan was put to a referendum in 2004 and was defeated soundly by a vote of 76 percent on the Greek Cypriot side. The occupied side, aided heavily by the illegal settler vote (the UN shamelessly allowed colonizers to vote), accepted the plan with a vote in favor of 65 percent. However, scant and fuzzy statistics coming from the areas under the control of the Turkish army make it difficult to ascertain whether the "yes" vote was primarily from the illegal settlers.

Current ongoing discussions still have the Annan Plan as the prototype and model from which the Turkish side is not departing by a single iota, while the process continues to be controlled by the same actors as before; namely, America, Britain, and Turkey. This is a deplorable development considering that the plan under discussion was massively rejected by a democratic vote. Turkey is adamant that it will accept nothing less than the provisions of the Annan Plan (plus more); the original plan will be disguised and given a fancy new name to make it look different and democratic. In light of the above, if a solution to the Cyprus problem were to be announced tomorrow, the hard reality is that it would automatically mean the dissolution of the Republic of Cyprus and the creation of a Turkish satellite state on about 3,000 sq km. Mallinson (2005) asserts that an Annan Plan–type solution would be ideal for the US and the UK because Turkey would immobilize Cyprus's foreign policy, meaning that Russia, the traditional friend of the Greeks, would be pushed out of Cyprus once and for all.

The prospects for the Palestine and Cyprus problems

It is axiomatic that strong countries dictate terms to their weaker adversaries; this has been the pattern throughout human history (Strassler 1988). It is equally true that strong countries are always concerned about how long they can keep their adversaries down. Even though the Israeli Defense Forces rule in the Middle East, the Israelis continue to be concerned about their future and the fact that they are surrounded by multitudes of antagonistic Arabs, hostile neighbors that are many times larger than Israel by territory and population.

One assumes that Israel would be willing to sign a two-state solution provided it were convinced that this would mean the real end of its troubles. It would not sign an agreement if it felt that only a new adventure would follow. This position has been repeatedly stated by Israel and is irrevocable. One also surmises that it is in Israel's benefit to sign an agreement now from a position of invincibility, rather than later under conditions that cannot be predicted, particularly regarding the future balance of power. On the one side we have the Israelis, who long for sustainable long-term security, and on the other we have the Palestinians, who long to have their own truly independent state. In between stands suspicion over the other side's intentions.

The situation of Cyprus is very different to that of Palestine because the vastly stronger of the two sides has heavyweight backers and little or no reason to accept a fair solution. Turkey now holds all the cards and is not worried about security vis-à-vis Cyprus. This situation is unlikely to change without a shift in the support of the big powers. Cyprus hoped that its entry into the EU would earn it a strong democratic ally in its struggle against Turkish domination and occupation, but it was quickly disappointed. Despite the many pronouncements on equality, fraternity, and the rule of international law, the EU has failed miserably to live up to its own declared ideals in the case of Cyprus. Indicatively, the EU continues to have a business-as-usual relationship with Turkey even though the latter does not recognize the Republic of Cyprus (an EU member) and forbids Cyprus's ships from entering Turkish ports. Worse still for Cyprus, some EU countries such as the UK, Sweden, and the Netherlands openly support Turkey, ignoring its occupation of 37 percent of the territory of a fellow EU member. Turkey is basically free to pursue its policy of ultimate control of the whole territory of Cyprus. While they are at Turkey's mercy, the vast majority of people on the island refuse to capitulate, choosing instead to press on with their demand for a democratic Cyprus. Short of being overcome by a mass suicidal trance, the Greek Cypriots are unlikely in a referendum to vote for their own demise and the end of the 3,500-year presence of Greeks in Cyprus. In all probability, the Cyprus problem will stay open for a long time.

History and trust

History has the capacity to propel people to great heights of forgiveness as much as it can create mistrust and keep animosity burning. The memory of World Wars I and II pushed Germany and France to create the High Authority in 1951, which brought peace to the two countries and ultimately led to the creation of the EU, now the home of countries that were formerly adversaries (for more see Gillingham 1991). The most outstanding example of magnanimity and generosity of spirit, however, was shown by Russia, who suffered nearly 28 million dead during World War II and yet found the courage and spiritual strength to forget this terrible carnage caused by Nazi Germany (Zhukov 1971). Thankfully, Germany and Russia now work in a peaceful and profitable partnership, even if at times they experience the occasional political hitch, mostly as a result of German membership in NATO and America's insistence that Germany follow US policy on Russia. Equally, the Chinese forgave Japan for the dreadful atrocities against them in World War II.

Vicious civil wars also provide us with examples of generosity of spirit and forgiveness on the part of the victor, which usher in a fresh and promising new beginning between old adversaries. One such example comes from the Biafran war in Nigeria, which ranks as one of twentieth-century Africa's most devastating and brutal fratricidal conflicts (Baxter 2014). This civil war saw thousands dead, hundreds of thousands injured, and millions starving and emaciated. The carnage lasted for more than three years until Colonel Olusegun Obasanjo surrendered with his Biafran forces. Immediately afterward, the victor and head of state General Yakubu Gowon gave his famous "no victor no vanquished" speech, followed by an amnesty and a program of reconciliation, reconstruction, and rehabilitation.

Thankfully, history is blessed with many such acts of largesse. Nelson Mandela is a world icon because of his vast kindness and his readiness to forgive the regime that incarcerated him with hard labor for nearly 30 years, just because he was fervently demanding one man, one vote. Incidentally, this fundamental human right for which Mandela paid a heavy price is denied to Cypriots in twenty-first-century Europe.

Regrettably, history also records conflicts and hatreds that are obdurate and keep coming back, causing confrontation between countries and in the process making building harmonious relationships difficult, if not impossible. Many of the oppressed find it very difficult to forgive their oppressor, particularly if the suffering has lasted for a long time, sometimes for centuries. Russians are often reminded what happened 400 years ago when Poland and Lithuania attacked Russia in the Polish–Muscovite War of 1605–18. Equally, historians remind the Poles and Lithuanians of their mistreatment by Russia. We see this antagonism surface even today in the context of the Ukrainian conflict, with Poland acting antagonistically and often belligerently against Russia, even though Poland is not part of the conflict.

Some formerly colonized countries in Africa and the EM (both these regions have seen more than their fair share of colonization) refuse to forgive their colonizer-oppressor even after centuries of peace (Pakenham 1992). The colonized simply find it difficult to trust their former masters, largely because of lingering fears that the colonizer is trying to return in another form using trickery and deception. Not many countries in Africa trust their former colonizer Britain, even if they gained their independence some 50 or 60 years back; it is similar for French-speaking former colonies. The people of Cyprus do not trust the British government, even if relationships between Cypriot and British peoples are exemplary and harmonious. Cyprus does not trust the UK not just because of some 80 years of colonization, but mostly because of recent untoward political behavior, such as insisting on having bases in a supposedly sovereign Cyprus, forcing an undemocratic constitution on the country, and lending unwavering political support to Turkey, which is violating Cyprus's territorial integrity that Britain pledged to protect as guarantor power. British tourists in Cyprus are always warmly welcome, just as Cypriots are in the UK, which hosts thousands of Cypriot migrants and students attending courses at its universities. When it comes to international affairs, it seems that harmonious relationships between the peoples of countries with different political interests mean little.

Turkey held the Greeks under the Ottoman yoke for an incredible 400 years (Brewer 2010). That is a long time to keep a nation in bondage, even if at times Ottoman rule showed glimpses of religious and language tolerance and Turkey at times employed Greeks in positions of high authority. This long, humiliating, and shameful occupation ended nearly 200 years ago, so one would have expected it to be long forgotten. Munificence could have been forthcoming, had it not been for the many other violent events that transpired after the end of Ottoman rule in Greece. Here, one is reminded of the horrific violence of 1922 that saw the forced and violent expulsion from Asia Minor of nearly 1,500,000 Greeks, the burning of Smyrna, and the peaceful transfer out of Greece and into Asia Minor of some 300,000 Turks. This event marked the end of a Greek presence in Asia Minor that dated back four millennia. Worse still, this carnage happened soon after the end of World War I, when Turkey sided with the losers and Greece with the winners. More conditions for mistrust were created some 30 years later, during "anti-Greek pogroms in 1955 and mass expulsions in 1964, [after which] the Greek community [in Turkey] was left in tatters. And so was the Orthodox Christianity they practised" (Lowen 2014). This recent BBC article speaks volumes about Turkey's attitude to Greeks and Christians.

In light of this discussion, unavoidably the question arises: How can trust, which is so vital to the creation of an HEA, be restored considering all that has happened between Arabs and Israelis, Greeks and Turks, and Arabs and Turks, bearing in mind that the Ottoman occupation of Arab lands also lasted for centuries? One understands why Egypt is antagonistic to recent Turkish attempts to lead the Sunni world (and thus most of the Arab world that was under Ottoman colonial rule). Memories of colonialism die hard. So what do the stronger nations in the region need to do to allay the fears of the weaker countries? It is sanguine to recall that it was the winner Russia that started the trusting relationship with Germany and the winner Gowon who forgave the loser Obasanjo in Nigeria. How does one reassure the Palestinians that Israeli bombing will not be repeated and the Israelis that rockets from Gaza will not rain down on Israel? Hilal Khashan (Chapter 6) believes that the building of trust requires first a period of peaceful coexistence between countries in the region. If this is the case, proof of peace would need to be established before an HEA can become a viable project. Although the odds are heavily stacked against a quick restoration of peaceful coexistence, the EM countries need soon to start the process of rebuilding relationships that ultimately could lead to trust.

High time for a High Energy Authority

Despite these mostly discouraging observations and the high probability that the HEA will not come to fruition any time soon, the concept still needs to be pushed forward with vigor. It makes sense and if finally applied could lead to vast benefits for the region and its people. The idea meets all the criteria of rationality, but stumbles on history and low levels of trust. Although on the surface trust seems to be a cognitive construct, in reality it has strong affective and emotional underpinnings. The Cyprus and Palestinian issues, two major hurdles in the way of an HEA, have both real and measurable cognitive aspects (e.g., number of wars and frequency of violence, number of deaths, lost lands and homes, number of refugees) as well as emotional aspects (e.g., attacks on religious faith, insult, hatred), probably in equal measure.

These two hitherto intractable political problems need to be resolved before any meaningful progress can be made. The most rational approach would be the strict application of EU principles on sovereignty, democracy, and liberty. The acquis communitaire (or the EU acquis, as it is commonly known) could be most helpful, as there one finds the accumulated legislation and court decisions on issues such as energy and justice.

The creation of an HEA could bring about a sea-change in the EM and could greatly benefit all countries in the region. Among others, the region stands to gain these advantages from an HEA:

- The HEA would act as an agent for peace, replacing aggressive competition between nations with cooperation.
- Action on exploration and exploitation of energy resources would move fast as emotional and other barriers to trust were gradually lifted.
- Each country in the region would get its fair share of benefits by agreement, thus taking away the need for antagonistic discussions that often lead to hardening of positions, deadlocks, and bullying by the stronger side.

- Each country would benefit by bringing to the fraternity its competitive advantages. In this way, each would have little reason to want to take away its neighbors' and partners' advantages, which would benefit the union collectively. Turkey, for example, would benefit greatly as an energy transit hub, because it has a competitive advantage in this matter even if it does not have energy reserves.

- The cost of security and protection of energy resources, exploration, and transport would be minimized as enmity between nations would be replaced by a spirit of cooperation and sharing.

- The role of superpowers in the region would be reduced significantly (history teaches us that such interference cannot be eliminated altogether). Britain as a former colonial power and its successor in the region, the US, would see their capacity to act as "independent" mediators for their own interests vastly reduced and with some luck one day their "services" would not be needed at all.

- The stability in the region would generate many important supplementary benefits. International investors, for example, would be more willing to invest in a stable and peaceful EM.

A High Energy Authority from the prism of holism

The propensity of countries in the region to work either as *closed* or *open* systems (two very important concepts of holism) or to adopt something in between will to an extent determine whether an HEA goes ahead or not, and whether it succeeds or fails if it does proceed. As countries battle to protect their energy reserves from predator neighbors, unavoidably the attacked will tend to take an inward-looking posture, becoming defensive (and aggressive as well). Equally, interaction with the neighbor will reduce, causing the system to become more closed. When there is little or no room for interaction (closeness) between Turks and Greeks or between Arabs and Israelis, the likelihood of them working together is infinitely diminished, particularly since most of their energies will be expended on driving out and isolating their adversary. Countries typically invest in defense either because they are afraid of their neighbor or because they wish to do harm to their neighbor and glean benefits from aggressive and expansionary policies.

Openness creates the preconditions for interaction between countries in the region, which in turn helps in the resolution of the problems that divide them. More significantly, openness tends to create trust, which in turn reduces the need for costly expenditures on defense. Openness and closedness can often make the difference between continued conflict and peace. They can also make the difference between economic stagnation and economic growth (through joint exploitation of energy resources, for example). Closed economies and nations are known to suffer the effects of inwardness and staleness, while open economies are known to work well with other economies for mutual advantage. Nevertheless, one needs to be careful before making generalizations. Greek businesspeople have invested in Turkey (a sign of openness on both sides) and trade between the two countries is growing, yet this has not stopped the militarily stronger Turkey from trying to impose its will on the Greeks using intimidation, threats, and violations of sea and air space. Although openness helps, it does not provide all the answers. The creation of an HEA will certainly be a strong sign of openness and interaction between countries, but it will clearly not be a panacea.

One also needs to consider the difference between *unified* and *splintered* approaches. Holism promotes the unification of divergent objectives into one, while atomism promotes individual objectives and interests. The EM suffers from the divergent plans and actions of individual nations that often work against the interests of the region as a whole. If countries decided to work more cooperatively and synergistically, then many of the issues that divide them would probably not even arise. The EM system is splintered in more than one way and this needs to stop. The following are some signs of system splinter:

- Countries blissfully pursue their own interests with little desire for true and honest cooperation with other countries in the region on the utilization of its vast resources.
- The economies are small by international standards; even the largest economy in the region (Turkey's) falls short of $1 trillion in GDP. Turkey makes up half of the GDP of the region and this gives its policy makers the wrong idea of their power and pushes them to want to overshadow rather than cooperate with others. It would be better to pool resources to allow the region to gain improved critical mass, which would be helpful to everyone.
- While citizens are clamoring for measures to enhance their quality of life, the political and economic elites of some of these countries have other worries to contend with, such as maintaining military dominance, squashing anti-government sentiment, and keeping their privileged position. One would think that the vast majority of people would support the cooperation that would improve their lives.

- Although the economies of large countries such as America and Japan are among the most heavily indebted in the world, they face no immediate threat, mostly because they are large, have their own currency, and government bond holders are locals rather than outsiders (more so in the case of Japan). Within the Eurozone the French and Italian debt is almost as troublesome as that of Greece and Cyprus, yet because of these countries' economic size, their treatment by the Euro group, the IMF, and the European Central Bank is much less harsh. If economic size matters, then it behooves the countries in the region to cooperate over their oil and gas finds in order to grow their economies more quickly. Acting jointly will put them in a better position to borrow at competitive rates for the necessary massive energy infrastructure.

Change is intrinsic to social systems, although sometimes it is forced on countries by external or unexpected events. The energy wealth provides just such an opportunity for change. Nature has done its work and provided the region with a windfall. Now it is time for the leadership to do what is expected of them. Now is the time to apply international law to solve outstanding problems and boost cooperation. This would pave the way for collaboration and economic growth. Unavoidably, change will need to be gradual and controlled and in line with the principles of dynamic homeostasis, as outlined in Chapter 8. The 1951 agreement between France and Germany for the exploitation of coal and steel that led to the creation of the EU is still work in progress. The fear of a Grexit and the possibility of the Eurozone experiment unraveling provide ample proof of why change needs time and good planning, as well as unfailing observance of the principles of dynamic homeostasis. The European Coal and Steel Community (ECSC) was first proposed in 1950 by the Foreign Minister of France, Robert Schuman, and was a two-country affair. The formal signing of the Treaty of Paris a year later brought into the French–German fraternity a few more countries in the form of Italy, Belgium, the Netherlands, and Luxembourg. It took over 60 years before the association was expanded to include all its current members. As the number of member countries grew the problems of the union also grew, calling for new measures to bring about the necessary unity.

In the best-case scenario, the interests of member countries of the proposed HEA will gradually converge with those of the new fraternity as it grows in stature. Great lessons can be learned from holism. The *Oxford English Dictionary*'s definition of holism is central to understanding the concept of an HEA:

> The theory that parts of a whole are in intimate interconnection, such that they cannot exist independently of the whole, or cannot be understood without reference to the whole, which is thus regarded as greater than the sum of its parts … the opposite of atomism.

The inter-connectivity between the countries inside an HEA would ultimately lead to the formulation of more unifying policies that will help bring the countries closer together in many fields for their mutual benefit. The bonding process could be contagious once the benefits of the whole began to manifest themselves. Countries should not worry about losing their independence, because by improving their economies and reducing conflicts, each would be better positioned to do more things on its own, provided that these did not contradict the HEA's principles.

Holism brings with it the warning that social systems are not free of weaknesses, because they are created by human beings who are imperfect, with passions and bounded rationality that make it impossible for them to see the picture correctly in its totality and to make perfect judgments. Cognizance should therefore be taken of the hard truth that the involvement of humans in the workings of systems also carries with it the risk of causing the system to generate unwanted consequences, because human behavior is not always rational.

With regard to a potential HEA, one needs to remember that policies and decisions will in the end be taken by people who are guided by their attitudes, perceptions, biases, sense of fairness, aggression, democratic values, egalitarianism, egoism, greed, and a host of other psychological constructs. Some of these attitudes can have a poisonous effect on cooperation and sharing, particularly when it comes to interpreting "national interest," which could mean one thing to one and quite another to someone else. To one person national interest could mean going it alone, dominating neighbors, stealing others' resources, or wanting the neighbor to serve as a vassal. To another it could mean, among other things, reduced conflict, good neighborliness, cooperation, joint project management, fair sharing of resources, egalitarianism, philanthropy, and so on. Lamentably, history teaches us that irrationality can often creep into decision making by the back door. Irrationality is capable of killing concepts that have great potential. Equally, it can cause countries to become victims of misjudgment and bad leadership. Irrational behavior can cause the strong to try to impose their will on others, with detrimental effects on the whole and with unpredictable future outcomes.

Efficiency is the hallmark of well-functioning wholes. *Management* is the primary tool through which efficiency can be achieved in social systems. The EM region could learn much from the experiences of other countries in the art of management and in this way avoid many of the pitfalls that will undoubtedly manifest themselves in the course of building an HEA. Germany, Switzerland, and Norway, for example, could act as good models provided that an eclectic approach is used. This might come in handy once EM nations decide to work together, because joint decision making would need to become part of the ethos of managing their combined energy resources. Good management would help tone down potential conflicts and allow for the convergence of interests.

One could legitimately ask: Is the creation of an HEA the best way to bring about efficiency, or would it be better for each country in the region to act alone and deal with its energy wealth as it sees fit? In answering this question one would need to take account of what acting alone would entail in the first place. As things stand, it could mean that the weaker states in the region, such as Greece, Cyprus, and Syria, would need to fight their common neighbor in protracted legal battles in international courts over EEZs and their delineation. It could also mean that these three small countries might never be able to exploit their resources without Turkey's approval, which is basically what is happening now. Greece is nervous about delineating its EEZ and the dream of offshore oil exploration in the northern part of Greece is now an apparition. Greece is now trying to sneak its way into energy exploration south of Crete, as far away from Turkey as possible. For now Turkey is keeping silent, but it will surely make its views known very soon and threateningly. Cyprus ceased to explore for gas once Turkey showed its teeth and it is not unreasonable to say that Cyprus's energy project is frozen for now; unless of course Israel provides the necessary security (an unlikely prospect, perhaps). With Greece and Cyprus out of the picture, Israel will probably content itself with working with those Arab states that are willing to cooperate despite the Palestinian impasse, while keeping the Turkey option open. Fortuitously for Israel, the ISIL-backed insurgency in the Sinai is bringing Israel and Egypt nearer in a common cause.

Under the go-it-alone scenario, much of the energy potential of the area looks like going to waste while conflict in the region continues. Clearly, the HEA option and its accompanying efficiencies and synergies are a far more attractive proposition for all concerned, even though difficult to achieve. Those not steeped in history and more particularly in the history of conflict and suffering may find it difficult to comprehend why a clearly rational and beneficial option could now take second place to one that is potentially conflict ridden and vastly inferior.

Undoubtedly, an HEA will require strong coordination (another definite trait of holism) considering the many countries and cultures involved.

With good coordination many of the vital and often controversial issues that will naturally arise will be easier to manage. Importantly, good coordination will help ensure proper execution of joint decisions. The degree to which coordination succeeds will depend on the willingness of member countries to allow professionals to do their job once the political decisions have been taken. Clearly, meddling at the execution phase will not help the project to go ahead as planned. It would of course be naive to think that the likelihood of inter-country grievances at the planning and execution stages will disappear overnight, but certainly one hopes that they will be kept to a minimum.

Serious legal issues are bound to arise in the process leading up to the creation of an HEA and more will surface as decisions are applied. One would hope that such legal problems will only be a fraction of those inherent in the go-it-alone option. The precedent of the legal arrangements over coal and steel in 1951, as updated, will be there to help the HEA with the maze of problems and complex decisions that need to be taken. There are, of course, mountains of EU legislation governing inter-country relations that could provide immense help to the project.

It goes without saying that the Law of the Sea would need to be applied strictly and violators sanctioned. This would mean all countries in a prospective HEA signing the Law of the Sea convention without any delays or hidden agendas. One appreciates that this legislation is still developing as new issues arise and as some of its provisions are contested (for instance, those of UNCLOS III are contested in the EM). Adoption of the Law of the Sea by all countries will certainly enhance the resolution of outstanding problems in the EM and reduce conflict. Clearly, when the exploration and exploitation of energy reserves come under an HEA, the legal issues that divide countries in the region will most likely diminish as well, in both number and severity.

The future lies in cooperation

The future of the EM and of the economies in the region will to a large extent be determined by the ability of these countries to cooperate on energy. If this issue is dealt with successfully, then those countries stand to earn a huge bonanza that will benefit their citizens, help grow their economies, and reduce potential conflicts. Equally, future generations will benefit from the creation of sovereign funds that will guarantee wealth. Every economy in the region is in need of a powerful financial boost, and energy can provide this. A brighter future lies ahead provided that current political impediments are managed wisely.

Relations between countries in the region need to improve significantly if the objective of cooperation is to stand a chance of being realized in a sustainable manner. Trust lies at the heart of the whole HEA exercise: trust between countries and particularly between current and former adversaries. Much of the burden for creating trust unavoidably falls on the shoulders of the stronger countries, because they have more to offer and can usher in trust by showing more goodwill to their weaker adversaries. Countries that hurt and bully their neighbors need to show genuine remorse and promise to themselves and others that they will no longer use their strength in that way. The strict application of international law and particularly the Law of the Sea must apply and this should be an irrevocable fact. The Palestinian and Cyprus problems need to be solved strictly in line with international law and the UN Charter, which gives equal rights to all citizens, forbids wars, and discourages the arbitrary behavior of stronger countries. After World War II we no longer have "Ministries of War," as these have been replaced by "Ministries of Defense."

All countries in the region stand to benefit from cooperating in the formation of an HEA. Getting them to cooperate may look like a tall order at this juncture, but it is clearly worth struggling for, because an inter-country energy alliance will, as far as possible, free countries from neo-colonial interference. Miguel Moratinos (Chapter 7) sagaciously sets this as a priority issue for all countries in the region. William Mallinson (Chapter 2) is less optimistic and takes the carefully considered position that for their own geostrategic interests, Britain and the US will do everything in their power to control events in the region and keep the British (American in effect) bases in Cyprus intact. In fact, he goes a step further and suggests that the impasse in the resolution of the Cyprus problem suits Britain (America) nicely, as it works as a buffer against possible moves by a peaceful unified Cyprus against the continued presence of British military bases on the island.

George Georgiou (Chapter 4) offers an intelligent review of the energy situation and concludes that countries in the EM need to genuinely cooperate if they are to capitalize on their energy reserves. He sees the relationship between Greece, Cyprus, Israel, and maybe Egypt as very encouraging, but predicts that Israel and Turkey will inevitably mend fences (the result of heavy American pressure), and as such Israel's relationship with the Greeks will weaken, even if both sides wish it to remain strong. He observes that countries in economic crisis such as Cyprus (more so in the case of Greece) need energy to regain their economic luster.

Hilal Khashan (Chapter 6) uses his vast and valuable knowledge of the geopolitics of the region to provide a comprehensive and integrated analysis of the relationships between countries and their willingness to break with the past and start working in unison on energy. He unhappily concludes that the EM countries are not yet ready for such a venture and that a golden opportunity to establish peace and create economic wealth will, for now, be missed. From his position as an authority on energy in the area, and more specifically on the EEZs of Greece and Cyprus, Solon Kassinis (Chapter 3) concludes that the vast energy reserves stand to make a huge difference to the economies of the region, most of which are now hard-pressed. The energy reserves in the EM could, according to Kassinis, rival those of the North Sea. On the issue of energy transport, he takes the position that Cyprus should not, under any conditions, allow its energy to transit through Turkey until further notice. A long period of peace and good behavior from Turkey would be needed before any serious thought could be given to doing so. Cyprus should have no problem working with Turkey once the latter lifts its military occupation, removes its colonizer-settlers, and starts applying international law.

Stephanos Constantinides (Chapter 1) gives the reader a masterful overview of the complex, and often shifting, relations between countries in the EM, the Middle East, and Saudi Arabia. Understanding the intricate and often erratic maze of relationships of the broader region is not easy at the best of times. Hopefully, the reader will now be in a better position to appreciate what the EM and Middle East regions are all about and how difficult it is to make predictions as to what will happen in the future.

Aris Petasis (Chapter 5) looks at the economies of the countries in the region, examines their competiveness, and notes their intrinsic weaknesses that explain why none (not even Israel) has managed to meet its economic potential. All need to redesign their economies (some marginally and some a great deal) to make them more sustainable and competitive in the long term. The enormous economic benefits that the region's energy can provide will offer breathing space to allow them to redesign their economies, reduce their energy costs, and make their products more competitive and therefore more exportable. Most countries in the region show disturbing current account deficits that need to be reduced in the first place and then hopefully turned into positive balances. The same holds for many of the other critical economic parameters, not excluding high sovereign debt. The creation of new jobs is fundamental for all these countries. The energy sector can create jobs in large numbers and this will hopefully make the attractiveness of public-sector employment (which weighs heavily on these economies) less alluring.

Well steeped in the science of medicine and the way in which the human body functions as a whole, Theodoros Kyprianou (Chapter 8) collaborates with Aris Petasis, who brings to bear his wide background in organizational development and strategy, to explain why the region needs to take a holistic approach to addressing its many ailments. They note that the region needs therapeutic care. Energy, economy, politics, strategy, geopolitics, beliefs, attitudes, and mindsets are all closely intertwined and this fact needs to be understood if attempts at addressing the ills of the region are to succeed. This set of parameters, and related others, affect the region in many and varied ways because of the inter-relatedness and inter-dependence of nations in the troubled EM. Due to that inter-relatedness, the establishment of an HEA would require the successful interplay of a vast number of factors and issues. In this holistic equation, countries would take the role of system parts that work together seamlessly to help the region (the whole) reach its potential. Kyprianou and Petasis avoid using the term "maximization of gains," however, because both agree that maximization is just a theoretical construct that does not exist in the case of social systems.

Perceived national interests, political positioning, geopolitics, and influences from the outside environment (e.g., big powers that have a great propensity to interfere in the affairs of weaker countries in pursuit of their own economic and geopolitical interests) need to be taken into account to arrive at a synergistic enterprise. The setting up of an HEA would require the alignment of an inordinate number of factors, sub-factors, sets, and sub-sets. Achieving this alignment is going to be difficult, but hopefully not impossible. The advantages of setting up an HEA far outweigh the sacrifices that individual countries would need to make. The citizens of these countries could be expected to want to see the management of energy in the region follow the paradigm of Norway rather than that of Nigeria. One hopes that they would support the establishment of an HEA given that it is natural for people to want their children to have access to high-quality education, good medical services, reliable transport, and a well-functioning civic society free of dependencies. Equally, one would assume that people in the region want to see their countries genuinely independent and free from neo-colonial practices and the irritating and costly meddling of outside powers. Cooperation offers the countries of the Eastern Mediterranean the hope of a better future.

References

Peter Bauck, Peter, and Mohammed Omer (Eds.) 2013. The Oslo Accords 1993–2013: A Critical Assessment. Lanham, MD: University Press of America.

Baxter, Peter. 2014. Biafra: The Nigerian Civil War 1967–1970. Africa@war series. Solihull: Helion.

Brewer, David. 2010. Greece, The Hidden Centuries: Turkish Rule from the Fall of Constantinople to Greek Independence. London: I. B. Tauris.

EIA. 2014. "International Energy Data and Analysis: Turkey." Washington, DC: US Energy Information Administration, April. http://www.eia.gov/beta/international/country.cfm?iso=TUR. Accessed August 2015.

ENI. 2014. "O&G World Oil and Gas Review 2014." http://www.eni.com/world-oil-gas-review-2014/sfogliabile/O-G-2014.pdf. Accessed August 2015.

Gillingham, John. 1991. Coal, Steel, and the Rebirth of Europe, 1945–1955. Cambridge: Cambridge University Press.

IEA. 2013. "Oil and Gas Security: Emergency Response of IEA Countries 2013." Paris: International Energy Agency.

Kyle, Keith. 2011. Suez: Britain's End of Empire in the Middle East. London: I. B. Tauris.

Lowen, Mark. 2014. "Pope Francis Visit: Turkey's Christians Face Tense Times." BBC.com, November 27. http://www.bbc.com/news/world-europe-30214805. Accessed August 2015.

Mallinson, William. 2005. Cyprus: A Modern History. London: I. B. Tauris.

Office of the Historian, n.d. "Milestones: 1993–2000 the Oslo Accords and the Arab-Israeli Peace Process." Washington, DC: US Department of State. https://history.state.gov/milestones/1993-2000/oslo. Accessed August 2015.

Pakenham, Thomas. 1992. The Scramble for Africa: White Man's Conquest of the Dark Continent from 1876 to 1912. New York: Avon Books.

Palley, Claire. 2005. An International Relations Debacle: The UN Secretary-General's Mission of Good Offices in Cyprus 1999–2004. Oxford: Hart.

Rabinovich, Abraham. 2004. The Yom Kippur War: The Epic Encounter That Transformed the Middle East. Berlin: Schocken Books.

Stockholm Peace Research Institute. 2015. "Military Expenditure by Country as Percentage of Gross Domestic Product, 1988–2014." http://www.sipri.org/research/armaments/milex/milex_database. Accessed August 2015.

Strassler, Robert B. (Ed). 1988. The Landmark Thucydides: A Comprehensive Guide to the Peloponnesian War. New York: Touchstone.

Thompson, Jason. 2009. A History of Egypt: From Earliest Times to the Present. New York: Anchor Books.

World Bank. 2015. "Unemployment, Total (% of Total Labor Force) (Modeled ILO Estimate)." http://data.worldbank.org/indicator/SL.UEM.TOTL.ZS/countries?page =2. Accessed August 2015.

Zhukov, Georgii C. 1971. The Memoirs of Marshal Zhukov. New York: Delacorte Press.

INDEX